Austrian Emigration   1938 to 1945

AUSTRIAN EMIGRATION
1938 to 1945

Franz Goldner

Frederick Ungar Publishing Co. / New York

To My Wife
The best companion
in good times and bad

Translated from the second German edition of
Die österreichische Emigration: 1938 bis 1945
by arrangement with Verlag Herold, Vienna

Printed in the United States of America

Designed by Stanley Rice

Library of Congress Cataloging in Publication Data

Goldner, Franz, 1903–
 Austrian emigration, 1938–1945.

 Translation of Die österreichische Emigration, 1938–
1945.
 Bibliography: p.
 Includes index.
 1. Austrians in foreign countries. 2. World War,
1939–1945—Austria. 3. Austria—Emigration and
immigration. 4. Austria—Politics and government—
1938–1945. I. Title.
DB34.5.G6513 1979   301.32′5′09436   78-4309
ISBN 0-8044-1303-7

Contents

Preface to the First German Edition

All historical writing is subjective. However determined the historian is to present his period objectively, he will still see events from a specific vantage point which influences his views of the processes of history.

In his classic description of the Peloponnesian War, Thucydides dealt with the momentous struggle between Athens and Sparta from the aspect of Athens's democratic institutions. This same war could also have been described from the point of view of Sparta's nondemocratic character. Nevertheless, and in spite of his ideological stance, Thucydides's history of the war is a highly factual one, a model for succeeding generations of historians.

By profession a jurist, I believe, with Theodor Mommsen, that history and law are closely allied. No legal, social, or economic institutions can be fully understood without taking into account their development in earlier ages. An understanding of the legal sources and institutions in a particular era is essential to the writing of general history.

Active political emigration is the main subject of this study. It can be best defined as the history of those émigrés who did not reconcile themselves to their emigration being irreversible. The particular subjects of this book are the émigrés who were obliged to leave Austria between 1938 and 1945. Their common goal was the overthrow of Nazism and their own return to their homeland; this was their stated ultimate objective.

To achieve this, one faction worked during their emigration for the establishment of an Austrian government in exile. Other émigrés set as their objective the prevention, or at least the obstruction, of an Austrian government in exile. They argued for the postponement of any such decision for as long as possible in order to leave to the population of their home country the determination of its own political future.

Both goals were pursued by the opposing groups of Austrian émigrés throughout the seven years here discussed. During this time the name "Austria" or "Republic of Austria" was blotted out, just as after the war of 1866 the one-time Kingdom of Hanover disappeared from the political map, its name thereafter applying to no more than a Prussian province. But since the Republic of Austria subsequently came into being again, the efforts of the politically active émigrés during the years 1938–1945 must be assigned positive value because of their insistence on the reconstruction of Austria's independence and the creation of a recognized Austrian government in exile. Conversely, from the standpoint of historical hindsight, a negative value is given here to the efforts of those circles of political émigrés who strove to prevent, obstruct, or postpone this goal.

To the extent that documents, records, letters, newspaper articles, and other written materials existed and were available, this study is based on them. To the extent that memoirs and autobiographical works by figures prominent in the emigration were available, they were also consulted.

Unfortunately, many documents and records were lost in the various countries of immigration, especially in France. Many written records were destroyed by the émigrés before or during their flight. Other documents are still not accessible, because in several countries of immigration the political archives will not be opened until thirty years have elapsed from the time of the events recorded therein. Others must still await publication of the writings of the political leaders of the emigration.

As added difficulty, research had to be carried out in several countries, and therefore in several languages. The profusion of sources was such that I had to separate the essential from the unessential and concentrate on telling the history of political emigration in those countries where actual political history was made.

The history of political emigration to France and to the United States requires the most comprehensive treatment; the short period available to the Austrian political emigration in France already manifests almost all the elements that were to characterize political emigration generally in this era. The history of political emigration into the United States, on the other hand, represents the acme of both positive and negative efforts, conducive or detrimental to the reestablishment of Austria's nationhood. Further, this is the period that can best be documented with the help of written records. The history of political emigration into Great Britain and Sweden will be treated following the chapters dealing with the United States.

With the fall of France and after the entry of the United States into the war, the wartime collaboration between the United States and Great Britain was so close that the most essential facts and events concerning political emigration into Great Britain as well as émigrés' activities can more easily be found in American sources than in the United Kingdom itself. The zeal to put pen to paper that exists in American consulates, embassies, legations, and political missions is admirable, as is the accuracy with which events dealing with the Austrian political emigration into the nations in question are described. Unfortunately, not all sources were accessible even in the United States. Reports in the Office of Strategic Services or the files of the Federal Bureau of Investigation, for example, are still considered "classified" material and are therefore withheld.

The history of political emigration into Sweden was also documented by American and British reports. Without an adequate knowledge of the Swedish language, it was therefore all the more important that I was allowed to make use of the numerous available diplomatic reports of the American envoy in Sweden.

The history of political emigration from Austria to Latin America is dealt with in a section toward the end of the book. Here, too, American diplomatic reports from abroad were a principal source.

The history of political emigration from Austria to the Soviet Union is limited to a few lines. Because of the notorious lack of accessible sources in that country, my remarks can only be partially supported by the reports of the diplomatic representative of the United States to the Soviet Union. However, use has been made of a recent and comprehensive study, *Erinnerungen und Reflexionen* [*Memories and Reflections*], by Ernst Fischer, an Austrian political émigré who lived in the Soviet Union. Written in 1969, the work offers a communist point of view of the émigré situation. Unfortunately, I have never had access to radio broadcasts from Moscow, but I have referred to those broadcasts as mentioned in the writings of the American ambassador in Moscow. In view of the lack of primary sources, discussion of Austrian émigrés in the Soviet Union occupies only a very short chapter.

For the most part two sets of records and documents have been consulted. The first includes the published and, more important, the unpublished files of the United States Department of State as well as the Departments of Defense and Justice. I am particularly indebted to Dr. Arthur Kogan, Assistant Chief of the Historical Department of the Department of State, for his support and expert advice. The second group of documents and records comes from the posthumous papers of Hans Rott, who died on December 30, 1962, in Vienna. Rott, a member of Kurt von Schuschnigg's government, kindly allowed me to examine these papers at the time he headed the Department of Organizations in the Austrian consulate in New York.

Other sources that were used are primarily the laws, decrees, and ordinances applying to émigrés in France, Great Britain, and the United States. Among the many writers I am greatly indebted to, special mention must be made of Joseph Buttinger, whose book *Am Beispiel Österreichs* [*By the Example of Austria*] was of invaluable help.

Special thanks are also due to Professor Robert Rie, a jurist from Austria, who, after the fall of his country, became an eminent historian. He has stood behind his work from the outset and has graciously offered both advice and sympathy. Last but not least, I am indebted to Ursula Gutheil for her untiring cooperation and help.

F.G.

Preface to the Second German Edition

Five years have passed since the publication of the first edition of this book. This passage of time has allowed me to develop further my preliminary observations on the Austrian emigration.

The new sources that have been made available since the earlier edition are primarily the files of the British Foreign Office covering the time under scrutiny. These are available at the Public Records Office in London. Unfortunately, in spite of a general release, some files of considerable importance to historians will remain classified for many more years.

Also now available are the files of the United States Office for Strategic Services in Washington and those of the Office for War Information. Many of these files were declassified at my request, while some remain restricted; there are others that cannot be found.

The files of the British Foreign Office were of particular significance. In compiling the first edition I had to ascertain facts and draw conclusions concerning British files from American sources, but the disclosure of the files of the British Foreign Office allowed not only use of new primary sources but also confirmation or disclosure of attitudes contrary to those found in American sources.

Also of great value are the files of the United States Office of Strategic Services in Washington, containing the secret reports concerning Austrian emigration into the principal countries of immigration—the United States, Great Britain, and, for the final year of the war, Sweden. Because of its late appearance on the scene, political emigration into Sweden clearly takes on a special position for the chronicler of the final year of the war, particularly in light of the newly discovered files on Austrian emigration.

New publications in the field of exile research have also been taken into account. One of the most welcome results of my first survey is that this area of investigation, which lay fallow for so long, has finally been plowed by historians. Some of the publications in this field that have since appeared have themselves opened new areas of emigration research.

I would like to thank the Federal Chancellor of Austria, Dr. Bruno Kreisky, for making available valuable records from his personal files. I wish to express my thanks to Dr. Herta Firnberg, Austrian Federal Minister, for her assistance. Special thanks are due to Dr. Ludwig Jedlicka, whose encouragement and expert knowledge of the period treated here have proven to be extraordinarily valuable.

Every attempt has been made to take relevant new publications into account. However, a survey of Austrian political emigration with the central object of an Austrian government in exile cannot consider all published materials, and especially not those for which the question of the Austrian government in exile is not a focal point.

New documentation was carefully incorporated as additions to the notes of the first edition. This did not necessitate changes in the sequence of textual indications to notes except for a few additional notes in Chapter XII.

F.G.

I

The Concept of Political Emigration from Austria, 1938–1945

An émigré is a person who has left his place of birth or residence or who was forced to leave his home for political or religious reasons. In a broad sense the name émigré applies to any emigrant, anyone who moves from a place and resettles elsewhere. Taken more narrowly, it applies to any person who has voluntarily or involuntarily left his place of birth or residence but who has not yet chosen, or has not been free to choose, a new place of residence. Among many other official pronouncements, a French law of May 2, 1938, defines a refugee as a "stranger" who is unable to leave French territory.

Emigration can be voluntary or involuntary. It can be permanent or temporary. The impetus behind it can be political, racial, or economic.

Emigration is considered racial in motivation if the émigré moves or is obliged to move because he belongs to a particular race. Economic dislocations, clearly, are the cause of economic emigration. And a political émigré leaves his place of birth or residence because of actual or potential persecution there.

A definition along these lines was used by the United States Department of State in anticipation of a stream of Austrian émigrés to the West, following the Anschluss of March 13, 1938. On March 23, the State Department summoned Joseph P. Kennedy, then United States Ambassador to the Court of St. James's, to a discussion of the situation.[1] Essentially the same definition of political emigration is given by the German legal expert Dr. Julius Weigert in his fundamental essay on the subject, "Soziologie der Emigration"["Sociology of Emigration"].[2]

The present study deals with the émigrés who did not accept their emigration as permanent, but rather considered it as the starting point in their struggle for the restoration of Austria and its liberation from foreign rule.[3] A further distinction must be made between "active" and "passive" political emigrants. The latter did not engage in political activity in their land of refuge. Active emigrants, on the other hand, aspired to the overthrow of the National Socialist regime, the reestablishment of their lost home country, and their own return.[4] But the active category also includes those émigrés whose activity, though including the goal of overturning the National Socialist regime and their own possible return, did not aim at the absolute restoration of the lost home within the previous borders.

In the present study the author restricts himself to the history of political emigration from Austria during the years 1938–1945, concentrating on the politically active emigrants.[5]

Early on, Dr. Paul Kris, a Paris lawyer and formerly an attorney in Vienna, established an *ad hoc* definition of Austrian emigration in the semimonthly publication *Österreichische Post* [*Austrian Post*], published in Paris. In a series of essays, "Zur Rechtstellung der Österreichischen Flüchtlinge in Frankreich" ["The Legal Status of Austrian Refugees in France"], he noted that the only émigrés who were to be considered refugees were those who had arrived in France after March 13, 1938—the day of the Anschluss—and who had identified themselves to the French authorities not as Germans, but as "Ex-Autrichiens." Of course Dr. Kris recognized that no legal definition as such existed.[6] But the label "Ex-Autrichien" made it possible for refugees to indicate that they personally did not recognize the Anschluss. The distinction became a tenet of French administrative practice.[7]

It is no accident that it was in France, the age-old sanctuary of European emigrants, that the special characteristics of political emigration between 1938 and 1945 were first identified.[8] During the short period between the Anschluss of March 13, 1938, and the Third Republic's armistice with Germany on June 22, 1940, France was the first country to set up a legal system that provided for a proper determination of the status of those émigrés entitled to political asylum. With the armistice, however, not only did France have to terminate the policy of granting asylum, but after her fall she was forced to hand over to the victorious Germans any person who might have requested political asylum.[9]

The Austriam émigrés who left their country after the Anschluss can be assigned to two groups. The first was united around the last two authoritarian governments, under Dollfuss and Schuschnigg, of the Christian corporative state of Austria from 1933 to 1938. This group also included the Austrian legitimists, as well as a great number of those who were persecuted because of the National Socialist regime's policy of hostility to their race. The second group encompassed those former Austrian Social Democrats who had emigrated after the February uprising of 1934, as well as the more radical group known as the Revolutionary Socialists.

In some respects, the second group were less harshly pressed politically than the first. During the period immediately after the Anschluss, the National Socialists still treated the former socialist workers with moderation. At the same time the numerous socialists of Jewish descent were, of course, excluded from this "benevolence"; they were persecuted as Jews, but not as socialists.[10]

The new rulers knew that the old Social Democratic party had long included in its own program an Anschluss of Austria to Germany. Though the party had abandoned this plank on April 12, 1933, after Hitler's assumption of power, it had been an essential aspect of its platform for fifteen years—that is, since the founding of the Republic of Austria in 1918. The National Socialists therefore believed that they, as those who brought about the actual Anschluss, could count on a certain amount of goodwill among Austrian workers. The more clever minds among them saw to it that the political terror was not immediately extended generally to the leaders and spokesmen of the socialist workers.[11] They also knew that the socialists had always doubted the viability of the Republic of Austria and that their views had influenced opinion on Austria in the English Labour party.

Although the Social Democratic party of Austria had clung to the idea of Anschluss for so many years, neither the National Socialists nor their opponents could ignore the fact that there was a split in the broader socialist masses, particularly evident after the right-wing attacks on the workers of February, 1934. Two of the workers' factions pursued their aims within the framework of the independent Austrian Republic and strove to preserve the state. The two groups were, first, the Revolutionary Socialists under the leadership of Joseph Buttinger (who used the pseudonym Gustav Richter), and, second, the spontaneous workers' movement of early March, 1938, which at that time strove to preserve Austria's independence in collaborating with the Schuschnigg government.[12]

While the Revolutionary Socialists, whose cadre and leadership were already known to the police of the Dollfuss regime, had good reason to leave the country, this urgency did not obtain for the great mass of former socialists except for those who were Jewish. It took a long time before the underground in Austria became aware of the difference between the relatively easygoing Schuschnigg police and the methods of the German Gestapo. But immediately after the Anschluss even the spontaneous workers' movement of March, 1938, was deliberately ignored, rather than prosecuted, by the National Socialists.[13] They wanted to create the impression that only a few communists in the workers' ranks had been prepared to cooperate with Schuschnigg. The question of whether politically prominent socialists who had not already emigrated after the February uprising of 1934 should now leave the country, however, was answered by the fact that many socialist leaders—for instance, the former Chancellor of the first Austrian Republic and later the first Chancellor and President of the second Republic of Austria, Dr. Karl Renner—declared publicly in advance of the plebiscite of April 10, 1938, that annexation by Germany was desirable. They felt that the issue should be affirmed by "yes" votes in the plebiscite (arranged by the National Socialists), arguing that historically annexation meant progress.[14] Many socialist leaders hoped, not without reason, that they would be able to avoid the dubious, risky life of the exile. If one simply renounced all political activity during the dictatorship, they reasoned, one could wait for politically better times.

One cannot speak of communist emigration into the Western countries, since the Austrian Communist party was politically meaningless because of its very small membership. After the communists went underground at the time of the Dollfuss regime, they continued to lag in membership behind the Revolutionary Socialists in spite of some gains after February, 1934. However, there was a small number of communist refugees. Once abroad, they either openly declared their allegiance to communism or tried to influence their respective countries of refuge to support the efforts of the Communist party, in particular to further the communist doctrine as propounded by the Soviets. In France and the United States, we cannot speak of communist emigration from Austria as such, since any open declaration of communism in those countries could have led to dire consequences for the émigrés. And in Great Britain, former Communist-party members and fellow travelers were reluctant to declare themselves as communists, though they could have done so. Only in Sweden, in the free world, was there an overt communist emigration from Austria.[15]

After the Anschluss, the National Socialists in power in Austria immediately adopted a harsh stance toward the followers of the overthrown Schuschnigg regime. Not only were they to be punished for their opposition to the Anschluss, they were also singled out as the presumed core of a subsequent movement for Austrian separatism. Prison, dismissal, and transfers were ordered for anyone from Federal Chancellor Schuschnigg down to the most lowly functionaries of the corporative state. Among prominent political figures, only Hans Rott and Guido Zernatto, a former high official of the Vaterländische Front [Patriotic Front], were allowed to emigrate—Rott because he had already endured five months of imprisonment. Followers of Schuschnigg must have been extremely frightened by the fate of prominent leaders of the Christian corporative state, such as the murder of the Minister of National Defense Zehner and the suicide of former Vice-Chancellor Fey.[16]

After the outbreak of war in 1939, political persecution turned also to the former leaders of the Social Democrats who were not Jewish.[17] Among the persecuted at this period, and even before, were Catholic emigrants from Germany who had fled to Austria after Hitler's seizure of power in 1933, as well as liberals and declared opponents of anti-Semitism. We need only mention Professor Dietrich von Hildebrand, Count Coudenhove-Kalergi, and Irene Harand as representatives of these movements. There was also a small Austrian Catholic emigration of various political shadings, mostly professional people who were welcomed as teachers and researchers.[18]

Little by little the conditions imposed on those who were persecuted and forced to emigrate became more inhumane, and as a result this group of émigrés no longer saw itself as political emigrants and Austrians, but simply as Jewish émigrés. They were so considered by Germany as well as by the various countries of transit and resettlement. The American *chargé d'affaires ad interim* in Vienna at the time of the Anschluss noted that racial persecution was the chief political weapon used by the National Socialists.[19]

As a result there was a clear imbalance between the far smaller number of those who were persecuted purely for political reasons as opponents of National Socialism and those former Austrian citizens who were forced to emigrate because they were Jewish. Among most Austrians there developed the distinct impression that the Anschluss had merely brought with it persecution of the Jewish population. It was seen as an imitation of the measures against German Jews taken as early as Hitler's seizure of power in 1933. The superficial observer, unacquainted with the facts, could easily be made to believe that, with the exception of the immediately affected Jewish citizens and the adherents of Schuschnigg's fallen government, the whole of the Austrian population had accepted the loss of Austrian independence and that a considerable portion of the population had even welcomed it. This view was further fostered when the Hitler regime immediately stamped as an "enemy of the German people" anyone who left his homeland for political reasons, thus making all emigration appear racial in motivation. It was widely thought that all emigration was Jewish, affecting individuals unconnected with the German body politic; that there was no Catholic, Protestant, or socialist emigration from Austria.[20]

It must be remembered that Jewish emigrants from Austria had not been politically active after 1934, since the collapse and the prohibition against the Social Democratic party had deprived them in effect of any institutional framework for political participation. After all, activity in the ranks of the Revolutionary Socialists remained limited to very few people of whatever ethnic background because of the underground structure of this organization. Further, as Buttinger reports, anti-Semitism had "increased enormously" among former Social Democrats.[21] Up to the banning of the Social Democratic party in February, 1934, Jewish citizens in Austria had found an arena for political activity within the framework of this party, since the Social Democrats constituted the only Austrian party—with the exception of the "bourgeois Democrats," who had not achieved a mandate since 1920—whose program assured equality to Jewish voters. Even the designation of the Christian Socialists as a specifically Christian party was unavoidably incompatible to those who thought of themselves as Jews, even if the party platform did not include any anti-Semitic program.

The Jewish population of Austria thus found itself without a political home after February, 1934. The Christian corporative state, which repeatedly attempted to justify its existence in the years 1934–1938 by reference to papal authority, was incompatible with Austria's Jewish population.

Admittedly, the day-to-day practices of the government and the administrative leaders in the Christian corporative state deliberately avoided discriminating against Austria's Jewish population as such. But the ideology of the Christian corporative state was not designed to attract or encourage the Jewish population to participate in the political process. During these years Austria opposed the official and nonofficial racial propaganda emanating from Germany. In the event that Austria were brought into conformity with Germany in the area of Jewish policy, German anti-Semitism would far exceed in intensity and pervasiveness any Catholic Austrian anti-Semitism. And the preservation of Austria's very independence was a primary goal of her authoritarian leadership in the years 1934–1938.[22] As an independent entity she had to prove that, although she was an authoritarian and Christian state, she could—as a democratic government—secure full equality to her Jewish citizens. In view of the inflexible posture of Hitler's Germany, the Austrian governments during 1934–1938 saw themselves compelled to apply willy-nilly special caution to one of the cardinal concerns of the National Socialist system—the Jewish question.[23]

Only within the framework of the Patriotic Front, a broad organization of all Austrian patriots which corresponded to the principles of the Christian corporative state, was political activity allowed, and this to everyone, including the Jewish population. Membership in the Patriotic Front, however, did not grant individual members access to meaningful participation in the political life of the country, as had been the case with both the old Social Democratic party and the many institutions connected with it. The Austrian Jews found just as narrow a field of activity in the defense formations and other government-sponsored leagues. For the majority of the Jewish population, therefore, there was no avenue of participation during these final years of Austrian independence except within the framework of Zionist organizations and in committees tailored only to persons of Jewish descent.

The governments of the corporative state found it fitting that the Jewish population of Austria should seek political participation only in such purely Jewish organizations. Those few representatives of Jewry appointed to the corporative bodies were either members or sympathetic followers of the Zionist movement in Austria. In no case were appointments made on the basis of prior participation in Austria's political parties or on the ground that the appointees had declared their foremost allegiance to Austria; the declaration of loyalty to Judaism as a national minority was held to be the decisive criterion.[24]

As a consequence of these policies, the Jewish émigrés from Austria, particularly the younger generation, were not at all accustomed to political participation. The older generation had had political experience only within the framework of the former Social Democratic party and now felt victimized by a hostile regime in the corporative state. As a result, the group that left the country for racial reasons saw itself as nonpolitical, unconnected with the ruling political groups in the final years of Austria. In addition, as a result of their overwhelming majority among the émigrés, they considered themselves as almost the only group affected by the annexation of Austria. Largely without ties to the ruling groups and of necessity nonparticipants in Austrian political life, once having left Austria, they hardly considered themselves Austrian-Jewish or Jewish-Austrian, but Jewish émigrés, pure and simple. Also, they were to keep their distance from the national policies of the host countries and pursue politics relating only to Jewish community affairs. In their host countries, the Jewish émigrés had as their objective carving out a new existence and being integrated in the economic and civic life of the countries of refuge.[25] Ties to their homeland seemed permanently severed, even if leading statesmen postulated a return to the country, from which they had been dispersed, as one of the objectives of the war.[26]

Thrown back on their own, and in many cases made conscious of their Jewishness with particular intensity through persecution, the émigrés found themselves searching for new human ties that would outlast even the trauma of Hitler's persecution. Stateless and often practically outlawed, the Jews discovered that they could realize their ancestral heritage only in the Zionist movement, which had no political interest in resettling Jews in their countries of origin after the fall of Hitler. The Zionists, of course, were promoting Jewish emigration to what was then Palestine.

The Jewish press in the host countries was well disposed toward Zionism. It did not show the slightest interest in maintaining old political ties, no matter what new forms these might take, between the new immigrants and their countries of origin. When this press took account of the origin of the German-speaking immigrants, it did so principally in order to satisfy their cultural and psychological needs. There was concern to foster the feeling of fellowship among immigrants coming from the same region, and the press emphasized the significance of German language and culture. Only occasionally did Jewish writers focus on the special characteristics of the Austrian émigrés as Austrians.[27]

Clearly, then, neither the Jewish émigrés from Austria nor their Zionist supporters wished to have any part in the objectives of political emigration. Only isolated individuals, acting on sentimental motives or expecting economic advantage, were prepared to collaborate with the political émigrés. As far as Jews from Austria were concerned, the restoration of the Republic of Austria, or its membership in a democratic Germany, or a political alliance of the successor states, were not problems crucial enough to move them to adopt a positive or negative position. Their expectations of the future were: integration into the country of refuge and consciousness of their origins and futures as Jews.[28]

From Austria's geographic situation at the center of Europe, the flood of refugees spilled first into the neighboring countries of Czechoslovakia and Switzerland and then into the easily accessible France, Belgium, and Holland, whose democratic forms of government seemed to offer asylum. A significant number of refugees, though, turned to Italy, Hungary, and Yugoslavia, countries under either fascist or authoritarian rule.

Czechoslovakia, however, was soon to fall victim to Germany's territorial amibitions. With the Munich agreement concerning the cession of the Sudentenland in September, 1938, the country ceased to serve as an asylum. This change had been predicted by the European political press and by the Austrian socialist émigrés of 1934 then residing in Czechoslovakia, and they had transferred their activities to Paris in good time.[29] After the fall of Czechoslovakia in March, 1939, the Austrian émigrés still there shared the fate of the native Czechs who were persecuted by the National Socialist regime.

Neighboring Switzerland feared being engulfed by the migrations, and the Swiss took early measures to stem the dreaded inundation of refugees by stiffening their requirements for residence. It is well known that Switzerland instituted a system of labor camps for the refugees. However, Switzerland retained in principle the status of asylum when the country was completely encircled by the Axis powers after the French armistice in June, 1940. After the Germans occupied all of France in November, 1942, Switzerland took in a considerable number of the émigrés who had previously lived in the unoccupied zone of France.

Belgium and Holland were also sought after as countries of refuge and transit, but the refugees in these countries did not escape the German invasion of May 10, 1940. The Austrian émigrés in Belgium were sent to France as enemy aliens and were placed in French internment camps. Because of the brief period of Dutch resistance and the sudden nature of the German invasion, the refugees in Holland were taken by surprise and could not be moved to an allied country, since Belgium was attacked at the same time and France was accessible only by way of Belgium.[30]

The nearby countries of Italy, Hungary, and Yugoslavia also offered sanctuary to the refugees streaming in from Austria, although Italy was under a fascist government, Hungary pursued an anti-Semitic policy, and Yugoslavia's authoritarian government was friendly to Germany. But to differing degrees these countries provided effective asylum. The anti-Semitic laws introduced by Mussolini's government in 1938, directed against alien Jews, were only occasionally enforced or were deliberately circumvented. Italy's population was sympathetic to the refugees, and even Fascist party members had no real enthusiasm for these emergency laws. To the end of the war, Italy remained an important shelter for Austrian refugees. After Italy's entry into the war, a majority of the Austrian refugees were either moved to internment camps or were obliged to remain in the places where they had first settled. But, in spite of administering harsh treatment, Italy was able to save the lives of many refugees.

Hungary also took in a significant number of Austrian refugees, although sanctuary there effectively ceased after the German occupation of the country in March, 1944; thereafter the Austrians were forced to share the fate of all those who were persecuted by the National Socialists in Hungary. Until the outbreak of hostilities with Germany on April 6, 1941, Yugoslavia was a significant country of asylum for refugees from Austria, even though a number of the emigrants there were interned.

The most sought-after country of refuge in Europe was France, the age-old antagonist of the German Reich. The Austrian refugees saw France as the traditional champion of human rights.

Because of its location, Great Britain was not easily accessible to the refugees. Nonetheless, by generously issuing entry permits, Britain enabled the salvation of very many. When, after the armistice of 1940, France ceased to be a country of asylum, Great Britain turned out to be the principal fulcrum of political emigration in Europe.

The Scandinavian countries, especially neutral Sweden, became valuable countries of refuge for a number of émigrés, most of them of socialist orientation. While Denmark and Norway came under German occupation in April,

1940, Sweden remained unharmed and managed to shelter Austrian refugees throughout the war.[31]

Spain and Portugal did not become significant countries of transit until after the fall of France in June, 1940, but they were important way stations during much of the war, and in a number of individual cases they became countries of asylum as well. Bulgaria, Romania, and Greece mattered only as countries of transit for those refugees on their way to settling in Turkey or Palestine. Romania was especially unsuitable for Jewish refugees because Hitler's racial persecution was shortly to be implemented there in its home-grown version.

Russia was not considered a country of shelter by noncommunist refugees. Even before the Anschluss it was known in Austria that a number of socialist refugees who had gone to Russia after the defeat of the February uprising of 1934 had fallen victim to the Stalinist terror of those years.[32] The Soviet Union did, however, become the country of refuge for a number of refugees of communist orientation. During the war in Russia and after the war in Austria, these refugees—among them the former Social Democratic party member Ernst Fischer—were to play a significant role.[33]

Among the permanent countries of immigration were the United States, Canada, Australia, and to a lesser degree the Union of South Africa, Kenya, and other British dominions such as India. The South American states and some of the Central American and Caribbean countries, especially the Dominican Republic, took in large numbers of refugees.

The Chinese seaport of Shanghai turned out to be a completely unexpected place of refuge for a broad stratum of Austrian Jewish émigrés. As persecution grew more severe and consequently emigration more urgent, this city was the only accessible goal for many. In spite of the well-known and frequently described difficulties emigrants had to face in Shanghai, the city remained a place of refuge even during the war. Many Austrian émigrés were confined in the infamous Shanghai ghetto in 1943, but a majority of them lived to see the dissolution of the ghetto after the Allied victory.

Immigration to the British Mandate of Palestine also constitutes a special case. Here immigration was exclusively Jewish, and admission, sometimes legal, sometimes illegal, was in the hands of Jewish organizations, especially the Zionists. We can therefore speak of political emigration to Palestine only in the broad sense, and no active Austrian political emigration is to be looked for here. Nevertheless, a number of the Jewish immigrants continued to think of themselves as Austrian refugees and took as their ultimate objective a return to a liberated Austria.

If we look at the countries through which the political active emigration passed (or where they stayed), we see that France, the United States, Great Britain, and in the last year also Sweden, provided the principal arenas for their activities. Political committees emerged also in all South American and a number of Central American countries, but large-scale success was possible for the émigrés only in the Atlantic democracies. We need only to remember that during the First World War, Czechoslovak and Yugoslav political emigrants who worked for the defeat of the central powers and for the creation of independent nations in Eastern Europe actually did their work in these same three countries. Even then, the extraordinarily skillful Czechoslovak emigrants realized where the center of their activity should be.

II
Austrian Political Emigration in France

1. Before the outbreak of war

The Austrian Anschluss confronted France with a fait accompli. During the entire period between the world wars, France had viewed the independence of the Austrian Republic as a pillar of her own security; as late as 1931 she prevented the attempted customs union between Austria and the German Reich. Invoking a provision of the peace treaty of St.-Germain, she opposed all movement for an Anschluss. Several factors contributed to France's posture *vis à vis* the Austrian émigrés after 1938: the deep, often unconscious uneasiness about a development (the Anschluss) that countered France's own longstanding view of her security in Europe; the desire to maintain her traditional role as the leading country of political asylum in Europe; the efforts of influential French circles to avoid conflict with a Germany that was growing increasingly powerful; and last but not least, the fear of being flooded with refugees, especially those of Jewish descent.[1] French opinion simultaneously favored and opposed free admission of refugees, and the course of events reflected this contradiction.

Officially France declared her willingness to remain a country of asylum,[2] but the French government found good reason to set legal limits on the influx of refugees. Of the roughly seven thousand refugees from Austria who arrived in France before the end of 1938, less than a thousand had immigrated through regular channels.[3]

France shared borders with Germany, Belgium, Switzerland, and Italy, all countries providing refugees from the Greater German area with ways to reach France. With so many governments involved, it was hard to restrict refugees without passports and visas from coming into France. This problem was very clearly described by the French Minister of the Interior Albert Sarraut in a speech delivered to police officials at the Sorbonne in January, 1939.[4]

Other countries, including the United States, also shared the fear of being inundated by waves of refugees. On March 23, 1938, shortly after the Anschluss, the American Secretary of State, Cordell Hull, sent a telegram to Joseph P. Kennedy in London, in which he suggested the formation of a committee with members from various countries to regulate the emigration of political refugees from Austria and Germany. There is little doubt that in using the term "political refugees" the American communication was meant to include racially persecuted refugees. But President Roosevelt, in his press conference of March 25, 1938, denied this interpretation and referred to the American tradition of harboring political refugees.[5] In any event, after the Anschluss a stream of refugees, not only from Greater Germany but also from the neighboring regions, was bound to begin. Concern about this movement doubtless played a part in policy formulation not only in France but the United States as well.

Observers familiar with the situation, such as the former Austrian Chancellor Schuschnigg or the correspondents of the *New York Times,* had understood long before the Anschluss that after the fall of Austria, Czechoslovakia would be the next danger point in Hitler's program of expansion. The French deputy Ernest Pezet was warned by the Austrian chancellor as early as July 1937:

> Tell President [Edvard] Beneš that, contrary to the opinion prevailing in Prague, it is not Czechoslovakia that protects Austria, but Austria that shields its neighbors. If our country should lose its freedom, Czechoslovakia would be in jeopardy within a year at most.[6]

This prophecy came true.

It can be said that the Anschluss and the passive stance of members of the League of Nations, when confronted with a member state's being eliminated by the unilateral action of a neighboring state, brought about a worldwide upheaval in the political consciousness of the times. The effects on France were to become clear all too soon. The law of May 2, 1938, concerning emigration (including Austrian political emigration) became the basis of French policy.[7] The introductory report on this law, which was sent to the president of the French Republic, maintains the concept of asylum in principle and establishes it as the guideline for the law.[8]

The concept of asylum enabled the politically active emigrants to pursue their aims on French soil. The French idea of asylum had always allowed the active political participation of refugees to the extent that their activities coincided with France's interests. This had been true in the period 1815–1848 and at the time of Napoleon III, when Italian refugees from the parts of the peninsula that were still smarting under foreign rule strove to attain Italy's independence by working on French soil; it was also the case during the First World War, when political émigrés of Slavic nationalities, especially the Czechs, pursued their political objectives in France.[9]

The former press attaché of the Austrian embassy in Paris, Dr. Martin Fuchs, was eager to create political benefits for the Austrian emigrants by capitalizing on the extraordinary divisions in French public opinion. The French saw the Anschluss as a severe diplomatic setback and were attempting to alleviate its consequences. Dr. Fuchs tried first to win for the Austrians a standing separate from that of the other German émigrés. Shortly after the Anschluss, and in spite of the French government's official recognition of that development, it was established that any Austrian refugees who had entered France on old Austrian or German passports and who were willing to renounce the protection due from the German consulates to German nationals abroad, could now call themselves former Austrians. Thus, by making a declaration to the French authorities, a refugee who had been an Austrian citizen before 1938 could declare himself an "Ex-Autrichien." He would hand his passport over to the French authorities, thereby relinquishing its acceptance, extension, or renewal by the German authorities abroad. In effect, any Austrian who declared himself an Ex-Autrichien was renouncing, at least for himself, the constitutional consequences of the Anschluss, no matter how the legal consequences of such a declaration were to be judged.[10] With this provision, the first step was taken toward giving recognition to the entire Austrian emigration as being a political emigration, as distinct from the general German emigration.[11]

While the French government gave not only *de facto* but also *de jure* recognition to the Anschluss, the administrative practices of the country allowed individual former Austrians to refuse to recognize the change in citizenship that the Anschluss had created. Instead, they were free to choose, in effect, citizenship in a nonexistent state. The Ex-Autrichiens were listed separately from the Germans both in their police dossiers and in their identification cards; and, in spite of actual statelessness, they were not marked as stateless persons.

Though this anomalous position was different from the status accorded German émigrés, it was not elaborated upon, nor were the consequences of statelessness specifically taken into account by the French administration. Developments took a contrary course. Clearly many contributors to French public opinion were not well disposed toward the refugees, and this tendency increased. But the overrriding motive here was a growing concern about the sentiments of the German Reich, especially after the Munich agreement of September 30, 1938, and the desire to avoid conflict with a powerful neighbor over a matter of principle. Open support for a group of refugees, which could hardly be agreeable to Germany, had to be avoided by French agencies, since at this particular time the policy of appeasement reached its climax. Always underlying these considerations was the growing fear of inundation by refugees from countries occupied or menaced by Germany and a growing, general sense of alienation and discontent in public opinion, which could be viewed as a symptom of emerging xenophobia. In spite of its commitment to asylum, there existed in France also a pervasive distrust of all foreigners.

Aside from the designation Ex-Autrichien, the Austrian émigrés in France were legally treated just like the other stateless aliens with rights of asylum. With the outbreak of war, they were accorded the status of enemy aliens along with the other foreigners from Germany and those parts of Greater Germany with a German-speaking population.

The decree of May 2, 1938, of the French Ministry of the Interior set into motion a series of legal regulations affecting refugee existence. The trend toward more detailed control of refugee life continued with the decrees of May 14 and June 17, 1938. The situation of the refugees worsened as each law was passed.[12]

A decree of January 21, 1939, also from the French Ministry of the Interior, established a specific detention center for all aliens subject to the law of

May 2, 1938. This legal resolution was to have far-reaching consequences in wartime—and it was applicable to refugees from Austria.[13] Thus, from a strictly legal standpoint, Austrian political emigration shared the fate of the entire Austrian emigration.

But, although they were covered by these decrees, the Austrian political emigrants were not impeded in their movements and activities. Even for active political refugees, France continued to remain the country of asylum as before, if only in principle. The introductory report to the fundamental law of May 2, 1938, which aimed at regulating the expected waves of refugees, including Austrian émigrés, nevertheless spoke sympathetically of the "persecuted idea and ideal."[14] A former minister of the last Schuschnigg government, Hans Rott, entered France with a foreign, non-German passport and was nevertheless immediately granted a residence permit; a nonpolitical refugee would have had to pay dearly for entering with false papers. None of the leading political refugees were confined, nor was political activity forbidden. Thus, increasingly harsh official rulings referring to the duties of those entitled to rights of asylum were not applied to the leaders of the active political emigration. When, after the outbreak of war with Germany on September 3, 1939, there was initial hesitation, the Austrian refugees almost without exception were interned in camps as enemy aliens. However, most of the leading personalities of the Austrian political emigration—such as Federal Minister Hans Rott and the socialist leaders Julius Deutsch, Oskar Pollak, and Karl Hans Sailer—retained their freedom. They were permitted not only to continue their political activities but did so with the encouragement of the French ruling powers.[15]

Nor did the French authorities place any obstacles in the path of the organizations founded after the Anschluss to further Austrian interests, either for political gains or as relief organizations for Austrian refugees. April, 1938, saw the establishment of a semiofficial relief organization for Austrian refugees, named Entre-Aide Autrichien.[16] The Accueil français aux Autrichiens was founded in Paris with the participation of the Catholic writer François Mauriac. The Ligue Autrichienne, 30 rue St.-Augustin, Paris, and the Fédération des Émigrés provenant de l'Autriche were founded in Paris in May, 1938.[17] The office of the Austrian socialists abroad moved from Brno (Czechoslovakia) to Paris and settled down at 20, rue de Trudaine.[18] As of April 3, 1939, there was also a special committee for Austrian refugees who pursued intellectual professions.[19]

From the beginning of the emigration into France, two lines of policy crystallized among the Austrian political emigrants. They differed on the question of whether the independence of the Republic of Austria, as it had existed before the Anschluss, should be reestablished, or if another solution should be found. The crucial point here was whether Austria was to remain part of the German Reich, should Germany be freed of National Socialist rule.

A third political line was pursued by Otto von Hapsburg. But this direction—discussed below—could not be considered an emigrants' policy aimed solely at the restoration of an independent Austria, although the restoration of Austria was one of its objectives.

The ideological quarrel began with a resolution drawn up by the Austrian socialists abroad, meeting in Brussels in April, 1938. An executive committee composed of Otto Bauer, Friedrich Adler, Otto Leichter, Oskar Pollak, Karl Czernetz, and Manfred Ackermann had been established in the Belgian capital, and this group considered itself authorized to guide foreign socialist policy because of an "internal mandate" from illegal groups in occupied Austria. Thanks to an essay, published in the Parisian newspaper *Der Sozialistische Kampf* [*The Socialist Struggle*] on June 2, 1938, by the leading Austrian socialist theoretician Otto Bauer, the principles of this resolution were made public. The essay "Nach der Annexion" ["After the Annexation"], was to have grave consequences for the policy of the Austrian political emigrants for seven years, not only in France but also in Great Britain, the United States, and other countries of immigration. Otto Bauer died soon after in Paris, but in this essay the longtime leader of Austrian Social Democracy plainly and clearly laid down the basic belief that the liberation of Austria could only come about through an All-German revolution.[20] In the context of Bauer's influential formulation, anyone holding a brief for the restoration of Austria—by itself—was a reactionary.[21]

Such a thoroughgoing policy of necessity led to the rejection of all other possibilities, and it was decisive in dividing the Austrian émigrés into two groups on the issue of restoring the Austrian Republic.[22] But Otto Bauer's solution was expected to result only from the efforts of Austrian workers as part of an All-German revolution; it would not come from revolutionary activity by other strata of the population. This meant, both in France and in other countries that admitted the émigrés, that the socialists abroad rejected any overt revolutionary activity by their own efforts or in conjunction with non-socialist forces, accepting instead a passive stance of waiting for the hoped-for All-German revolution. This basic principle of the Austrian socialists abroad and the passivity resulting from it were further developed by Joseph Buttinger, the leader of the Revolutionary Socialists, who was active in the office of the Austrian socialists in Paris. It was his idea that socialist participation in émigré politics was impossible and that all political activity by the socialist émigrés was to be abandoned.[23] It followed that if the socialists in exile decided to leave all decisions to the native population in the Greater German Reich, then the only active political task that remained to the émigrés was to prevent the restoration of Austria's independence, even if this aim could not be clearly spelled out during wartime.

On the other side stood those groups that aimed for the restoration of an independent Austria. Their leading representative in France was Hans Rott, who had arrived in Paris after months of imprisonment. He called for the unification of all political émigrés, including the Austrian socialists abroad, as the basis for the recognition of an Austrian government in exile. It will be remembered that Rott was one of two representatives appointed by Schuschnigg to negotiate with the workers in March, 1938. In France, the Ligue Autrichienne was particularly active in pursuit of the goal of Austrian independence. The former Viennese art dealer and art connoisseur Dr. Otto Kallir made possible the publication in Paris of the semimonthly *Österreichische Post*. Published from December, 1938, to September, 1939, it became the organ of the faction of political émigrés within the Ligue Autrichienne.[24]

The concern of Austrians abroad, especially the Austrian émigrés, focused chiefly on the areas of welfare, legal aid, procurement of residence permits, and counsel in continued migration. Since the leading members of the Ligue Autrichienne understood clearly that the demand of the French government for unification of all Austrian political factions was perhaps the crucial point and even a precondition for the recognition of an Austrian government in exile, the Ligue Autrichienne and the *Österreichische Post* engaged in vigorous actions urging a unified front of all Austrians. In this endeavor they profited from the Czech experiences during the First World War. The Czechs had learned that collaboration among all important political factions was a precondition for a representative government in exile.[25] Hans Rott was to prove himself an ardent champion of an Austrian unified front. That he never wavered in this conviction is shown by his narrative complied at the end of the war, which relates his struggle for the unified front of all Austrian party factions.[26]

One of the outstanding personalities of exile politics in France was Otto von Hapsburg; shortly before the Anschluss he wrote to Chancellor Schuschnigg demanding the cession of the chancellorship—a demand Schuschnigg rejected.[27] Without ever taking the limelight, Otto von Hapsburg was in constant contact with French government agencies and with those factions of political émigrés working toward the restoration of Austria's independence, especially the Ligue Autrichienne. After the Anschluss, which occurred without any resistance by France, the subsequent collapse of the French system of alliances through the Munich agreement of September, 1938, and the transformation of the rest of Czechoslovakia into a German protectorate in March, 1939, it is not surprising that the views and suggestions of a representative of the house of Hapsburg were found worthy of consideration by French statesmen.

Otto von Hapsburg—for whose capture an arrest warrant was issued by the National Socialists—was considered a reliable opponent of the prevailing state of affairs. He was seen as the possible unifier of a constellation of states that might protect France's security more effectively than the alliance with the Little Entente, which had lasted a mere twenty years. It did not escape notice that Schuschnigg considered the monarchist movement the last trump card in the struggle for the independence of an autonomous Austria, even if it were never played. There were reports that in the final months before Austria's fall, sentiment for the monarchist movement had expanded considerably, even among wider circles of workers, and that at the end a monarchist coup d'état had been discussed.[28]

William C. Bullitt, the American ambassador in Paris, also took a lively interest in Otto's efforts. A personal letter from the ambassador to President Roosevelt, dated September 5, 1939, makes clear the close contact between the ambassador and the Hapsburg heir.[29] In a telegram of November 14, 1939, to the United States Department of State, Bullitt reported advising Otto to stand above party politics, since there was a possibility that after the war he might head a government not only of the Austrians, but also the Hungarians, the Czechs, and possibly even the Poles.[30]

We can conclude that the Austrian political emigrants in France consisted of two broad groups whose objectives were in opposition—one united around the Ligue Autrichienne and the other centered on the agency of the Austrian socialists. As a political power associated with the group of the Ligue Autrichienne, Otto von Hapsburg pursued his own objectives. The other organizations mentioned in this chapter primarily served as relief agencies for the striving Austrian refugees, and their sympathies insofar as they concerned the restoration of Austrian independence lay generally with the Ligue Autrichienne.

2. From the outbreak of war on September 3, 1939, to France's armistice on June 22, 1940

The outbreak of war opened a new and crucial chapter for all the Austrian émigrés in France. During the months preceding France's declaration of war, when it became clear that war against National Socialist Germany was inevitable, French legislation began to exercise administrative curbs on the refugees' right to asylum. They also began to stress police surveillance of refugee activities. A French governmental decree of January 21, 1939, created the concept of the "Centre spécial de Rassemblement," based on the alien legislation of May 2, 1938; the order furnished a legal basis for detaining in internment camps refugees entitled to asylum. It was made clear to the refugees that in case of war they could expect to be interned.

On August 26, 1939, a delegation of refugees called on the Minister of the Interior: The group consisted of Paul Hertz, former secretary of the socialist faction of the German Reichstag; the French member of parliament Jules Moch; the German political émigré Willi Münzenberg; and the Austrian socialist Julius Deutsch. The delegation learned that provisions had been made for general internment of the émigrés in case of war. The planned measures turned out to be more stringent than those actually carried out a few weeks later.[31]

Following the outbreak of war, internment was ordered for large numbers of Austrians living abroad, including those who were long-time residents of France and married to French citizens. Persons up to the age of sixty-five were subject to internment. Though an official declaration was issued on September 16, 1939, stating that these internment measures were only temporary, they brought unexpected hardship and economic difficulties to groups of persons who were either completely integrated into French life or who believed that they could rely on their right to asylum.[32]

When, after the outbreak of war, public placards called on citizens of the German Reich, including those entitled to the right of asylum, to assemble "voluntarily" for their internment in the camps de rassemblements, the Ex-Autrichiens were uncertain whether they too were affected by these measures. They had renounced all connections with the German Reich, specifically in terms of seeking protection from that government. In fact, some Parisian police commissariats had turned away Ex-Autrichiens who had reported for internment; the argument given was that these persons were not to be considered denizens of Greater Germany. Other commissariats interpreted the instructions to mean that Ex-Autrichiens were to be interned along with other refugees. This ambiguity was quickly resolved by the ruling that Ex-Autrichiens were indeed subject to the internment decree. Such an extended application of internment showed that at this critical time the decision not to recognize Austria's annexation by Germany had no legal effect on the Austrian refugees' status as enemy aliens. The internment decree equated former Austrians with German citizens and refugees from Germany.

Equating the Ex-Autrichiens with aliens and refugees from Germany meant that people were interned who legally and ideologically should have been regarded as stateless. Stateless persons in France were not interned at the outbreak of the war; but, according to French decrees of asylum, they were obligated to serve in the French armed forces. The Ex-Autrichiens had handed their passports over to the French police authorities and had voluntarily forfeited protection by Germany, and this declaration had been accepted by French officials. The princpal difference between the Ex-Autrichiens and other German citizens residing on French soil or refugees with German passports was that the Ex-Autrichiens had for the most part entered the country with passports issued by Austria before the Anschluss and were now considered to be German citizens only because of Germany's annexation of Austria. Interning the Ex-Autrichiens represented not only a violation of the right of asylum but also a breach of the special position guaranteed to the Austrian refugees by the French government.

From the standpoint of French policy, which aimed at blocking the National Socialists' plans for conquest, the interning of all émigrés from Germany, but especially the interning of the Ex-Autrichiens, was politically one of the many serious mistakes made by France at the beginning of the war. Indiscriminate interning of virtually all émigrés caused the collapse of the right of asylum, and the French authorities no longer profited from the support of the overt opponents of National Socialist Germany. Paul Hertz made this clear in an essay of January 5, 1940. He spoke for all émigrés when he wrote: "I reject the underlying assumption—which is both false and defaming to all refugees—by which the German and Austrian refugees are treated, not as Hitler's victims, but as his allies."

Paul Hertz, a German Social Democrat, was, of course, not concerned with the special problem of the Austrian émigrés. The more specific question therefore remained why France took recourse to these general internment measures and why, through internment of the Ex-Autrichiens, she voided the special position that had been offered these refugees. At the same time, France was breaking her promise to treat the former Austrians as distinctly different from the Germans. These new regulations were early signs of French defeatism. Internment exemplified the political attitude of influential segments of French society who, accepting at Munich the dissolution of Czechoslovakia, were eager to avoid war with the German Reich and who pursued the goal of collaboration with Germany. An important detail supporting this view is the provision that no émigré, especially no Ex-Autrichien, was to be admitted to military service against Germany, even if he volunteered.

It can be convincingly shown that if the French government had continued the policy of classifying Austrian émigrés as Ex-Autrichiens, it could easily have pursued the practice of the Entente powers during the First World War. Then, soldiers of Czech nationality were taken from prisoner-of-war camps and called up for military service against their former homeland, although these soldiers not only held citizenship in an enemy nation, but had also participated in armed warfare against the Entente powers. The Ex-Autrichiens, on the contrary, neither ideologically nor legally remained citizens of an enemy nation, nor had they ever offered armed opposition to France. It would have been far simpler to enlist the Ex-Autrichiens against the German Reich.

The regulation that former Austrians who had volunteered for the armed services were not to be enlisted against Germany showed that the French wanted to avoid making the war against National Socialist Germany an ideological struggle, with the possibility of political actions that might jeopardize an early peace. Even after the beginning of the war, a defeatist strain in French politics never abandoned the hope of arriving at a settlement with Germany. The Ex-Autrichiens were given the opportunity of serving France only in the French Foreign Legion in Africa. Of course a majority of the refugees were interested in the struggle against National Socialist Germany but had little commitment to the Foreign Legion's purpose of preserving French interests in Africa and Indochina; this practice shows that French military policy intentionally tried to eliminate any political motivation in its conduct of the war. In particular, they tried not to stress either the particular situation of the Ex-Autrichiens or the question of Austria's restoration.

Release from the internment camps was possible under three conditions: volunteering for the Foreign Legion, emigration overseas, or performing forced labor as a prestataire or bondsman. In view of these choices, it is hard to believe that France looked upon the war with National Socialist Germany as an ideological struggle. Instead the French saw it as merely the action of one country that threatened to jeopardize the interests of another. By interning the Austrians, France deliberately forfeited the opportunity of conducting war against Germany with the aim of liberating Austria from Germany's forced rule and of availing herself legally of the help of the émigrés. It was not the same France that, in 1859, had made war against the old Austrian monarchy with the intent of revolutionizing Hungary and Croatia. France did not even follow her own example from the First World War, which had been extremely successful. Then, even tsarist Russia had managed to separate the Slavic prisoners of war from the German- or Hungarian-speaking prisoners of the old Austro-Hungarian monarchy in order to reach the enemy's vulnerable spots.

France renounced all these posssibilities in 1939. The native Austrian population, called up for war duty in the Greater German Reich, was informed by the German propaganda machine that Austrians in France were treated as enemy aliens, no differently from citizens of the Reich. The only possible conclusion to be drawn from this was that by waging war, France wished to check Germany's threatening superiority but never intended to annul the Anschluss as one of its objectives. On November 23, 1939, Vladimir d'Ormesson, writing in the Parisian daily, *Le Figaro,* called his countrymen's attention to these German propaganda efforts, stressing the paradoxical situation of the interned Austrian refugees.

How did the political émigrés react to this problem? In this first year of the Second World War, what did the political émigrés do for all the emigrants from Austria who had been driven to France by a similar fate? What conclusions did they draw from their common fate?

While so many of the Austrian émigrés were placed in camps after the outbreak of war, the recognized leaders of the active Austrian political emigrants—such as Hans Rott, Julius Deutsch, Oskar Pollak, and Karl Hans Sailer—were not interned.[33] And it was not long before all the rest of the émigrés who had played an active role in the political emigration were released.[34] Still other internees, too, were gradually released,[35] although the overwhelming majority were forced to remain in the camps.

If we consider the successful political work performed by the Czech emigrants in France during the First World War, surely we can say that the Austrian political émigrés missed a unique opportunity to perform important political work for their own aims among the camp internees. The only requirement would have been to give up privileges and advantages temporarily and to volunteer for internment. As principals among equals, the political émigrés would have had the opportunity to win adherents to their cause, especially to the creation of an Austrian troops unit or legion. If such leading political personalities as Hans Rott and Julius Deutsch had shared with the emigrants the suffering of internment, then public opinion in France and other Allied nations might have recognized the total absurdity of a policy that treated Austrians as German citizens. Furthermore, in this way the representatives of political emigration would have demonstrated that they felt a common bond with their fellow citizens. But any camp internee who read in the French newspapers that Otto von Hapsburg was making social advances to Edouard Herriot, the French Prime Minister, could have had no doubt about the imposed distinction.

It can justifiably be claimed that even Otto von Hapsburg could have far better advanced his political objectives by voluntary internment than through all his efforts to gain the goodwill of French political figures. The internment camps of the émigrés and the camps of Austrian prisoners of war offered a natural sounding board such as was never again to be found in the history of Austrian political emigration. Not only did the émigrés furnish a captive audience, but also the prospect of recruiting men in their prime. In France, where at the beginning of the war attempts were under way to create an Austrian political representation abroad, the time was indeed favorable. Viewed from the standpoint of Otto's efforts, many of the internees still retained a vivid memory of the uncompromising attitude of the Austrian monarchists in the final years of the National Socialist onslaught.[36] Chances for winning over a sizable number of adherents to some form of pro-Austrian activism were especially favorable in France, since the majority of the internees had to remain here, lacking any opportunity for further emigration.

The argument also applies to the other leading political émigrés—principally to Hans Rott—for whom the objectives of creating an Austrian representation abroad and an Austrian fighting unit were important programmatic items close to their hearts. Even a short period of internment, even voluntary internment, would at least have been of symbolic value. The incomprehensible avoidance by all active and committed factions of the Austrian émigrés of sharing the fate of the interned masses; the lack of understanding in failing to draw out the common objectives throughout the spectrum of political emigres; the division of the émigrés into one groups whose precious freedom was left to them or restored after a brief period, and another, larger group of people who were interned for an indefinite time—all these considerations evoke the question: Why was this unique opportunity overlooked or, if it was recognized, not made use of?

Many believe that anti-Semitism was involved here.[37] We cannot completely reject this possibility. At a time that was critical for the restoration of Austria, the consequence of this destructive attitude has to be compared unfavorably with the Czech emigration. The latter, under the leadership of Beneš and Jan Masaryk, advanced a consciously pro-Semitic policy and assured total equality to the Jews in Czechoslovakia in the event of the country's liberation.[38]

The Austrian socialists abroad were not interested in winning over the interned Austrians to their political goals, but viewed internment only as a humanitarian problem and did not perceive any political tasks for the broader circles of the nonpolitical émigrés. Rather, they were eager to be distinguished from the nonpolitical, racial émigrés. While Julius Deutsch, the socialists' spokesman, still recognized an obligation to offer their services to France, the host country, such generosity was attributed to vanity by another leader of the foreign agency, Joseph Buttinger.[39] Buttinger was totally unwilling to consider any kind of political activity during emigration. He left France soon after his release from the internment camp; only the sudden outbreak of war had delayed his planned departure.

Though the Austrian socialist émigrés worked for the release of individual refugees, especially internees who were close to them, the group showed no interest in winning release for all of those who had been detained. Nor was there any connecting link between the émigrés who aimed at creating a political representation with the large mass of internees who, although listed as Ex-Autrichiens, were treated as enemy aliens. The Austrian political émigrés drew no political conclusions from the internment of the Ex-Autrichiens, which was bound to be damaging to their own aims and therefore should have been unacceptable to them. Such an attitude is all the less comprehensible since shortly before the outbreak of war, at an open mass meeting in Paris, the Ligue Autrichienne had called upon the internees to take up the struggle for Austrian independence.[40] Not the slightest public move was undertaken by the Ligue Autrichienne or any other of the groups collaborating with it in favor of the internees. Also, no one acknowledged openly that internment of the Ex-Autrichiens was incompatible with the negotiations, carried on at the same time, toward establishing an Austrian political representation abroad. These negotiations were admittedly carried on in a vacuum, although the groups around the Ligue Autrichienne and Hans Rott did their utmost to achieve the recognition of an Austrian representation abroad.

Until the day of the Anschluss, Austria's independence had been an axiom for every French party. None of them would have characterized the Anschluss as anything but damaging to France's political position in Central Europe. The consequences were made clear to every politically minded Frenchman when, barely seven months later, the Anschluss was followed by the separation of the Sudetenland from Czechoslovakia and—almost a year later to the day, in March, 1939—by the fall of the rest of Czechoslovakia and the dissolution of the French system of alliances in Central Europe.

By the time war broke out, it had become clear to the French leaders that if the restoration of Austria were to be achieved, the first step would be the creation of an Austrian representative agency abroad or a government in exile, along with an Austrian troop unit.

Immediately after the beginning of the war the Conseil National Autrichien was established. Hans Rott was its president, Karl Hartl its secretary, and Martin Fuchs secretary for foreign and press relations. The French government looked with favor on the efforts of the organization to gain recognition from the Allies.

The United Kingdom, however, waited to see what would happen, an attitude that subsequently changed into a negative one. A report to Lord Halifax, dated October 12, 1939, noted that as of September, 1939, Daladier's government was prepared to recognize the Conseil National Autrichien, provided there was no objection from the British government. Daladier was ready for a new diplomatic move, since objections had been raised that the French and the British were being too conciliatory, and that neither government wished the Germans to believe that attempts were afoot to destroy German national unity. But the British put forward the argument that a nonrepresentative organization of émigrés could not serve as a recognized representation abroad. This argument led to attempts to ensure that an Austrian exile agency would be representative. At the same time, greater stress was placed on the close identification of the Conseil National Autrichien with Hapsburg legitimism.

Meanwhile, the Ligue Autrichienne and Hans Rott were conducting discussions with representatives of the French government in order to attain the desired Austrian representation. The political émigrés surrounding them immediately encountered resistance from the Austrian socialists in Paris, although the French government would have welcomed the chance to recognize the Conseil National Autrichien. But they expected no help and support from the majority of the interned émigrés. The socialists were determined to prevent the formation of any Austrian political representation abroad.

Joseph Buttinger left no doubt on this in his book *Am Beispiel Österreichs* [*By the Example of Austria*] (1953). According to his description of the last session of the representation of the Austrian socialists abroad—on the day war broke out—this body and all its members were forbidden to take any official position

> . . . that signifies a direct or indirect commitment of the party to the so-called restoration of Austria's independence. . . . A final proposal further sought to prevent this body or any of its members from participating in discussions toward the formation of a kind of Austrian émigré government which were supported, in concert with the monarchists and nationalists from Austria, by the reactionary bureaucracy of the French Foreign Ministry and the French propaganda and espionage apparatus.[41]

Joseph Buttinger's description has the merit of straightforwardness and candor.

By 1953 this approach was no longer popular even in socialist circles. Buttinger was right, however, to have perceived a common German and Austrian socialist revolution as the only "proper" solution to the problem of removing the Hitler regime from Austria. Buttinger's view appears all the more credible as it was rendered by a man who had foresworn all ambitions in the postwar Socialist party and who was not kindly regarded by this new Socialist party of the second Austrian Republic.[42] The historian whose task it is to evaluate the pros and cons of his sources must therefore conclude that Buttinger has given the facts of socialist opposition to any Austrian foreign agency in France in their correct sequence.

His recollections set forth the facts far more clearly than does the tortuous account by another member of the representation abroad, Julius Deutsch. In his book *Ein weiter Weg* [*The Long Road*], Deutsch claims that the decision not to participate, either directly or indirectly, in any action to restore "the so-called independence of Austria" had already been established by a party resolution of the main body of Austrian Socialists at the outbreak of war in September, 1939. According to Deutsch, this resolution was honored until the dissolution of the foreign agency at the time America entered the war, December 7, 1941.[43]

Since the socialists abroad viewed the restoration of Austria's independence as a reactionary goal, it is not surprising that Buttinger and other members of the representation considered the bureaucracy of the French Republic equally reactionary. The French government aimed to foster an Austrian government in exile in order to further France's own best interests. It must also be noted that, following Otto Bauer's early statement, all adherents of the restoration of Austria's independence were considered reactionaries—this formulation acquired the status of a demonstrated principle. Hans Rott repeatedly mentioned this equation in his correspondence dating from shortly before the end of the war.[44] According to Otto Bauer's broad definition, however, reactionaries were not only the monarchists, the members of the Patriotic Front, and the semifascists, but also any nonpolitical émigrés who wished to see Austria's independence restored.

But Hans Rott seems to have overlooked that it was only Julius Deutsch who, in spite of the executive resolution of the representation, carried on serious negotiations with the radical socialist French government and with representatives of the Ligue Autrichienne in Paris—Deutsch frankly admits as much in his memoirs. It is even his opinion that during the first few months of the war the governments of England and France were very much in favor of the plan for an Austrian political representation abroad and that the difficulties lay more with the Austrian emigrants than with the two countries of refuge. Joseph Buttinger's work details the moves and countermoves in the camp of the socialists abroad.[45] It is not unimportant, as Buttinger reports, that old party leaders controlled the disposition of the salvaged funds of the former Social Democratic party, enabling them to bring recalcitrant members into line.[46]

There can then be no doubt that it was the socialist organization that blocked the formation of an Austrian government in exile or a representation abroad, since both the French and the English governments demanded a united front of all Austrian political factions in the emigration as a precondition of recognition. Julius Deutsch, who is unjustly accused by Joseph Buttinger of having offered his services to the French government at the outbreak of war, was forced to bow to the veto of the socialist group; after such members as Joseph Buttinger had returned from the internment camps, Deutsch was no longer allowed to take part in any government in exile. By taking this resolution, the Austrian socialist emigrants also acted against the interests of the government of France, their host country.

Buttinger's policy of refusing to participate in any émigré government would have been logical if, when the war broke out, he had not himself put through the resolution not to participate either directly or indirectly in an Austrian government in exile. By this action, he took a crucial step in disregarding his own precept of remaining passive and abstaining from any kind of action during the emigration. Such a decision must be incomprehensible to any politically minded person since politics implies activity, and passivity is in effect just another form of activity. By his proposition not to participate in any efforts leading to a restoration of Austria, Buttinger decisively determined the orientation of Austrian socialists abroad generally during the emigration, as Otto Bauer had earlier done in his essay in *Der Sozialistische Kampf.* The socialist veto of participation in further discussions about the establishment of an Austrian representative agency in France is directly traceable to Buttinger. According to his own account, he could see no possibility of any socialist activity except in collaboration with the German socialists; cooperation with nonsocialist forces among the emigrants he never considered as a possible option. His total lack of understanding of the power relationships prevailing in Europe after the Anschluss is evident.

Buttinger adhered to the views he had formed within the framework of his political activities in Austria from 1934 to 1938. He kept those views even after the Anschluss, and his clinging to the principle of passivity during the emigration makes him a principal exponent of those socialists abroad who offered bitter resistance to all efforts to restore Austrian independence. It is not surprising that Buttinger's position enjoyed the sympathy of Dr. Friedrich Adler; the latter eagerly defended these principles even at a time when the three Allied powers, preparing the Moscow Declaration of November 1, 1943, were about to include the restoration of Austria as an objective of the war.[47]

The resolutions of the socialist representation abroad beg the question of the organization's objectives after the outbreak of war. Buttinger's proscription of politics during the emigration and, following Otto Bauer's specifications, his injunction to look for the liberation of Austria through a revolution of all of Germany could have only one result: fighting the "reactionary" principle of the restoration of Austria's independence. But might not these resolutions of the socialists abroad also allow for the opposite conclusion—that the desired German revolution of necessity demanded a Greater German solution to the problem of Austria? That is, ought not Austria be part of a German republic—as the socialists had demanded as early as 1918? Is it not true that the refusal to participate in any efforts at restoring the independence of Austria positively called for another solution, that of a socialist Greater Germany? The decision to revolutionize the German workers and to renounce cooperation with the nonsocialist segments of the German population, including nonsocialist Austrians—did this not mean a further handicap to the Allied efforts to achieve the liberation of Germany and Austria from Hitler's tyranny. The answer to these questions demonstrates that during all the years from 1938 to 1945, those segments of the Austrian emigration that advocated the restoration of Austria's independence regarded the official socialist policy as being Greater German and favoring the Anschluss.

Julius Deutsch's attempt in his memoirs to play down this position of the socialists abroad is untenable, and his claim that "from no quarter was an Anschluss with Hitler's Germany ever even considered" borders on the ludicrous. Everyone was aware that any representative of the socialist movement abroad would have risked his life had he dared to set foot on the soil of Hitler Germany, nor was there any real possibility of a socialist Anschluss to Hitler Germany.[48] In 1960, Deutsch wanted very much to mitigate the idea that Anschluss was a motive for the socialists abroad; he preferred to stress "the varying evaluations of the total course of social development" as the principal topic of internal discussion during the emigration. This claim only serves to substantiate that the principal objective of the socialists abroad remained the Anschluss of Austria for as long as there was even the slightest possibility of its happening.[49]

Julius Deutsch's particular attitude was that of a political pragmatist who tried as a guest of France—which desired the restoration of Austria—to participate in the efforts toward this restoration during the early phases of the war. It is impossible to accept Buttinger's view that craving for personal recognition and "his immeasurable vanity" induced Deutsch to negotiate with other factions of the political emigrants and representatives of the French government. Rather, his readiness to enter into negotiations after the outbreak of war was based on a practical politician's conviction that he must remain involved in a struggle in which he wished to maintain a part. At the time he could not know with certainty whether the restoration policy would be successful even without the collaboration of the Austrian socialists abroad. In fact his primary motivation here was his belief that as an émigré he had to make himself useful to his host country. There is no question but that Julius Deutsch was not entirely free of vanity or ambition. But Buttinger is being unjust when, determined to find nothing good to say about Deutsch after February, 1934, he identifies both these traits as the principal motives behind his actions.[50]

Hans Rott points out that the Austrian socialists in France knew perfectly well that their cooperation in establishing an Austrian representation abroad and a government in exile would mean the restoration of Austrian independence after the war. From the time he arrived in France, Rott was the most fervent advocate of collaboration with the socialists to achieve this objective.[51] The importance interested political figures assigned to socialist participation, particularly in the establishment of an independent Austria, is shown by a telegram dated November 14, 1939, from Ambassador Bullitt to his country's State Department. He reports that at last an Austrian committee under French influence had been established in which monarchists, bourgeois, and socialists would each have a one-third representation.[52]

Hans Rott also pointed out that the socialists' readiness for Anschluss was the principal reason for their rejection in principle of the efforts to bring about the unity demanded by the Allied governments, especially France.[53] Rott's view is in part confirmed by Deutsch, who noted that the obstacles to establishing a united front lay with the socialists, who refused to join with "monarchists and Austrofascists," as the Allied governments demanded as a precondition for granting recognition to a government in exile.[54]

Negotiations by the French government proceeded without any appeal to the émigrés in the internment camps. No participant in the negotiations attempted to induce the internees to support his position. Only insofar as it appeared opportune to allow political émigrés to participate in the discussions were certain individuals speedily released from the camps. One of these was Buttinger, the leader of the Revolutionary Socialists. After his release he immediately and most emphatically brought his influence to bear in opposition to any efforts at unification. No attempt was made to create a second committee with neutral, nonpolitical personalities, especially the racial émigrés, and to win the support of the great majority of the émigrés in France. Nor did the negotiators attempt to win the support of this majority by persuading them that their unqualified release from the camps depended on their recognizing the restoration of Austria as one of the objectives of the war and on the creation of a provisional Austrian political representation.

The Czech émigrés in France enjoyed total freedom, in spite of the German annexation of the Sudetenland and the protectorate over the remainder of Czechoslovakia. In spite of their similarities to the Czech group, the Austrian émigrés, as we have seen, were treated differently. Not until all hopes had dwindled for a representative committee of the Austrian émigrés was the proposal made to create a simple Bureau Autrichien under the direction of the nonpolitical former Viennese university professor Dr. Richard Wassitzky; Hans Rott and Julius Deutsch were to be members of this group and act as political advisors.[55] This proposal is first mentioned in a report of November 13, 1939, from the British embassy in Paris to the Foreign Office in London. Letters of recommendation for Austrian political émigrés fleeing from Paris from the French department chief, Charles Rochat, as well as the Archdiocese of Paris reveal how imminent was the official recognition of this nonpolitical organization, so modestly conceived.[56]

Recognition of the Bureau Autrichien, however, never came about. Without furnishing any proof at the time, Julius Deutsch claimed that the monarchists had conspired against the committee because they were not represented in it.[57] It is my belief, however, that recognition was withheld because of efforts then under way to bring about peace with Germany. It was in March, 1940, that the American Undersecretary of State, Sumner Welles, on a tour of the countries at war, also called in at Paris to learn about France's war aims.

Substantial segments of French society were always in favor of arriving at a negotiated peace with Germany. Any political action that might have jeopardized this objective was to be avoided. Though Deutsch noted without regret that "nothing came of the Office Autrichien," he nevertheless mentioned in the tortuous account in his memoirs that a chance had been lost; he believed that it would be hard to say whether the failure of the project should be regretted, for "this official agency of Austrians abroad would in any case have been little more than a symbol. On the other hand, it is obvious that for oppressed peoples even symbols have some meaning."[58] Looking back eighteen years later, he too arrived at the conclusion that the most insignificant political committee, even under nonpolitical leadership and with the objective of fulfilling only administrative chores, would have been an important symbol for oppressed Austria.

With the fall of Paris in June, 1940, and the armistice of June 22, every political activity of the Austrian émigrés had to cease for the time being. Flight from both the occupied and the unoccupied section of France became the principal concern for the émigrés; they had to fear for their lives. The armistice agreement obligated France to hand over the refugees demanded by Germany. Everything seemed lost. The country considered to be the country of asylum in Europe no longer offered refuge. France herself had become helpless; the political refugees she had admitted were exempted of their right to asylum by the armistice and were now legally outlaws. For the Jewish émigrés the prospects were still gloomier.[59]

The leaders of the political émigrés could escape: for them, ways and means were found. For the political émigrés left behind and for the many Jewish émigrés, the only remaining possibility was to participate in the French resistance movement, which gradually grew in significance. In spite of all the dangers it offered, the best chance of surviving the years of occupation was participation in the underground. Not until after the liberation of France did the Austrian émigré circles in France and Algeria once again organize as Austrian political groups. Then they played a crucial role in the further development of Austria when they found in the person of one of their representatives, Dr. Ernst Lemberger, a man of leadership quality. Countless émigrés, however, had been placed in concentration camps or had been deported.

It is deeply regrettable that as a consequence of the collapse of France numerous sources and important documents were lost. A significant amount of material seems to have been destroyed even before the occupation of France, an understandable precaution. Other records are said to have been carried off.[60] Because of the suddenness of events and frequent change of location, the fleeing émigrés were in no position to take along written materials. They also had to fear being caught in possession of compromising documents. For example, the posthumous papers of Hans Rott, which were made available to me contain no documents, letters, memoranda, nor any other records from the time of his emigration in France. Rott's posthumous papers do not include any document relating to the negotiations concerning the formation of an Austrian government in exile. The only accessible sources to rely on include: newspaper articles, reports from American archives of United States diplomatic representatives in France, interpretations of the sequence of French laws and regulations to the extent that these deal with emigration and the right of asylum, as well as recollections and subsequent accounts by prominent political émigrés.[61] Only when most of the records of the British Foreign Office were released in 1972 did new documents pertinent to the history of this period become available for research.

The history of Austrian political emigration in France, brief as it was and suddenly as it ended, is nevertheless the crucial prelude to the history of Austrian political emigration in the years from 1938 to 1945. Not only is it the point of departure for all efforts by the leading political émigrés of this period, it is also in itself a climax, containing the seeds of future developments, under political circumstances that were favorable in a way never to return.

Because of her geographical position on the European continent, no other nation in the Allied camp had the same interest in Austria as France. No other country offered the same possibilities for political activity to political émigrés. Neither Great Britain nor the United States—the major countries where, after the fall of France, the Austrian political emigrants continued their efforts— could even come close to furnishing an equally favorable climate. It is my belief that the history of Austrian political emigration—and the development of the second Republic of Austria—would have taken a quite different turn if it had not come to such an abrupt halt as early as the first year of the war.

Had the Bureau Autrichien, which was deliberately conceived with such modest aims, been realized, it would have furnished the basis of an Austrian political agency abroad. The composition of this small Bureau Autrichien, designed only for administrative tasks, combined in itself all the elements that would have bridged the irreconcilable antagonism of the opposing émigré factions through the chairmanship of a nonpolitical personality. Such a neutral figure could have represented those who were not tied to political parties, including the Jewish émigrés. Never again in the years that were to follow and nowhere, least of all in Great Britain and the United States, did anyone ever resort to this simple solution: a nonpolitical personality entrusted with the leadership of an Austrian committee, with prominent émigrés as political consultants. It remains an unanswered question why even ardent advocates of the unification of all Austrians during political emigration never returned to the example of France. But precisely because all the criteria for the future direction of political emigration were already present in France, the history of political emigration in that country is of considerable significance. The subsequent development of Austrian emigration cannot be understood without this prologue.

III

Austrian Political Emigration in the United States to America's Entry into the War, 1941

Political activity in France by émigrés from Austria came unexpectedly to an end. After June, 1940, such activity was out of the question even in the unoccupied sector under the Vichy regime. The Austrian émigrés were obliged to find a new refuge, and many of them tried to reach the New World by way of Portugal and Spain.[1] They were aided by influential persons as well as by American organizations set up to facilitate the emigration of endangered individuals.[2]

Spain and Portugal proved to be, for the most part, friendly countries of passage and subsequently granted permanent residence to a considerable number of refugees. Portugal provided a strategic location: the refugees could gather there and emigration overseas could be organized. It was from Portugal that most of the Austrian political émigrés reached the American continent. Federal Minister Hans Rott settled in Toronto; Julius Deutsch arrived in the United States by way of Cuba; Otto von Hapsburg—who had been received by President Roosevelt in March, 1940, on the occasion of a visit to the United States—was granted an unlimited American residence permit on the basis of a Belgian passport.

Despite the legal and financial difficulties prevailing in Lisbon and other Portuguese cities, the political programs begun in France were continued there. On September 24, 1940, a group of Austrian émigrés, composed of Baron Hano Friebeiss, Walter von Schuschnigg, Major Albert Hartmann, and Peter Paul, sent a memorandum to the British government requesting permission to form an Austrian legion and to make radio broadcasts. To support the first query, the memorandum mentioned the two thousand Austrians then serving in the French Foreign Legion, suggesting that they could be recruited at a moment's notice.[3]

Also, in Portugal were initiated the first plans for the Free Austrian Movement. Discussions took place between Otto von Hapsburg and such prominent political émigrés as Hans Rott and Wilhelm Wunsch, who was later to become Secretary General of the Free Austrian Movement in Toronto; these talks were to affect the course of émigré efforts in the United States and Canada. The model for the proposed Free Austrian group was General Charles de Gaulle's Free French Movement, which was committed to continue fighting the war at the side of Great Britain against Germany in spite of France's armistice with the Nazis. The Free French considered themselves the genuine government of France, in defiance of the Vichy regime which collaborated with Germany.

It must be borne in mind that in France Otto had been deliberately kept in the background. Both the friendly French political authorities and the American ambassador, William C. Bullitt, hoped that if he were untainted by internal party struggles, he might be in a position to be the ruler, not only of Austria, but also of other successor states that might be created after the war.[4] After the fall of France, the Austrian émigrés pursued similar lines of thought. Some of the political émigrés who favored a restoration of Austria's independence became convinced that they would not be able to achieve their goal without Otto's support.

Hans Rott shared this belief. A spokesman of the left wing of the old Christian Socialist party and a close collaborator of the Christian Socialist labor leader Leopold Kunschak, he had been Secretary of State after the July agreement with Germany in 1936 and a member of Schuschnigg's last cabinet. In Austria it had been his assignment to win over the former Social Democratic labor force, which after February, 1934, assumed a hostile stance toward the Schuschnigg regime, and to persuade the workers to cooperate within the country and help defend it against the increasing pressure of National Socialism. Hans Rott was an ardent democrat, a commitment acknowledged even by his socialist counterpart in the emigration, Julius Deutsch. And Leopold Kunschak, Rott's close ally, had attempted a last-minute rescue of democracy in Austria just before the February uprising. For all his democratic convictions, Hans Rott, never an enemy of the monarchists, was willing to cooperate with Otto von Hapsburg.[5]

Nevertheless, Rott regarded the monarchist, or legitimist, movement in Austria as a sort of last resort, a reserve position and political trump card to be played at some propitious future juncture in the struggle for the preservation of the country. The same powerful historical associations that lent the Hapsburg name its power also made it an incalculable gambit in the years of the emigration. The émigrés acknowledged all the risks that had persuaded Chancellor Schuschnigg even at the moment of utmost danger, on March 2, 1938, to reject Otto's offer to make an attempt to save Austria by transferring the chancellorship to himself.[6]

In Portugal Hans Rott and other political refugees could command little attention and were obliged to rely on uncertain financial support. For them increasingly, Otto von Hapsburg, with his worldwide connections, represented their last and only hope. It was known that he was offering himself far and wide as a lecturer and that he was receiving an increasing number of invitations to lecture and to attend conferences. In Portugal and overseas generally he possessed the kind of security—including financial security—that was the yearning of every political émigré. In addition, after the fall of France not only the émigrés from Austria, but also wider Western circles with political concerns felt a new urgency concerning the question of whether the fall of the old Austro-Hungarian monarchy in the First World War might not have removed the one Central European bulwark that could have acted as a dam against an overly powerful Germany and, if reestablished, could do so again. The fall of France had deeply disrupted the basis of European balance and the security system based on the peace treaties of the First World War. If France, a victorious power of 1918, whose policies underlay the rearrangement of Europe after the First World War, had fallen as the result of an inadequate security system, then political circles, especially the political emigration from Austria, had to raise the question of whether it might not have been better to re-create the old power structure in Central Europe, i.e., the Austro-Hungarian monarchy, in a new shape; whether the error of 1918 should not be rectified. With France's elimination as a field of political activity for the Austrian émigrés, they had also to regroup in terms of their more immediate undertakings and goals. Some notes included in Hans Rott's posthumous papers indicate that Portugal was the place where he and Otto von Hapsburg agreed to organize the Free Austrian Movement.[7] They intended to establish it in the United States, and it was specifically meant to be a broad-based movement rather than a party with particular objectives. The goal was the restoration of Austria's independence; the form the government was to take—republic or monarchy—however, was to be determined by the Austrian people themselves after the country's liberation.[8] Otto von Hapsburg was seen as something like the "chief" of the movement, since it was dependent on his support.[9] Hans Rott was to be the day-to-day leader, with Wilhelm Wunsch as his deputy.[10] The Free Austrian Movement aimed at encompassing Austrians of every political stripe, like its Free French model. The movement was obliged to turn to Otto and his followers to ensure access to his financial and political help; in return, they guaranteed not to exclude the possibility of a monarchic form of government after the liberation of Austria. But it was equally important that even the most fervent adherents of the republican form of government for Austria be represented in the ranks of the movement. In any event, it could not be long before all the émigré factions understood that Otto von Hapsburg was furthering the Free Austrian Movement, and that, if only by its neutrality in the question of the future form of government, the organization did not run counter to his interests.

When the Free Austrian Movement was actually established on October 18, 1940, in Toronto, Austrian émigré political activity moved its effective focus to the Western Hemisphere. But before describing the various political trends among émigrés in Canada and the United States, it seems essential to describe the political, social, and economic conditions that confronted the Austrian political émigrés in their new environment.

The most pervasive difficulty encountered by the Austrian émigrés was the lack of information about Austrian conditions and the massive ignorance about Austrian history—though public opinion was by no means favorable to Germany.[11] The picture Americans had of Austria had been formed by emigrants from regions formerly subject to the Austro-Hungarian monarchy. Commencing with Hungarian revolutionaries under Kossuth in 1848, a very one-sided account had been offered to American public opinion.[12] The emigrants of 1848 could hardly feel any great love for an Austria they perceived as absolutist, and neither could subsequent waves of emigrants who had lived through the nationalist struggles within Austria-Hungary. Given, also, a bias toward national self-determination, it was hard for Americans to view the old multinational Hapsburg state as a benign guarantor of the balance of power and peace in Europe.[13]

Even after Austria had become a republic, this one-sided opinion did not change significantly.[14] The new Republic of Austria was burdened with all the mistakes of Austrian history. As a result, the American public saw no significant disadvantage to Europe or the United States in the elimination of Austria as an independent nation in March, 1938. Only few observers understood at once what such changes in the map of Europe, first in 1918 and most especially in 1938, meant also for the United States.

It was even more difficult for the American public to understand that the old monarchy held a historically justified place in Central Europe, and that monarchy was not the bondage various groups of emigrants accused it of being.[15] It has been argued that the persuasive propaganda of Tomaš G. Masaryk and Edvard Beneš during the First World War convinced President Wilson the Czechs must be liberated from the Austrian "prison state."

Not a single group of American emigrants from the region of the old Austria considered itself purely "Austrian"; none championed Austria as a supranational state. The German-speaking emigrants who, as the foremost ethnic group of the old Austrian state, should have felt called upon to explain the supranational nature of their country, considered themselves merely as Germans and were thought of only as German and not as Austrian immigrants.

In addition, the official diplomatic representatives of the old Austria had had difficulty adjusting to American thought patterns. There had been a lack of understanding in official Vienna for conditions in the United States going back to Joseph II's attitude during the American War of Independence.[16] The last Austro-Hungarian ambassador had not been given full information even about the Austrian ultimatum to Serbia in 1914, and he could not justify his government's position at that crucial juncture.[17] It was quite in line with the unfortunate policy of the old Austrian government to take little heed of public opinion in the United States, which was and is, after all, a primary factor for determining the direction of American policy.[18]

Thus, while the old monarchy was a kind of terra incognita for the American public, the Austrian Republic did not fare much better. The political public in the United States kept on believing that the Republic was a kind of artificial successor state brought into being by the victors of the First World War for the sole purpose of not strengthening the new Germany.[19] Given the constant political and economic crises during the almost twenty years the independent Republic had lasted, restoration of a new independent Austria did not seem a particularly desirable objective.[20] Politically sophisticated circles therefore suggested that after an Allied victory Austria be merged in some form or other with Germany or southern Germany or Bavaria; alternatively, it was planned to bring Austria into a politically and economically permanent association with other successor states of the old monarchy.[21] The American public had no clear picture of which of these possibilities was preferable; the proposals all started from the generally prevailing assumption that Austria as an independent state had not proved herself to be economically viable; and the question of Austria's economical independence had become an axiom. That postwar Austria must be economically viable was also semiofficial opinion in Great Britain. "We imagined Austria and Germany could remain joined, with this new Germany governed out of Vienna"—so thought Dr. Lewis Mumford of the Inter-Allied Information Center in New York in November, 1940.[22]

The uprising of the Austrian Social Democrats in February, 1934, and the ensuing repression by the government of Chancellor Engelbert Dollfuss, including the dissolution of the Social Democratic Party, were decisive—and harmful—in forming the Americans' opinion of contemporary Austria. The Social Democrats had always been considered the center of the Republic and of its democratic institutions, and the formation of an authoritarian, corporative Austria with the elimination of traditional institutions clouded Austria's image in all democratic countries after 1934. From then on, Austria was considered a nondemocratic, semifascist, or clerical-fascist country.[23] Overlooked was the fact that an independent Austrian state, as established by the peace treaties of the First World War, remained, regardless of its system of government, a political necessity for the maintenance of the European system of balance, most particularly in the interests of France and Czechoslovakia.[24]

In the United States, however, Austria and its authoritarian regime (even before 1938) were seen only as having turned away from traditional parliamentary democracy. The United States was still under the influence of the Wilsonian idea that democracy was everywhere and at all times the most desirable form of government; this was also the reason for the high regard in which Czechoslovakia was held—the Czech Republic had been established on the American model.[25] The American public's uneasiness about the disappearance of parliamentary institutions in Austria and their dislike of the undemocratic system at the helm since 1934 made them forget geographic, historical, and political considerations with significance for the maintenance of the European peace, and world peace along with it.[26] The Americans ignored the teachings of an earlier republican form of government—that of ancient Rome, where in times of a national emergency a "dictator" might replace the republican consuls until the state of emergency has passed.

The Soviet Union was realistic enough to see the maintenance of Austria's independence as a crucial question. When the new Soviet ambassador, Lorenz, first called on the American chargé d'affaires in Vienna in 1935, the newly accredited diplomat declared that Austria's independence must be supported, by force of arms if need be. In answer to the American's comment that under Schuschnigg and Prince Ernst Rüdiger Starhemberg the country was ruled by a dictatorship, the Soviet ambassador explained that unfortunately even these leaders had to be supported. When the American diplomat hinted that the Austrian communists might raise objections to such a policy, Ambassador Lorenz replied that his government would make certain that no such difficulties would arise. In contrast to such realism, in 1934 Americans saw only the forced demise of Austrian democracy, which itself might have been avoided had the polarization of the active political forces in Austria not prevented it.

But America did not see that the Austrian dictatorship had made a desperate attempt to preserve the political independence of Austria in the Danube region, which had already largely turned fascist or semifascist. This Austrian government believed it could obtain Italy's much-needed help against the growing pressure of National Socialist Germany only by smashing the Austrian Social Democratic party. A detailed account of these developments, published August 27, 1941, at Balliol College, Oxford, concluded that if France and England had stood by Dollfuss's government, the events of February, 1934, might not have happened.[27]

After Hitler's seizure of power in Germany, the pressure on Austria steadily increased. The American public did not realize that only the deployment of Italian troops at the Brenner foiled the Austrian National Socialists' Putsch of July 25, 1934. Also, for several more years the independence of Austria could be maintained solely with Italy's support. Only after the dissolution of the so-called Stresa Front between Italy and the Western powers in 1935 did this support gradually weaken, until at last, in the midst of the Abyssinian campaign, Italy was forced to choose between Germany's help in her confrontation with the Western powers and the maintenance of Austria's independence.

When, on March 13, 1938, Germany effected the Anschluss of Austria with only Mexico protesting in the League of Nations, neither the democratic nor the nondemocratic member states took a stand in favor of Austria's independence.[28] It is unlikely that even an Austria that had remained democratic would have received any help from the League of Nations and its member states because of the Great Powers' favored policy of appeasement.

Thus, the demise of Austrian democracy is the primary reason for the evident American animosity against that segment of the Austrian emigration that included officials and adherents of the corporative state. The Austrian socialists, in the United States as in France, continued to refuse any kind of cooperation with the objective of restoring independence; but, as we shall see, their opposition could not have had lasting results had it not been for the ingrained assumptions of many Americans.[29]

Of great significance was the attitude of the Jewish émigrés toward the entire spectrum of political emigration from Austria.[30] By immigrating, the Jewish émigrés had as their principal objective the establishment of a new existence—to be integrated into the economic and social life of the United States and also to acquire citizenship. Time and again these objectives were announced in columns entitled "Explanations of an Immigration Policy" in the weekly *Aufbau,* published in New York, which was achieving the status of semiofficial organ for the German-speaking emigrants.[31] The same objective was also urged on the immigrants by the Jewish-American aid organizations, while the United States Department of State encouraged them not to participate in the undertakings of the politically active emigrants.[32]

The German Jews who had immigrated since 1933 and their press had significance for the work of the politically active Austrian emigrants as well. As a result of their common language and because Austria was now a part of Greater Germany, the Austrian-Jewish emigrants, far inferior in numbers, were forced at first not only to form a close alliance with the German-Jewish group, but to rely on it. The differences between the two groups of émigrés, so evident to the Austrians, were occasionally acknowledged by the German-Jewish group as well. Nonetheless, it was inevitable that the German group would control the Austrian segment, especially since for some time all German-language émigré journalism had been in the hands of German émigrés.[33] Part of the German-Jewish emigration had formed regional organizations, while other groups banded together in religious congregations or in organizations based on their common mother tongue and their shared Jewish faith. The Germans were ambitious and purposeful, and, by comparison with the Austrian emigrants arriving after 1938, in sound financial circumstances. Thus it came about that the German-Jewish immigrants in the years 1933–1938 were frequently able to enter into American life with sufficient funds. The emigration originating in Germany, which was able to rely on the liberal tendencies of earlier German immigrants to the United States, in many cases encountered a fair, often even a friendly, attitude on the part of German-Americans. The newcomers were seldom thwarted in their aims by the old German immigrants, and often they were encouraged. Since 1934 the German-speaking Jewish emigration from the German Reich had found its journalistic expression in the *Aufbau,* which was published first as a monthly, later as a semimonthly, and finally as a weekly, always edited by Manfred George. Under his purposeful leadership, the publication developed into the recognized organ, not only of the German-Jewish émigrés, but also of the Jewish immigrants who came from Austria, and altogether of the German-speaking Jewish emigration from other nations.[34] The *Aufbau* quickly became acknowledged as such a semiofficial organ by the American public.[35] Throughout the period 1938–1945, the publication was a significant influence on the Austrian emigration.[36]

All the editors and the publisher of the *Aufbau* had emigrated from Germany. For them, the former Weimar Republic, in which many of them had held leading positions, was the most desirable political settlement for the German Reich. In spite of the Weimar Republic's failure and the Nazis' seizure of power, these émigrés felt that the form of government the Weimar Republic represented was the best goal for post-Hitler Germany as well. The *Aufbau,* of course, was obliged to consider the composition of its total readership, particularly the commitment of some German Jews to the creation of a

Jewish national home in Palestine and subsequently a Jewish national state. But as far as Germany was concerned, the newspaper fostered the esteem of the Weimar Republic current in the United States and supported all efforts directed to the restoration of a German republic. In spite of recurrent editorial statements that the *Aufbau* was only an organ of the German-Jewish immigrants, the periodical also had to defend itself against the accusation of aiming—along with other representatives of pre-Hitler Germany—to preserve the integrity of Germany in spite of the expected defeat.[37]

A careful perusal of the *Aufbau* between 1938 and 1945 leaves the impression that all political events and movements were seen from the viewpoint of the Weimar Republic. Certainly this is true in the treatment of the various objectives of the Austrian political emigrants and also of the Free Austrian Movement and other, similar movements. Any reader of the periodical cannot help but notice that at the beginning a cautious neutrality prevailed, but that subsequently this developed into a position in favor of those émigré factions that shared the thinking of the *Aufbau*'s publisher and editors. For example, the Beneš Plan for a Central European federation was repeatedly supported by the *Aufbau,* which praised the plan as "daring" and contrasted it with Otto von Hapsburg's efforts, although Soviet war objectives should have made it plain that any kind of federation in Central Europe would have to remain a utopia.[38] The *Aufbau's* preference for the Czech political figures Tomaš G. Masaryk and Edvard Beneš led the paper to favor proposals that did not fit the real political conditions.

The desire for a union of the German Reich with the German-language territories that had emerged as the Republic of Austria from the demise of the Danube monarchy was a policy favored by the Weimar Republic; the prospect of union was uncongenial to imperial Germany and had been opposed by the founder of the Reich, Otto von Bismarck. This political objective was even more urgently striven for from the Austrian side, where it was generally seen as a national objective, though not one essential to the survival of the state. There had been movement in the direction of union; we need only recall the negotiations of 1931 to bring about a German-Austrian customs union. Though not a political annexation, such an agreement would very likely have meant economic annexation. The history of the unification of Germany during the nineteenth century amply proves that a customs union—or a tariff union— was often the forerunner of a political merger.[39] In the Weimar Republic the idea of Anschluss had been a rather abstract national aim—possible but distant. When the Anschluss was actually effected, in 1938, the German-Jewish immigrants and their journalistic representatives saw the annexation of Austria, though it came about by force, as a political and economic matter of course. Although the Anschluss had not come about in the ideal form envisaged by the Weimar Republicans and the Austrian Social Democrats, it was nevertheless difficult for the republican defenders of a German union to consider that the Anschluss should be annulled. The German-Jewish emigration therefore considered the Austrian-Jewish emigrants as another segment of the total emigration from greater Germany even if occasionally they took note of the Austrian immigrants' idiosyncracies.[40]

The German-Jewish emigrants thus tended to view the Anschluss as a permanent situation. Though the National Socialist actions related to the Anschluss were rejected, it was impossible in principle to oppose all the policies of National Socialist Germany, especially the fact of the successful Anschluss of Austria. Convinced that the Austrian Republic was not a practicable entity, the German immigrants rejected, both covertly and openly, the Austrians' aim of restoring an independent Austria. The socialists among the German immigrants in the United States, close to the *Aufbau* in ideology, favored Anschluss on principle, as did the socialist emigrants from Austria.[41] These circles were reluctant to acknowledge that at least half the Austrian population had already come to terms with Austria's independence as a permanent condition after 1918 and that a significant segment of the Austrian population had actively opposed the National Socialist efforts to annex Austria in the years 1933–1938. The same groups, influenced by the jubilation in Vienna at the time of the Anschluss, ignored observers' assertions that the majority of Austrians would have rejected the Anschluss if they could.[42] The prounion immigrants pointed to the plebiscite on the Anschluss to justify their point of view, but it is hard to see how such a plebiscite can be equated with a free vote, especially given the results of the earlier plebiscite on the return of the Saar and the general methods of the National Socialists.

The Austrian émigrés arriving in the United States also had to contend with the old Czech immigrants' dislike of Austria dating from the time of the Austrian monarchy and from the Republic of Czechoslovakia after 1918. Regardless of whether they were of Jewish or non-Jewish descent, the Czech immigrants instinctively rejected the republic that was seen as a successor of the old Austria, and they showed little liking for or interest in a restoration of a newer Austria. Outstanding representatives of Czechoslovakia, such as Jan Masaryk, the son of the late president Tomáš G. Masaryk, who enjoyed great respect in the United States, did indeed early on express support for the restoration of Austria.[43] The significance of the Czech and Slovak immigrants' influence on the fortunes of the Austrian immigrants cannot be overestimated. Even before 1918, as we know, they had laid the basis for an independent Czechoslovakia. This group therefore took a hostile position toward all efforts that might even remotely be seen as impairing the interests of their country, but most especially all efforts that might lead to the restoration of the old Austrian monarchy or the return to power of the house of Hapsburg.[44]

An equally strong rejection of Austria's restoration and an even greater hostility to the house of Hapsburg could be found among the immigrants coming from the South Slavic parts of the old monarchy—Serbs, Croatians, Slovenes—inhabitants, after 1918, of the Republic of Yugoslavia. For a long time, the Yugoslavs were indifferent to whether their borders abutted the Republic of Austria or National Socialist Germany. They did not understand that a Germany become too powerful through annexation could not but threaten the Yugoslav state in the same way that it threatened independent Czechoslovakia and Hungary.

The attitude of the Hungarian emigrants must be seen as neutral. Various leftist groups of immigrants turned against the political emigrants who were in contact with the Hapsburgs. Others, considered right-wing, were inclined to support the right-leaning Austrian groups. In addition, Otto von Hapsburg was clever enough to support, not only Austrian, but also Hungarian interests.[45] The right-wing Hungarian groups, however, did not aim for the simple restoration of the former Republic of Austria; instead, they proposed to reestablish lateral communications between a German-language area and Hungary, a policy reminiscent of arrangements under the old monarchy. The Hungarians' broader aims made them less a help than a hindrance for those Austrian emigrants who aimed at nothing more than the restoration of the Republic of Austria in the 1938 borders.[46]

Bad memories of the old monarchy in the former Italian territories of the empire made Italian emigrants unwilling to support the Austrians' efforts. There was one exception to this situation: The antifascist Italian emigrants were prepared to work with similarly minded groups of Austrian emigrants, especially the Austrian socialists, in their opposition to the prospect of the Hapsburgs' participation in postwar plans.[47]

In contrast to the divisiveness described above, we must stress the cordial attitude toward everything Austrian of the emigrants coming from Galicia—Poles and Jews as well as emigrants of Jewish descent who originated in Bucovina. These immigrants revered the memory of Emperor Franz Josef I, who had been well disposed toward them,[48] and they brought to their new home the conviction that the time of Franz Joseph had been happy for them. In contrast to the suppression of the Jewish population in the bordering territories of tsarist Russia—Austrian rule had granted the Jews of Bucovina and Galicia protection from the Polish and Ukranian populations of the area. Jewish emigration from these old Austrian crown lands was occasioned more by economic than by political causes, and the Jewish emigrants were without any resentment against the land from which they came; they retained good feelings about Austria and were emotionally prepared to support the restoration of the country's independence in the old form of the Republic or in a new form suited to new conditions.[49] Those few among the immigrants who had pursued political aims—such as socialists, Zionists, and left-wingers—are exceptions; but the broad mass of Jewish emigrants from Galicia and Bucovina were not hostile to the idea of restoring an independent Austria.[50]

If we examine the political and social conditions the Austrian emigrants encountered in the United States, we can categorize them as not favorable but negative, at best indifferent, concerning the restoration of an Austrian Republic. Grave as these circumstances were, the crucial problem for the emigrants was financial weakness, and sometimes simple poverty. After the occupation of Austria, the Nazis stopped taking into account Western public opinion and increased their harassments of would-be emigrants. Thus it came about that a majority of the Austrian émigrés entered the United States without possessions; these emigrants were not allowed to take with them anything but the bare necessities—in the end, only the clothes on their backs.

Considering that even the most limited political activity in any country, but most especially in the United States, requires financial resources for the most routine expenditures—such as office rent, telephone and postage fees, stationery, and especially staff honoraria—the desperate position of the Austrian political emigrants is clear. Lacking any financial resources of their own and without recourse to the broad masses of an earlier wave of immigration, the new immigrants were nevertheless eager to get to work. Membership dues, no matter how minimal, could be collected only with painful efforts and countless reminders; often they went unpaid. One of the early emigration periodicals in Paris had already issued a public reminder to its subscribers to pay up their membership dues, noting with dry irony that the Nazi Gestapo in Paris always paid its subscription to the paper on time, while the émigrés remained in arrears.[51] Every organization of Austrian émigrés dedicated to political objectives had to worry about procuring funds and about the necessary living costs for the leaders; this was true from the moment the organization was founded to the day it suspended activities. Members of almost all the émigré factions had to carry on their activity without pay and were only rarely able to hire paid staff. Every accessible relative, every friend or acquaintance had to be approached for a contribution.

Except for those political groups with access to private means, funds for political activities are generally raised through donations and other contributions from the likely beneficiaries of the programs planned or from those for whom election campaigns are conducted. In any case the basis of all political activity in the United States consists of contributions from the parties for whom an action is undertaken.

Given the poverty of the political emigrants from Austria, the seemingly near-hopeless position of the little band of Austrian émigrés is surely evident. If they wished to pursue their aims, they were confronted by an overwhelming number of political opponents and an overwhelming majority of indifferent immigrants. Aside from their financial problems, they lacked a wide circle of interested persons from whom contributions might have been solicited. Indeed, their financial difficulties seriously impeded all the emigrants' political activities. At the most basic level, it was impossible to secure the indispensable publicity that can only be achieved with paid staff.

For the most part, the Austrian political emigrants had access to only a few sources of aid. The only exception was the Austrian socialists, whose leader could call on financial resources including unions through his connections with the international labor movement. Further, "the old leaders controlled all the party funds that had been taken out of the country," as Joseph Buttinger, himself a member of the socialist representation abroad, has noted.[52] Doubtless it is precisely this circumstance that freed the Austrian socialists from depending on other emigrants. The author believes that the socialists would have paid a great deal more attention to the needs of the wider political emigration in France, Great Britain, and the United States if they had been forced to consider the interests of this larger group as well as their own.

Among that sector of the political emigration that strove for the restoration of Austria's independence—the Ligue Autrichienne in France and the Free Austrian Movement of Hans Rott in the United States and Canada—the opinions and interests of Otto von Hapsburg had to be considered, if for no other reason that that his support was a vital factor. The leaders of the movement—who also had to consider the republican-minded members and at first planned nothing more than the restoration of Austria's independence—could nevertheless not help but see Otto as a political liability. But, in their view unfortunately, Otto was the sole source of available support. There is no question but that he supported the Free Austrian Movement.[53] It is interesting to note that though Otto and Hans Rott sought to restore the independence of Austria through this association, Rott had received his political education in the left, republican-minded, workers' wing of the old Christian Socialist party in Austria. During the entire period of emigration he never ceased to reject the accusation that he was a monarchist and he never wished the Free Austrian Movement to be seen as a monarchist organization.[54] Instead, he consistently laid down the principle that the form of government for a restored independent Austria should be decided only by the liberated Austrian people; but he insisted that the monarchists be allowed to participate in the struggle, and that the Free Austrian Movement was justified in accepting the support of Otto von Hapsburg.[55] Rott himself professed to be a democratic republican, and this attestation was subsequently confirmed by Julius Deutsch in his reminiscences, where he noted, "Hans Rott was acceptable to us."[56]

Other emigrant groups had their own problems of securing support while preserving their independence. One of them, however, Austrian Action, attracted a very broad range of members and so, in comparison to the socialist groups and the Free Austrian Movement, achieved the relative freedom of action of a true mass movement.[57]

Another politically oriented emigrants' group gathered around the former Vienna deputy mayor, Dr. Ernst Karl Winter, who had left Austria as early as March 18, 1938. And it was Winter who, in January, 1939, established the first organization of Austrians in New York. At that time a professor at the New School for Social Research, Winter accepted the leadership of this new group, the Austro-American Center. He also participated in the American Committee on European Reconstruction, established in June, 1940.[58] Winter's political goal was to combine all the Austrian émigré forces into a "Holy Union" against National Socialism. His organization was intended to devote itself only to cultural goals that could be pursued in the memory of Austria's independence and in the hope of restoration, but not political objectives such as the creation of an Austrian representative body abroad or a government in exile. Thus, the Austro-American Center was established on a strictly nonpolitical basis, and the preservation of the values of Austrian culture was its highest goal.[59]

In spite of this restriction to cultural efforts, there soon arose confrontations between the Austro-American Center and members of different political factions, such as Professor Robert Heine-Geldern, the renowned Indologist. These wanted to see the organization used for political activity. The controversy over this question led to a grave conflict as early as the first anniversary of the occupation of Austria, in March, 1939. This dispute led Heine-Geldern to resign from the Austro-American Center in April, 1939, and he subsequently established the Austrian-American League in New York.[60]

Within a few months a number of socialist and communist members of the Austro-American Center left to found the Austrian-American Society in New York. Thus at the outbreak of war in Europe, in September 1939, three cultural organizations existed among the Austrian émigrés in New York, their members embracing different political views on the question of Austria's future.

As the United States moved closer to direct involvement in the war, it became risky for non-American citizens to engage in political activity if they intended to take up permanent residence there. Jan Masaryk, speaking with Austrian emigrants in New York on March 30, 1939, urgently advised them to work through Americans in all crucial matters, even including Austrian political concerns, since it was not well received in the United States for foreigners to become politically active.[61]

After the outbreak of war in Europe, all three Austrian organizations in New York held a joint session. The question on the agenda was whether a resolution prepared by the Austro-American League asking for the restoration of Austria's independence should also be signed by the other organizations. While the Austro-American Society was prepared to sign, Dr. Ernst Karl Winter proposed wording that called only for the right of self-determination for Austria. He hoped in this way to win over the leaders of the Socialist party, who were in New York at the time. Only after this attempt had failed was a joint resolution of the three organizations published, calling for the restoration of Austrian independence.[62] After the occupation of the remainder of Czechoslovakia in March, 1939, Professor Heine-Geldern also attempted to establish connections with the Czech émigrés who were now sharing the fate of the exiled Austrians and to initiate some joint action. On March 30, 1939, in New York, he succeeded in reaching Jan Masaryk, who was to become foreign minister in the Czech government in exile. Their discussion demonstrated in a most heartening way the understanding each had for the other's problems, and the account of the meeting is still worth reading today. Masaryk dared to admit that at Versailles in 1919 the nascent Czechoslovak Republic had taken too much territory from Austria and still more from Hungary. And the Czech statesman was far more objective than his compatriots in understanding Otto von Hapsburg's significance for the Austrian emigrants. He was not opposed to collaborating with Austrian political emigrants in exile but suggested that caution be employed about monarchism, "for the Czechs and Dr. Beneš had not yet arrived at that point."[63] Professor Heine-Geldern continued his efforts even after the outbreak of the war and subsequently took an active part in the efforts of the political emigrants to create a foreign agency in the United States.[64] But it was not until after the fall of France in June, 1940, and the arrival of the leading political émigrés from France that the Austrian emigrants began concerted political activities in the countries of the Western Hemisphere.

The first organization with the declared objective of an Austrian political representation abroad and a government in exile was, of course, the Free Austrian Movement. The organization's central office was in Toronto, and the group's leader intended that offices should be opened in all the free nations of the world. A statement of principle explained that the Free Austrian Movement was not a party and that its only objective was the liberation of Austria and the restoration of its independence.[65]

But representatives of the other side in the controversy over Austria's future had also come to the United States. The proponents of incorporating Austria into a democratic Germany gathered in New York and formed a socialist committee. In New York, unlike the socialist representation in Paris, the leaders of the former Social Democratic party were from the outset the leading group, while the Revolutionary Socialists formed only a small minority. Julius Deutsch was quick to reassure the United States Department of State about the committee's ideology, and he soon took his place as the spokesman for the socialists abroad.[66]

The third force in the political emigration was Otto von Hapsburg, who had remained in the background in France. He took up political activity in the United States with support from Ambassador Bullitt, who opened all doors to him. It was Bullitt who arranged Otto's first meeting with President Franklin D. Roosevelt on March 9, 1940. And Bullitt furthered Otto in other ways as well, using his connections in American society. It was not long before Otto von Hapsburg was a sought-after figure for conferences, lectures, and expert advice on Central Europe. He was often a guest of the President in the White House, and his mother, Empress Zita, and his brothers also received invitations. In spite of all political ups and downs on the question of Austria throughout the war, Otto maintained close ties to President Roosevelt.[67]

On April 5, 1941, another active political organization was founded, the mass-oriented Austrian Action, which sought support among the large number of liberal and nonpolitical immigrants. Its president was Ferdinand Czernin, son of Count Ottokar Czernin, the foreign minister of the old Austro-Hungarian monarchy in the government of the Emperor Charles.[68]

At least one of the groups established in New York even before the politically active émigrés arrived from France, the Austrian-American League, discontinued its activities after America's entry into the war. Its chairman, Professor Heine-Geldern, began to work closely with Hans Rott in his efforts to achieve an Austrian political representation abroad. The Austrian-American Center, too, ceased to play a significant part, while the Austrian-American Society, under another name, went on to form a left-wing organization with the objective of Austrian independence.

The circumstances and possibilities confronting the political emigrants from Austria in the United States were fundamentally different from those prevailing in France. As we have seen, France considered Austrian independence an important plank in any French security system. But for the United States, Austria was only a small country lying at the periphery of its interests, at best a building block for a future European balance of power.

In America, Hans Rott's efforts continued, just as they had in France, to be directed toward achieving a united front of all Austrian political emigrant factions, but this time he was proceeding with the participation and support of Otto von Hapsburg. In a fundamental appeal to the former Viennese university professor Dr. Willibald Plöchl in Washington, dated February 17, 1941, he explained the necessity of this tactic. He pointed to the example of the Czechs during the First World War; they had won recognition for an independent Czech Republic only by presenting a united front. Tomaš G. Masaryk had attributed the Czech success to three activities: having encompassed all Czech and subsequently also all Slovak forces abroad; having kept the Allied statesmen and governments constantly informed on the Czech independence movement; and having campaigned assiduously for the program of Czechoslovak statehood. Hans Rott wished to follow this successful example.[69] But Plöchl had already written him laconically on January 12, 1941, that there was "no danger of such a unification."[70]

In spite of his understanding that unification was essential to his aims, Hans Rott could not overcome the pattern revealed in France, where, in spite of pressure from the concerned French government, the representation abroad could not be incorporated because of opposition from within the emigrant body. Only a modest Bureau Autrichien, under nonpolitical leadership, was the narrow outcome of all efforts. And even this limited agency, as we know, was never properly established.

In America, Hans Rott determined to overcome the obstacle of disunity in spite of the emigrants' discouraging record. He worked out a new tactic for achieving the old goal of a representative Austrian representation abroad. The basic idea, which he developed in cooperation with Dr. Plöchl, a renowned expert on ecclesiastical law, was to form a legitimate government in exile by interpreting applicable articles of the constitution that had been Austria's fundamental law at the time of the Anschluss. Dr. Plöchl well knew that he was the only minister of Schuschnigg's last government now living in freedom. He reasoned that, given the enforced incapacity of the legitimate organs of government, he was entitled to carry on the government of the federal state of Austria. This seemed a valid interpretation, especially as the United States had not granted de jure recognition of the Anschluss. Hans Rott assumed that the Austrian federal constitution guaranteed that the functions of a government could be exercised at any time and in all circumstances. No state could allow affairs of state to be paralyzed because constitutionally assigned state functionaries had been eliminated. During the debates on the Austrian federal constitution of 1920, on the amendments of 1929, and on the constitution of the federal state of Austria in 1934, no one could have foreseen the precise pattern of subsequent events: that the country would be occupied by another nation, that the federal president would be isolated, that the last federal chancellor would be arrested, and that the members of the last Austrian government would be put in jail or relieved of their offices through intervention by the occupation forces. No one could have foreseen how the representatives of independent Austria would be prevented from exercising their functions through an action that ran counter to the law of nations. It was Hans Rott's legal opinion that, exiled and out of the reach of National Socialist Germany, he could implement—at least abroad—the Austrian laws existing at the time of the Anschluss, especially the constitutional articles concerning the prevention of governmental functions. In this attempt he and Dr. Plöchl relied on Article 81, Paragraph 2, and Article 77, Paragraph 1, of the constitution of May 1, 1934.[71]

In his considerations of how to set up a provisional government abroad through interpretation of the federal constitution, Rott worried that other Austrian émigré organizations would then have no motivation to oppose any provisional foreign representation, but also would not start on their own well-intentioned efforts toward creating a foreign office.[72] That his fears were justified was demonstrated by the establishment of Austrian Action on April 5, 1941.

This group's incorporation under the leadership of Ferdinand Czernin was immediately hailed by the *Aufbau* as "a new combat unit of Austrian emigrants."[73] Earlier, under the sponsorship of the New World Club, a New York organization, Czernin had given speeches appealing for aid for the victims of National Socialism.[74] Because of his name, he was seen by the nonpolitical factions as precisely the right representative of a group aiming for the restoration of Austria's independence. The elder Czernin, Count Ottokar, had taken part in Austria-Hungary's negotiations with the Entente powers during the First World War. Thus, Ferdinand Czernin was the heir, both literally and figuratively, of a statesman of the old monarchy who at the same time had not been hostile to the Western Entente powers. Even in drastically changed circumstances a generation later, the son considered himself uniquely qualified to lead the politically active Austrian emigration in the United States.[75] Since Czernin was allied with none of the former parties of the Austrian Republic, it was understandable that his newly established organization would direct its program to the broad unpolitical strata of the emigration and to exclude partisan activists. At its foundations, Austrian Action announced that only naturalized American citizens and Austrians holding first papers would be allowed to join the organization. Many refugees were concerned about the new Foreign Agent Registration Act, and to assuage their fears, the founders of Austrian Action made sure that the new organization would not be obliged to register as a foreign agent. In effect, the requirement that members must either be naturalized or hold first papers was Ferdinand Czernin's way of acknowledging the refugees' fear that they might fall within this American statute.[76] He also hoped that the composition of the membership would make possible collaboration with the Austrian socialists abroad, who tended to keep their distance. To reassure them, his organization immediately spoke out against any action in which Otto von Hapsburg took a part, direct or indirect.[77]

The reason why Ferdinand Czernin remained irreconcilable to the house of Hapsburg may never come to light. The explanation may well be his close relations with the representatives of the successor states, especially Czechoslovakia.[78] Czernin's dislike of Otto must have been known to Hans Rott and Willibald Plöchl. Even though Rott accepted Otto's support in the administration of the Free Austrian Movement and therefore had to fear the inevitable confrontation with Czernin and the Austrian Action group he had established, the way chosen by him and Plöchl made it possible from the outset to condemn to failure Czernin's attempts to establish a foreign representation. His efforts must be viewed from this perspective as well.

Meanwhile, Rott and Plöchl translated into action their legal theory of attempting to continue in exile the last Austrian federal constitution. In September, 1941, they established the Free Austrian National Council with Hans Rott as acting federal president and Willibald Plöchl as chancellor and representative in Washington. The Free Austrian National Council was to be the legal Austrian representation abroad until the formation of a newly elected government after the liberation of Austria. Plöchl also published a newsletter in Washington, *News of Austria*. To support it, the American Friends of Austria was organized, also in Washington. On September 19, 1931, Plöchl informed the United States Department of State that the Council considered itself the successor and continuation of the last legitimate government of Austria. At the same time he also informed the State Department that Hans Rott, as the oldest surviving member of the last Austrian government, had assumed the duties of acting federal president of Austria while he himself was acting as federal chancellor.[79] To justify this action further, Plöchl also referred to a statement by President Roosevelt, of May 27, 1941, to the effect that the attack on Czechoslovakia had begun with the conquest of Austria. Plöchl therefore tried to connect Austria's political situation with that of Czechoslovakia, and he urged collaboration between the new Austrian government in Washington and the representatives of other states in the Danube area.

In spite of Hans Rott's and Dr. Plöchl's roundabout route to achieve recognition for an Austrian agency by continuing abroad the last Austrian government, Dr. Plöchl was obliged to hear from his opposite number in the discussions, Assistant Secretary of State Adolf A. Berle, Jr., that United States interests in any matter concerning Austrian independence presupposed the joint efforts of all groups of Austrian emigrants.[80] This statement meant turning back to the old way: the unification of all emigration groups, which had been tried before. It meant, especially, renewed collaboration with the Austrian socialists abroad. These groups had remained aloof even in the United States, but they, too, understood that the American government required total unification as the basis of any recognition of a foreign agency of Austria.

Foreseeably, as soon as Rott's and Plöchl's move had been announced in the *New York Times* of September 28, 1941, it was immediately attacked by other groups of émigrés. An Austrian Coordinating Committee, which had been formed in New York a short time before, protested in the *Aufbau* of October 3, 1941; Rott was accused of lacking contact with the existing Austrian organizations, and his plan was characterized as "a childish attempt."[81] A "Statement of Austrian Social Democrats" followed in the same publication on October 17, 1941, signed by an impressive number of former officials and functionaires of the Austrian Social Democratic party. It declared that the formation of an Austrian government "through Herrn Hans Rott" and Willibald Plöchl could not be borne in silence. These men were, the statement went on, simply representatives of a monarchist splinter group, a small segment of the emigration, while the signers of the declaration of the Austrian Social Democrats represented 42 percent of the votes in the last Austrian elections—those of 1930. Under no circumstances could the political future of Austria be erected on the difficult years from 1934 to 1938.[82] Ferdinand Czernin and Austrian Action raised an objection to Otto von Hapsburg's assumed support of the newly established Austrian National Council.[83]

This storm of newspaper articles mobilized both American public opinion and the thinking of the Austrian emigration. This first wave of protests also served to demarcate the opposing fronts. From the outset, it was clear that the newly formed Austrian Action wished to cooperate extensively with the Austrian socialists abroad.

In retrospect the attempt by Rott and Plöchl to achieve an almost unattainable goal through legal interpretation of constitutional articles appears to have been anything but a childish undertaking, as the above-mentioned newspaper article tried to make it appear. The attempt may have been far-fetched and daring; it may even have had little chance of success in trying to apply Austrian legislation in a foreign country. Nevertheless, Rott's and Plöchl's failure must be seen in the same perspective as President Beneš's success in continuing the Czech government. Rott was accused of being simply "Herr Rott"— that is, no longer a proper federal minister—but from a historical standpoint this argument is not convincing. Dr. Beneš, the former president of the Czech Republic, resigned his office after the Munich agreement, while Rott was a member of the last recognized government of independent Austria and never officially left his post; his departure from Austria after months of imprisonment under the National Socialist regime can surely not be called voluntary. In any case, an attempt, like Hans Rott's, to circumvent a political roadblock in the pursuit of a worthy goal represents a justified political strategy, even if this particular strategy had to stand on shaky grounds. Time and again, when all other attempts to achieve a united front of the Austrian emigration failed, Rott and his coworkers referred to the articles of the federal constitution. In organizing the Free Austrian National Council, they applied these articles in petitions and applications to the United States Department of State.

Hans Rott and Dr. Plöchl gave up their participation in the Council as early as January, 1942, since after the American entry into the war Rott tried to form a united front with the other Austrian political organizations. The legal argument was then taken up by Professor Heine-Geldern in a detailed report to Congressman Eberharter.[84] Further, as will be shown below, he continued even after the Moscow Declaration of November 1, 1943—yes, even after the July Putsch in Germany in 1944—to refer in further applications to the State Department to the articles of the Austrian federal constitution. Even American attorneys who, toward the end of 1943, worked to gain recognition from the State Department for Rott and his associates as legitimate representatives of Austria in line with the Austrian constitution in effect at the time of the Anschluss, based their arguments on this legal position.

At the same time that Rott and Plöchl were setting up the Austrian National Council, a first joint initiative was taken by Austrian Action and the Austro-American Center (then still in existence), under the leadership of Dr. Ernst Karl Winter and the Austrian Section of the American Committee for European Reconstruction, which he had formed. This initiative attempted to raise the Austrian question once again. A declaration signed jointly by these organizations and dated June 21, 1941, stated that they would never recognize the occupation of Austria and demanded a solemn declaration by the government of the United States that America had never recognized the Anschluss.[85] The occasion for this step was the intended closing of the United States General Consulate in Vienna scheduled for July 15, 1941. The letter of the three organizations was acknowledged by the State Department, which, however, took no position either for or against the petition.[86] Aside from the declaration, cast in general terms and issued at the outbreak of war in September, 1939, by the three Austrian organizations then existing in New York, this document of January 21, 1941, must be judged the first joint action of the Austrian emigration in the United States, as far as groups of émigrés aimed at the restoration of Austria at all.

During the months preceding America's entry into the war a number of individuals also called at the State Department to present various views and proposals for the future of Austria after an Allied victory. In extraordinary times, when an established polity such as Austria disappears in the maelstrom of history, individuals and groups will appear and try to bring private initiative and private influence to bear on the situation. Efforts were made to attain goals and exercise functions for the vanished state that had previously been exercised by its governmental institutions. In the case of Austria, which, in contrast to all other nations overrun by Hitler, had disappeared without the last government's having been able to represent the interests of its former citizens through a government in exile or some similar expedient, it was almost bound to happen that former citizens would try to preserve the interests of the vanished state and its citizens. For the most part these were former diplomats, statesmen, writers, and university professors, who felt it their responsibility to present their opinions concerning Austria to the American authorities.

This last statement cannot be applied so directly to Otto von Hapsburg; his standing in the United States among the political emigration was unique. Thus in October, 1941, George M. V. Alexich, the former Austrian ambassador to the Netherlands and Belgium, inquired whether the Free Austrian National Council had been established, under Hans Rott's leadership, with the approval of the American government.[87] At the same time he offered his own services to the United States, but not without mentioning the chairman of Austrian Action, Ferdinand Czernin, in less than laudatory terms because of some financial transactions that lay far in the past—apparently intending thus to prevent Czernin's participation in official Austrian matters.

A survey of the personalities and organizations of the worldwide Austrian political emigration is given in a report of December 9, 1942, of the British Postal and Telegraph Censorship, issued under the title "Free Austrians— General Trends." Here we find a noteworthy remark summing up the core of the apparently unbridgeable differences among the Austrian emigration groups: "There is a noticeable division between those who place the independence of Austria first on their programme and those for whom democracy comes before anything else."[88]

Julius Deutsch also began to emerge in the United States as the principal spokesman and journalistic representative of his political friends in the Austrian socialist emigration. In a petition to the State Department he pointed out that there existed in New York a club of Austrian Social Democrats and Revolutionary Socialists, as well as a joint foreign representation. Cautiously he added immediately that the Revolutionary Socialists accounted for only a small minority, meaning that the Social Democrats of the old stripe played the leading role in the foreign representation and that one would have to deal with them, rather than with the Revolutionary Socialists. Today, however, we know from the far more reliable leader of the Revolutionary Socialists, Joseph Buttinger, a fact Deutsch withheld: At the time of his memorandum the foreign representation was inactive as a consequence of opposition from the Revolutionary Socialists, and its dissolution followed on the outbreak of war.[89]

Count Richard N. Coudenhove-Kalergi, the well-known spokesman for Pan-Europe, the utopian movement, exhibited a lively interest in the organization of an Austrian government in exile. As early as September 19, 1941, he had approached the father of the Secretary of State Henry Morgenthau in order through his good offices to be received in the State Department. He submitted to the State Department a detailed memorandum entitled "Austrian Independence in the Light of the Atlantic Charter," contrasting the legal recognition of a Czech government in exile to the anomalous position of the proposed Austrian government in exile.[90] He also conveyed to the State

Department his firm conviction that the Austrian socialists abroad favored a Greater Germany and that in his opinion the legitimists, who were calling for the restoration of Austria, were the strongest party. He proposed to change the international situation of Austria by revoking the Anschluss to the extent that Austria would be recognized by the Allies as no longer a German province but as an occupied country. Such recognition, he insisted, would have to take effect before any peace conference could be held.[91]

As his contribution to the question of Austria's situation, Guido Zernatto, the former Austrian minister without portfolio, presented his opinion in a document of April 18, 1941, to the State Department. He believed that rather than establishing a political organization for Austria, there was a need only for a central administrative committee to support the host country in case of war by assisting in the screening of Austrians threatened with internment and their classification into those who were not opposed to National Socialism and those who were its avowed opponents. Not surprisingly, he also offered his own services as a member of such a central committee. It was astonishing that Zernatto assumed that in case of war the United States would resort to general internment of enemy aliens. He was apparently not aware that, when the First World War broke out, citizens of the old Austrian monarchy were not considered enemy aliens and that their treatment differed fundamentally from that accorded citizens of the German Reich. In any case, his proposal was certainly not advantageous for the emigrants from Austria.[92]

Speaking of the activities of individual figures in the interest of Austria during this early period of the war, we must deal with the most outstanding one, Otto von Hapsburg, and with his significance for Austrian legitimism, which he represented.[93] Otto's relations with President Roosevelt and Ambassador Bullitt have already been mentioned. His efforts to raise the Austrian question had not remained without success. As is vouchsafed in his letter of September 5, 1939, to President Roosevelt, Ambassador Bullitt while still in France had shown an interest in all questions of an Austrian government in exile; he may even have suggested them.[94] In addition, during the final years of the Republic of Austria, legitimism as a movement had made considerable progress and had come to be seen as a reliable support in the struggle for Austria's independence. The significance of legitimism during these years is evident from the reports of the American diplomatic representatives in Vienna.[95] Otto's opponents, especially the Austrian socialists abroad, repeatedly asserted that the monarchist movement in Austria had been meaningless and had never received a mandate; but this argument failed to convince because legitimism became significant only in the years after the destruction of the Social Democratic party, in February, 1934.[96] The argument leveled against legitimism—that it was insignificant in numbers in comparison with the Social Democratic party—does not hold. It is true that the Social Democrats had emerged from the 1930 elections as the strongest party, with 42 percent of the votes. But this plurality certainly deteriorated during the 1930's, just as Austrian democracy itself deteriorated. Surely any argument based on the election of 1930 is not relevant to the occupied Austria of the years after 1938. Time changes circumstances: It is interesting to note in this connection that the socialists within Austria had long since declared the Anschluss no longer desirable, while the socialists abroad were still in favor of it.[97] The socialists' argument wholly overlooked the fact that in 1930 National Socialism played no role in Austria either as a movement or as a party, while eight years later at least one-fourth of the Austrian population had turned to National Socialism. In *Am Beispiel Österreichs,* Joseph Buttinger bluntly admits that after the suppression of the February rising, many workers preferred to become National Socialists. During the same eight years, legitimism, too, attracted an increasing number of Austrians.

In Austria and, later, in exile, Otto's name attracted the hopes, strivings, and goals of those political figures who believed in the necessity of reviving, even if in altered form, the cooperation or collaboration of all the successor states in the Danube area, splintered since 1918. Also in the United States, the question was raised how to check Germany's drive for expansion. Since with the exception of the German-speaking and Hungarian-speaking sections of the old Danube monarchy, the successor states had failed as cornerstones and supporters of a European security system, the question arose also in the United States whether the destruction of the Danube monarchy had been necessary or useful. Before America's entry into the war, it was Otto von Hapsburg with whose name the concepts of the old Austrian monarchy became associated. More and more he was considered the expert and consultant for Austrian and Hungarian affairs.[98]

Otto, however, never became popular with the American public or with most of the Austrian emigrants. An Austrian political writer, Alexander Vodopivec, has pointed out the reason for this circumstance: "The roots of all subsequent evil lay in the fact that Otto von Hapsburg never personally experienced conditions in Austria. For him they are a mosaic composed of many small chips, each of which he knows, each of which is correct in itself, but from which he has put together an incorrect total picture."[99] It seems that Otto did not attach much importance either to public opinion in the United States or to the broad Austrian emigration. He preferred to use his personal connections to win over personalities whom he deemed important and neglected to cultivate an influence on public opinion. We shall see that subsequently this precise accusation was leveled at him from the American side.[100]

A comparison of Otto's efforts in France with those in the United States shows that he was forced to pursue his aims under fundamentally different conditions in the two countries. In France, a Danubian federation of all the successor states of the Austro-Hungarian monarchy, or at least of some of the successor states, headed by Otto von Hapsburg or even without him, seemed a valuable substitute for France's security system after the Little Entente—consisting of Czechoslovakia, Yugoslavia, and Romania—had turned out to be worthless in an emergency. Organization of a new security system was one of France's principal war objectives, and the idea of a strong power in the Danube basin was attractive in this connection. At the time plans for a Danube federation were discussed also in the United States. But here the principal question was how to frustrate Hitler Germany's plans for world domination and to reverse its conquests. The question of Austrian independence, of a Danubian federation, or of a new combination in the Danube area could be seen only as a subsidiary aspect of the larger objective.

In the final analysis, this is the reason why Otto had to fail in his efforts not only to assist in the restoration of the independence of Austria in the borders of 1938, but also to achieve political aims that went beyond this purpose. In France conditions were different from those in the United States. In France, his name was a symbol of a political objective in France's interest, and there he was a figure to be reckoned with even if, for tactical reasons, he was kept in the background.[101] In the United States he was only a private person striving to achieve the restoration of Austria's lost independence. His role was emphasized by the name he used, particularly in the United States, of "Otto of Austria." Although "Austria" is part of the official name and titles of the house of Hapsburg, this nomenclature stressed the word "Austria," connecting him with the Republic of Austria.[102]

In the United States, Otto von Hapsburg became *primus inter pares* in the strategies of the emigration factions, but in France it had been an advantage for him to be able to stand above party. French statesmen and Ambassador Bullitt, who took an interest in him, could keep him in the background as a symbol of a Danubian federation, so that he could stand above party later on because France wanted a Danube federation; but none of these considerations were of any advantage to him in the United States. Here Otto was seen as standing for Austrian legitimism. He did not represent any political party, since the legitimist movement, which had attained political significance only in authoritarian Austria in the period 1934–1938, did not "count." Legitimism could not be projected onto a party level in relation to other parties in Austria, as the guidelines of American politics required and as was considered legitimate according to American public opinion.[103]

It is incomprehensible to any retrospective observer that the American authorities, such as the State Department, where the Austrian political emigration organizations pleaded their cause, could have accepted the socialists' claim that they represented the strongest Austrian party. That claim was based on an anachronism; there was no standard of comparison between the elections of 1930 and the political conditions in Austria after the occupation of the country in 1938, and even less so during wartime. Since 1934 there were no longer political parties in the democratic sense; under the authoritarian regime there existed only one political organization, the Patriotic Front, and by no means did it express the country's true political opinion.

Equating German National Socialism with a Greater-German state, after the Anschluss, did not reflect the true political will of the former independent state of Austria. In authoritarian Austria, movements had partly replaced parties, but under National Socialist Germany the fiction was maintained that all Germans were represented in National Socialism. Therefore, citing the party policies of ten years before, as the Austrian socialists did in pointing to the elections of 1930 or 1932, was not reasonable. The only suggestion that, after ten years, under totally different conditions, it was not possible to work on the basis of the old election results is found in a polemical statement by Ferdinand Czernin in the weekly *Aufbau* in 1944, at a time when he himself, who had always sought collaboration with the Austrian Social Democrats, had had to give up any hope of being able to work with them.[104]

That Otto von Hapsburg himself and his circle never either recognized the socialists' contradictions or publicly opposed them may be considered one of his most serious political mistakes. Especially in the United States, with its deeply rooted concepts of majority and minority parties as the basis of a democracy, taking a clear position would have been in order. It can justly be stated (and could also have been confirmed by the diplomatic representatives of the United States in Vienna) that the legitimist movement in Austria, in the final years before the Anschluss, was of far greater significance than its opponents asserted.[105] But Otto followed another rationale. He was naturally one of the many individuals who called on the State Department in "the matter of Austria." A note on one of his conferences, of October 16, 1941, is in the records. According to this memo, he claimed that he could unite 85 percent of all Austrians in the Western Hemisphere. This claim was clearly unrealistic and was evaluated as such.[106]

In the months preceding America's entry into the war after the attack on Pearl Harbor of December 7, 1941, the Austrian question was discussed ever more frequently. Austrian political organizations sprang up in many places. Mergers were the order of the day. Attempts at detailing political principles and aims in reports and memoranda increased. In the traditional manner, attempts were also made to exploit personal connections and so to attain a sphere of action where one might use his knowledge and former position to aid the new country in case of war.

Around the same time the United States authorities, especially the State Department, began to concern themselves with the Free Movements from various occupied countries, which could no longer be ignored. They were organized on the pattern of Charles de Gaulle's Free French Movement and now began to spread out on the political stage. When the war broke out, the State Department could therefore send out a press release, apparently prepared long beforehand, under the title "Policy Concerning the Free Movements." This document includes the wish and also the directions that the leadership of the Free Movements should lie in the hands, not of United States citizens, but of nationals of the respective countries. A State Department official was even assigned to keep in touch with these movements and supervise them, although this should have happened much sooner if the State Department's idea was to keep up with the development of the Free Movements.[107]

The significance of the political emigration organizations and the Free

Movements for possible help in the struggle against the Axis powers was differently valued at different levels. One of the strongest supporters of the movement for a free Austria was, as we have seen, Jan Masaryk, the son of one of the most successful political emigrants of recent history. He had a deep understanding of the advantages the Free Movements could offer to a host country.[108] At a discussion in the State Department during the months before the outbreak of war, Masaryk pointed out that, as a consequence of the dissension within the political emigration in London and in the United States, unfortunately no proper progress toward recognition of Austria's independence had been achieved. But Masaryk did not fail to emphasize to the State Department the great significance of political organizations abroad; he stressed the Austrian question's high importance for Czechoslovakia.[109] In this period there also began intense consultations between the British Foreign Office and the State Department concerning the treatment of the Free Movements. In a memorandum of November 13, 1941, the State Department noted that the British government had permitted the organization of Free Movements but added that there was little chance of financial support by Great Britain. The British government, on the other hand, held that in the question of the Free Movements the United States and Canada, with their large number of foreign-born citizens, had to assume leadership. In this communication Great Britain passed the leadership to the United States. It was noted moreover that in Great Britain including small units of Free Austrians in existing British military units had caused difficulties—apparently this article was intended to stress the problems of mobilizing members of the Free Movements.[110]

It must be remembered that the leadership role assigned shortly before the war to the United States in its collaboration with Great Britain was not desired and that the State Department was not prepared for such a role. At that, the American authorities ought to have found it easy enough to prepare themselves on this point from their own resources or by consulting recognized experts, such as Jan Masaryk. The records of the State Department from the time of the First World War were available, as were comprehensive memoirs. It is true that pertinent questions concerning treatment of the Free Movements of the Second World War were on a different plane from any similar efforts during the First World War with which they could be compared. But in this question an active policy of the two Western powers had become inevitable. The United States and Great Britain could have anticipated their coming role with a high degree of probability if they had considered the strivings for independence of the Slavic peoples in the period 1914–1918. As a consequence of their shortsightedness, the Free Movements could not function effectively because they received no financial help. Memoranda from various sections of the State Department intended to remove this passivity went unnoticed. Not even access to radio facilities, for propaganda, was granted to the various Free Movements, including the Free Austrians.[111]

IV

Austrian Political Emigration
in the United States after 1941

After the United States entered the war, a Presidential proclamation of December 8, 1941, declared "all natives, citizens, denizens, or subjects of Germany not actually naturalized" to be enemy aliens. The Austrian émigrés found that, just as in France, their new designation as enemy, hence undesirable, aliens separated them from their environment. From a legal standpoint they were treated like German nationals.

But even in those critical days the question of general internment of all the undesirable aliens did not arise. This was in marked contrast to the general internment at the beginning of the war in France or in Great Britain when a German invasion seemed imminent. The émigrés in the United States were merely requested to register with the authorities and were not permitted to carry weapons, shortwave radios, and cameras. Before traveling any great distance, they had to receive permission from the authorities.[1] Only those aliens whom the authorities considered dangerous to national security were arrested at the beginning of the war, and most of these were released within a short time. The United States had applied the same liberal principle during the First World War, when Austro-Hungarian citizens were not interned at all and only about four thousand Germans were confined.[2] The treatment of all German and Austrian émigrés by the American authorities was benevolent—as was stressed in a letter to President Roosevelt from the Methodist Church of Chicago's Commission on World Peace.[3]

Alone among the active Austrian political organizations in the United States, Austrian Action, under the leadership of Ferdinand Czernin, understood immediately that the question of classifying Austrians as "enemy, neutral, or friendly aliens" was of the utmost gravity for its members. Their concern can be readily explained; they were doing their utmost to reach the large numbers of apolitical Austrian émigrés in America, and an unappealing classification would be a liability in this endeavor. Austrian Action also correctly saw that the possible reclassification of the Austrians as friendly aliens offered a superb opportunity to increase their membership through overt activity.

Under Czernin's adroit leadership, Austrian Action became the strongest Austrian organization in the United States.[4] For obvious reasons the other organizations were reluctant to publish their membership figures, but neither the Free Austrian Movement nor the Austrian Labor Committee could show a membership list that came anywhere close to that issued by Austrian Action.

In spite of the cooperation of the American authorities, a number of the émigrés were afraid to take a position on the "question of Austria" or to participate in overt political activities after America's entry into the war. They were seriously concerned that they would incur difficulties in obtaining American citizenship. Even before America's entry into the war, such fears had not been entirely groundless. In answer to an emigrant's query whether participation in the Free Austrian Movement was agreeable to the American authorities, a State Department official expressed his "personal opinion" that "though there is no legal grounds opposing membership in an organization such as the Free Austrian Movement, aliens in the naturalization proceedings should direct their efforts toward complete assimilation as United States citizens. This would be better than working in the interest of the former homeland." This letter even mentioned "divided loyalties."[5]

A radio address by Attorney General Francis Biddle revealed that there were in the United States 1.1 million nationals of the Axis powers. Compared to the number of German and other enemy aliens, the Austrian émigrés represented only a small fraction of the total.[6]

As early as four days after the attack on Pearl Harbor, Austrian Action sent to the State Department a circular originally addressed to three thousand Austrians in New York that provided proof of the Austrians' loyalty. It called upon them to join a legion of foreign voluntary blood donors,[7] and the organization continued its efforts with a press release headed "Austrians Rally to US Flag." This communication included a listing of all efforts undertaken by Austrian Action to change the classification of Austrians as enemy aliens.

Further efforts included a letter to the State Department of December 13, 1941, and a telegram to President Roosevelt the same day. Both requested a "reconsideration of the classification" of Austrians generally as enemy aliens.[8] The publicized loyalty rally took place in New York on December 22, 1941. Attended by one thousand people, it culminated in dispatching telegrams to President Roosevelt and Prime Minister Churchill professing their loyalty.[9]

Thus Austrian Action launched energetic actions on behalf of its membership. But the same cannot be reported of the other Austrian political émigré organizations in the United States. The Free Austrian Council in Washington, established by Hans Rott and Dr. Willibald Plöchl, did send the State Department a memorandum requesting that the Austrian question be considered a fundamental part of U.S. policy.[10] But since none of the members of the Free Austrian Council was really interested in a change in the classification of Austrians, this question was not felt to be urgent, and no attempt was made to reopen the problem of classification.

Nothing was heard from the other Austrian organizations. Just as in France, the political émigrés did not take an active part in the question of classifying Austrians as enemy, neutral, or friendly aliens. The Austro-American League, the Austro-American Center, the Austrian Society, the Austrian socialists abroad—none issued declarations like that of Austrian Action to demonstrate to the American public the loyalty of their members. These organizations did not consider it worth their while to write petitions or letters to newspapers in the hope of influencing American public opinion. The Austrian socialists abroad advocated the view, clearly stated by Karl Hans Sailer, that the problem of classification was the concern not of the emigrant groups but of special refugee organizations and that it was their job to make it clear to the authorities that the refugees could not be equated with those who had made them refugees—the Nazis. Sailer's article titled "Aufgaben in der Emigration" ("Tasks in the Emigration") concluded: "But this [i.e., classification] is not a political question and has nothing to do with the future fate of Austria."

Of course the question of their treatment as enemy aliens touched the émigrés far more closely than did matters concerning Austria's future. The newly established Austrian Labor Committee in New York petitioned the State Department for the right of self-determination for Austria in a letter of January 16, 1942, signed by Dr. Fritz Adler, Hugo Breitner, and Julius Deutsch. Of even less importance for them was the announcement by the socialists abroad that monarchists and semifascists had no significance whatsoever for Austria and that, on the basis of the 1930 elections, the socialists abroad represented the strongest party. The socialist position was an exact continuation of their attitude at the time of the French internments. The classification of Austrians as enemy aliens was, for them, a logical consequence of the position that Austria's liberation should come about in conjunction with that of Germany and that until then no support should be given to any "reactionary" action that could be considered as a first step toward Austria's independence. The socialists saw removing the Austrians' classification as enemy aliens as just such a tendency. Therefore, the last diplomatic representative of the United States in Vienna, John C. Wiley, could state that as late as 1942 various groups still wanted to consider the Anschluss as an unalterable fact. The groups in the United States that he named included doctrinaire socialists led by Dr. Adler; Greater-German nationalists; radical groups such as Neues Beginnen (New Beginnings) with Dr. Paul Hagen; and, in England, leftist Labour circles of the London Bureau Socialists. Sailer's view—that the refugee problem was only a humanitarian one and not one of citizenship—fitted logically with the Greater-German views that the right of self-determination for Austria meant remaining part of the German Reich.[11]

Otto von Hapsburg, for his part, submitted to the State Department a list of persons for whose loyalty he was eager to vouch.[12] Neither the State Department nor the Justice Department archives, however, make it clear who was responsible for the decree of February 5, 1942, reclassifying Austrians as nonenemy aliens. With this ordinance, announced to the public on February 9, 1942, Austrians were released from the obligation to register as enemy aliens.[13] Both Austrian Action and Otto von Hapsburg claimed credit for the successful reclassification. With the exception of Otto's list of trusted Austrians, however, no memoranda or petitions from him are in the records.

No previous mention has been made of the crucial efforts of one Austrian émigré, the former Viennese university professor Dr. Arthur Lenhoff. Working with Dr. Adolf Homburger—who was subsequently appointed professor of law at the University of Buffalo—Dr. Lenhoff compiled a thorough treatise entitled *Legal Status of Austrians in the United States*. In a convincing manner it explained to the Justice Department why Austrians should not be considered enemy aliens in the sense of the Presidential proclamation of December 8, 1941.[14] The documentation of this study was so exhaustive that it, rather than the political efforts of Austrian Action or of Otto von Hapsburg, laid the legal groundwork that convinced the Attorney General to change the classification of Austrians as early as February, 1942.[15]

The treatment of Austrian citizens at the outbreak of the First World War— when they were not classed as enemy aliens—was probably a significant factor in the reclassification of the Austrian émigrés.[16] This point was stressed at the time by Estelle M. Sternberger, a well-known radio commentator. Her comments on the position of the enemy aliens is included in the posthumous papers of President Roosevelt.[17] For the apolitical émigrés, it was of no concern who had achieved the success. But the universally known activities of Austrian Action on this issue meant that the prestige of the organization increased among the émigrés. The organization had created a political springboard for itself. The question was only whether it could make proper use of it whenever an opportunity arose.

The Attorney General's declaration of February 9 laid the groundwork for recognition of Austrians as an independent nationality. Now the struggle for the future of Austria could begin, even though efforts continued to void the reclassification of Austrians as nonenemy aliens and to rescind this first step toward Austria's independence.

Consistent treatment of Austrian aliens in the United States was slow in coming. Before the war registration rules for Austrians had been interpreted in several ways, and even after the beginning of the war Austrians were treated variously. In California their situation was complicated because of the harsh treatment meted out to the numerous Japanese residents who were evacuated after the outbreak of war; the Austrians generally feared that the military authorities might also evacuate the "German aliens," including Austrians. In San Francisco, for example, an effort was made to exempt from enemy aliens status only those Austrians who had entered the country before Hitler's advent.[18] While the Justice Department had exempted all Austrians from the obligation to register as enemy aliens, the Selective Service System, in a memorandum of March 16, 1942, did not include Austria in a recommendation directed to draft boards on the treatment they were to apply to foreign nationals according to their citizenship. Such directives created the impression that Austria was a province of Germany.[19] On the other hand, a law of March 28, 1942, included Austrians in approving the naturalization of aliens in the armed forces.[20]

The varying treatment of Austrians prompted John C. Wiley to take a sharp look at Austrian history. His detailed memorandum of March 21, 1942, to Secretary Hull states that the majority of Austrians did not want the Anschluss. He asserted that the plebiscite following the occupation of Austria was a fraud and proved nothing, and he argued that classifying the Austrians as enemy aliens would mean a German propaganda victory in southern and eastern Europe, and that recognition of the Anschluss would inevitably be a step toward losing the coming peace. Wiley also addressed the ambivalent attitude of the Austrian émigrés themselves toward "the Austrian problem." He referred particularly to the Austrian socialists in New York and London—who were intent on upholding the Anschluss—as proponents of Greater Germany. Certainly he was accurate when he emphasized that the classification of Austrians as enemy or friendly aliens was a crucial question of great political import for the United States and a question decisive for the restoration of Austria's independence.[21]

In spite of or because of Wiley's frank attitude in the question of classification—and of his intervention to prevent their reclassification as enemy aliens—the treatment of Austrians still continued to vacillate. In a memorandum of Assistant Secretary of State Berle of May 22, 1942, classifying Austrians as "neutral" in the Selective Service System is recommended.[22] But in a circular of June 3, 1942, issued by the visa division of the State Department, on the other hand, Austrians are considered to be enemy aliens with regard to immigration and naturalization.[23]

On June 4, 1942, the government finally took a decisive stand. A memorandum from the Foreign Nationality Branch of the Coordinator of Information declared that Austrians were not to be classified as enemy aliens. The memorandum referred to unrest among the Austrian refugees and to British indecisiveness in connection with the question of reclassification, as well as to the activity of the Neues Beginnen, which supported the Anschluss; it was considered unwise to play into the hands of this group.[24] Finally a joint conference of all American governmental authorities was called and the status of Austrians was "definitively" decided.[25] Nevertheless, the legal status of former Austrians remained uncertain for some time more. The American attorney John W. Davis, who appeared as *amicus curiae* in a lawsuit for Austrian Action, had to prove the special position of the Austrians before the war.[26] Finally, in a decree of May 15, 1943, the Justice Department declared once and for all that Austrians were not Germans.

This classification was also significant for the legal position of Austrians in Great Britain, its dominions, and the other member states of the United Nations. Soon after the Austrians had been removed from the ranks of enemy aliens, the British Foreign Office inquired whether this might not be the first step toward "nonrecognition" of Austria's Anschluss to Germany.[27] The possible consequences of the Justice Department's decision had been correctly assessed by the British authorities. Prime Minister Churchill referred to Austria as the first victim of National Socialist aggression and expressed the hope that after the Allied victory Austria would find a place of honor in the international polity. This statement implied nothing more than liberation from Nazism and made no provision for Austria's future and independence.[28] But since the German Reich was the adversary, logically only a restored independent Austria could assume the place of honor. On February 15, 1942, the Free Austrian Movement thanked President Roosevelt on behalf of émigré organizations in London for recognizing Austria as a conquered nation and as the first victim of National Socialism.[29]

The attitude of the British government, however, remained ambiguous. Shortly before the war, as we have seen, the Foreign Office expressed the opinion that the United States and Canada should assume leadership in dealing with the Free Movements. But with regard to the treatment of Austrians, the British authorities did not follow the American example. In the course of a debate on the position of Austrians in the United States and in Great Britain, the Home Secretary, Herbert Morrison, declared that he could not advocate the exemption of Austrians as a group from the category of enemy aliens. It was only after the Moscow Declaration that Austrians in Britain were able to reregister.[30] When we come to discuss the entire history of political emigration in Great Britain, we will examine the reasons for this ambiguous stance on the part of the British authorities. Their attitude also accounts for the long time it took the American authorities to abandon any idea of reclassifying the Austrians as enemy aliens.

We must therefore conclude that in the treatment of Austrians as nonenemy aliens, the interests of the Austrian political emigration generally coincided with the wishes of the Jewish emigrants among them. The politically active emigrants—especially Austrian Action—were fully aware that recognition of an Austrian nationality, separate from German nationality, was a prerequisite for the recognition of independence and the creation of an Austrian government in exile. It is worth noting, though, that even Assistant Secretary of State Berle, who, in his memorandum of May 22, 1942, considered Austrians as neutral aliens, took a negative attitude toward the restoration of Austrian independence and the creation of an Austrian agency during the wartime.[31] In 1943, after a conference with a representative of the British government, Berle still felt that it would be best to stay away from all Free Movements with the exception of the Free Italian Movement.[32]

At the time of America's entry into the war and with the change in the treatment of Austrians, the Allied powers' attitude toward the Free Movements took on new meaning. All Free Movements—that is, organizations of former citizens of the countries now occupied by the Axis powers—aimed at liberating their homelands. The policy favored by Assistant Secretary Berle—to keep a distance from all such organizations—was not universally shared by other American government bureaus. The attitude of the State Department generally, issued as ''Policy in Regard to the Free Movements'' on December 10, 1941, was to ensure that the Department was kept informed of plans, activities, and day-to-day developments; the ultimate aim was to prevent surprises. Indeed there was some concern that the activities of these Free Movements could run counter to the national interests of the United States, and additional causes for worry were the continuing discords within these organi-

zations and the often undiplomatic behavior of many of their representatives.[33]

The exchange of ideas with the British government on the question of the
Free Movements after the outbreak of war turned into a close collaboration
between the State Department and the Foreign Office. It was hoped that the
collaboration would enable them to deal with the problem of the Free Movements as a single entity. A report from the American embassy in London to
Secretary Hull on December 19, 1941, provides a detailed survey of the attitude of the British government toward the Free Movements. The report chron-
icles the early attempts by the émigrés in Great Britain to secure Austria's independence.[34] In this document the British government establishes two
fundamental preconditions for judging the viability of a Free Movement.
First, any Free Movement must include someone who is not only well respected, but can be considered a potential leader. Second, the particular organization abroad must represent a significant number of people within the
home country who share their political direction, even if the people in their
home country are condemned to silence. Also, the various groups within a
Free Movement must arrive at a meeting of minds and form a unified body
before Great Britain would take a stand. But—and this qualification was to
have the most serious consequences in the future—the British government
would under no circumstances assume a binding obligation to "solve" the
Middle European and Danube problems.[35]

As far as the Austrian Free Movements in Great Britain were concerned,
the same report to the Secretary of State noted that no single Austrian emigrant in Great Britain could be viewed as a potential leader. The fifteen
thousand Austrians in England split off into thirteen different groups that were
supposed to work together. On September 3, 1941, eleven groups had issued
"The Declaration of the Austrian Society in Great Britain," announcing that
they would jointly pursue the following goals: nonrecognition of the
Anschluss by Great Britain; recognition of the right of self-determination; a
change in their classification as enemy aliens; and the creation of an Austrian
fighting unit in Great Britain. Two groups—the "Pollak Socialists" and the
group around Count Czernin—refrained from signing this declaration. ("Pollak Socialists" refers to the London Bureau of Austrian Socialists, led by
Oskar Pollak; Count Czernin's group, of course, was Austrian Action.) The
Association of Austrian Christian Socialists in Great Britain, which represented the former Christian Socialist party, was not mentioned.[36]

"The Declaration of the Austrian Society in Great Britain" coincided with
the objectives of those in America who aimed at the restoration of Austria's
independence. It is equally clear, though, that Austrian Action, an American
organization, could not sign a British manifesto. The American embassy
should not have mentioned their not signing at all, let alone have drawn infer-
ences from the absence of their signature. It appears, then, that the Pollak Socialists were only one of two Austrian organizations in Great Britain that did

not sign, the other being the Association of Austrian Christian Socialists in Great Britain—an error on the part of the Embassy. But this means nothing more than that this foreign group (the Pollak Socialists) was not in agreement with the statements laid down by other Austrian groups in the declaration. They did not believe that the majority of the émigrés wished to see the Anschluss annulled. Nor did they want reclassification of the émigrés into nonenemy aliens. And it is obvious that the Pollak Socialists rejected the restoration of Austria's independence.[37]

On the American side, mention must be made here of a memorandum issued by the State Department on January 26, 1942. The document set out three possible policies relating to the Free Movements: giving them an entirely free hand; exercising government scrutiny over them; and finally, effecting a compromise solution between the two options. A year later, as we have seen, Assistant Secretary of State Berle asserted that it would be best to sidestep the Free Movements.[38] In a reply to the American envoy in Ottawa on April 2, 1942, Berle argued for keeping an eye on developments within the Free Movements without officially or unofficially recognizing them. The same attitude is found in a State Department memorandum of December 24, 1942, in response to an inquiry from the Office for War Information. Ultimately Berle found a fourth way of dealing with the Free Movements—to keep as far away from them as possible, excepting the Italian movement. The question remains, however, why the State Department would assign one of its own officials as liaison officer to the Free Movements if after more than a year of war no policy in this area had been developed.[39]

Nevertheless, in January, 1942, a "gentlemen's agreement" was achieved between Undersecretary Welles and the British ambassador in Washington, Sir R. I. Campbell. The two governments were to keep each other informed about the Free Movements. This agreement is acknowledged in a memorandum of November 2, 1942, concerning a discussion between the ambassador and Assistant Secretary Berle; we will return to this memorandum in the chapter on the Austrian batallion.[40] The question may be raised why both governments found an exchange of information important if neither intended to use these movements for their own political aims.[41]

Both the American and British foreign offices were hoping to postpone any decision concerning the treatment of the free movements and thus passively to delay answering the question of what was to become of Austria. Nonetheless, the new more intensive treatment of the question of Austria's restoration could not be overlooked.

In line with both countries' preconditions for recognizing Austria's independence and establishing a provisional foreign agency, the nonsocialist political organizations in the United States attempted to create a committee without reference to party lines and modeled after the Austrian Society in Great Britain. This group, named the Austrian National Committee, was established in New York on February 14, 1942, calling upon all Austrian factions, especially the socialists abroad, to cooperate.[42] Representatives of Austrian Action and Hans Rott's Free Austrian Movement—which had transferred its headquarters from Toronto to New York—joined the Austrian National Committee, as did members of the Young Conservative party, headed by Dr. Martin Fuchs, the former press attaché of the Austrian embassy in France. Hans Rott and Guido Zernatto were copresidents of this umbrella organization. Just like the Pollak Socialists in London, the Austrian socialists in New York refused to collaborate with this new committee. In February, 1942, they founded the Austrian Labor Committee, and beginning on April 20, 1942, they published their own periodical, *Austrian Labor Information,* enabling them to oppose all efforts at unification.

In the first issue Karl Hans Sailer published an article, "Aufgaben in der Emigration" ("Tasks in the Emigration"), which outlined the official political program of the Austrian Labor Committee. He too opposed all attempts at unification with other émigré factions. The principal task, he maintained, was "to ward off the sallies of the Austrian reaction."[43] If one remembers that Otto Bauer's programmatic essay, which was crucial to the ideology of the socialist emigration, had declared reactionary the policy of restoring Austria's independence, then it appears that Sailer, too, was disguising his true motive behind a rhetorical label. It is clear that the Austrian Labor Committee was established simply to counter the efforts of the Austrian National Committee.

The cordial welcome given to the Austrian Labor Committee by Ferdinand Czernin in his newsletter *Österreichische Rundschau (Austrian Review)* on March 7, 1942, met with no response from the socialists. Czernin's statement that the Austrian Labor Committee had clearly come out in favor of Austrian independence was equally ineffectual. It is understandable that Austrian Action was hoping to form closer ties with the Austrian Labor Committee. But it remains incomprehensible how, given Sailer's lead editorial, Czernin could claim that the Austrian Labor Committee had committed itself to Austria's independence.

Meanwhile, Julius Deutsch, once he had learned that there was no talk of recognition of the new organization, informed the State Department that the Austrian Labor Committee would not join the Austrian National Committee.[44] Thus the fronts, for and against Austrian independence, were established in the United States and in Great Britain at the same time.

In spite of Czernin's courtship of the Austrian socialists abroad, the Austrian National Committee remained a rump group. It began by attempting to settle differences in its own ranks. To place all Austrian organizations under a common roof, Hans Rott dissolved the Austrian National Council, which he had founded in Washington with Dr. Plöchl; he also dismissed his former collaborator as his representative.[45] Czernin also deleted the subtitle "Free Austrian Movement" as a sacrifice to the attempted unification of his organization (Austrian Action), since Rott's Free Austrian Movement had been the first to use this designation.[46]

But the unity of the nonsocialist groups in the Austrian National Committee did not last long. Czernin thought it more important to take a stand against

Otto von Hapsburg than to emphasize the unity of the émigré groups. Dr. Plöchl was annoyed that he had not been invited to take part in the Austrian National Committee. Furthermore, a new Austrian organization—Assembly for a Democratic Republic of Austria—was founded under the chairmanship of Dr. Fritz Rager, former secretary of the Vienna Chamber of Labor.[47] This new association rejected Austria's incorporation into Greater Germany.

In the meantime, the various organizations and personalities that had been concerned before the war with the recognition of an Austrian nationality and the establishment of a foreign agency continued their efforts after the war broke out.

As early as February 25, 1942, Professor Robert Heine-Geldern submitted to the State Department a well-documented statement entitled "Austrians in the War." In it he pointed out ways in which Austrians might help the Allies and contribute to their victory. He demanded recognition of an Austrian provisional government, Austria's admission to the United Nations, Austrian consular offices abroad, an Austrian propaganda office, and an Austrian Red Cross.[48] Dr. Plöchl together with Professor Friedrich Engel-Janosi sent a letter to President Roosevelt urging that Austria be made an official subject of American policy and that an American commissioner for Austria be appointed. Aided by American and Austrian experts, such a commissioner would act as a trustee until such time as the Austrians could erect a government of their own.[49]

Otto von Hapsburg conveyed to the State Department the draft of a public declaration commemorating the assassination of Chancellor Dollfuss by the National Socialists on July 25, 1934. This draft was accompanied by a request that the declaration be used at the memorial celebrations on July 25, 1942, the eighth anniversary of the assassination.[50] The declaration was meant to stress that the United States had never recognized the Anschluss and that therefore the Austrian state continued to exist. Otto did not win the State Department's approval, however. In particular, Assistant Secretary of State Berle, who had a decisive voice on the Austrian question, bluntly stated that there was no American interest in equating Austria with Otto von Hapsburg.[51]

Nevertheless, these efforts did result in one success. On July 25, 1942, the radio commentator James J. McDonald interviewed Otto in Washington concerning the significance of the anniversary of Dollfuss's assassination; July 25 was proclaimed "Austrian Day" in four states. Senator Claude Pepper also delivered a widely noted speech on the question of Austrian independence.

In spite of this success, however, four Austrian organizations—Austrian Action, the Austrian Labor Committee, the Assembly for a Democratic Republic of Austria, and Free Austrian Youth—addressed a letter to Senator Pepper and Representative Eberharter in which they expressed their astonishment at Otto's participation. Through his active presence, they claimed, the memorial occasion had been turned into a monarchist propaganda action.[52] On July 27, 1942, Secretary of State Hull released a statement that read: "This government has never taken the position that Austria was legally absorbed into the German Reich.''[53] But Otto could not prevent Berle from asking Hull not to reply to a telegram of thanks for this announcement.[54]

Until this time Austrian Action, led by Czernin, seemed to have attracted more attention in the State Department than the other Austrian organizations. The group had the largest membership and had outdone all other associations in a fervent display of patriotism. For reasons that are no longer clear today, George M. V. Alexich had taken a stand against Czernin, and the influence of Austrian Action appears to have waned after April, 1942. The record suggests Czernin ceased to enjoy the State Department support about that time. A hand-written note in a State Department file states clearly that the writer will do nothing to promote Czernin, and the same document wonders who might be backing Czernin and why Czernin said that his hands "were unfortunately tied."[55]

Also, since Otto was not a favorite of Assistant Secretary of State Berle, we must assume that Berle was significantly swayed by the views of Julius Deutsch, who worked in the Office for War Information. Deutsch continued to emphasize to State Department officials the position of the newly established Austrian Labor Committee. In two documents—dated January 16, 1942, and March 10, 1942—the socialists took the position that they represented the strongest Austrian political party in the country and that all other organizations in the United States were nothing more than splinter groups.[56]

Hull's statement on July 27, 1942, was followed on September 5 by a declaration by Anthony Eden, the British Foreign Secretary. It stated that the British government did not feel committed by changes in Austria after 1938 to any particular position on the Austrian question. The statement did not, however, go so far as to declare the Anschluss null and void or to make the restoration of the Austrian Republic a war objective.[57]

A great part of 1942 was spent in trying to turn the Austrian problem into an object of national policy for the United States and Great Britain, to win recognition for the Free Movements, and to have their offer of cooperation acknowledged. Not until 1943 were the definitive juridical and administrative conclusions finally drawn—at least in the United States. At last it was determined that legally Austria had never been part of the German Reich. At the very least, three years of controversy established the significance of the Austrian problem in the minds of American and British officials. Thus, the period 1942–1943 can be deemed fruitful insofar as the efforts to restore Austria's independence were concerned.[58]

V
The Austrian Battalion in the Army of the United States

At a press conference held on November 19, 1942, the American Secretary of War, Henry L. Stimson, announced that an Austrian battalion was to be organized within the framework of the United States Army. The War Department had gratefully accepted an offer of assistance from Otto von Hapsburg, head of the Military Committee for the Liberation of Austria, to recruit volunteers for the battalion. Thus was set into motion the only successful attempt supported by the Allies to achieve full official recognition for an Austrian foreign representation, in the limited form of an Austrian troop unit. The following is a history of the formation of the independent Infantry Battalion 101 in the United States Army, its brief existence, and its quick dissolution.

Even in France, where Ernst Rüdiger von Starhemberg, the former vice-chancellor in Schuschnigg's government, had attempted to establish an Austrian legion, the émigrés efforts had proved unsuccessful.[1] Another group of émigrés while still in Portugal had approached the British government requesting its consent to the formation of a military unit of Austrian émigrés. In Great Britain, the Free Austrian Movement of London also advocated the creation of an Austrian military unit. But neither group was successful in mounting añ Austrian military unit under British auspices.

After the collapse of France, Otto von Hapsburg eagerly continued his efforts on this front in the United States. Not without justification, he and his associates saw in the prospect of an Austrian military unit a symbol of the singular situation of the Austrians. Furthermore, to set up such a unit was viewed as an important step forward on the road to the longed-for Allied recognition of Austria's independence and the establishment of a government in exile. The lessons learned from the growth of the Czechoslovak legion in the First World War, and its significance for the subsequent creation of Czechoslovakia, were obvious.[2]

Otto von Hapsburg's efforts to create the Austrian battalion must have required careful planning over a long period of time. Otto's adjutant, Count Heinrich Degenfeld, in a letter of November 14, 1944, to Grace G. Tully, President Roosevelt's private secretary, expressed his gratitude for all the goodwill shown to Otto von Hapsburg and his family during the preceding four years.[3] Any chronological study of the period must reveal that many discussions on this project, particularly with the President and with Undersecretary of State Sumner Welles, had taken place before the first written memorandum concerning the establishment of an Austrian troop unit gave concrete form to the project. Not only Otto von Hapsburg, but also his mother—

Empress Zita—and his brothers had talked with President Roosevelt.[4] The President's private correspondence, which can be inspected in the Franklin D. Roosevelt Library in Hyde Park, New York, includes a letter from Otto dated August 27, 1942, in which he expresses his gratitude for the reception granted him on August 26, 1942, and also mentions the plans discussed at that meeting for Austria's and Hungary's postwar disposition.[5]

The earliest document relating to the creation of an Austrian battalion—a memorandum from the Organization and Training Department, Division G–3 of the War Department, to the Chief of Staff of the United States Army—is to be found in the War Department's archives in Washington. This paper, dated August 29, 1942, records that at a conference with the Assistant Chief of Staff, representatives of an "Austrian government in exile" had proposed the establishment of an infantry battalion within the framework of the United States Army. According to the memo, such plans were being reviewed favorably both by the President and by the Department of State.[6]

In surveying the memorandum, it is curious to note that representatives of an "Austrian government in exile"—which never did exist—had participated in the negotiations. The question who might have passed themselves off as ministers-in-exile remains a beguiling puzzle that cannot be answered from the existing records. Could a high-ranking military official not have known with whom he was dealing? Was the American official speaking with a private person, a group of private persons, or a semiofficial committee? This last seems highly unlikely, for the author of the memorandum frankly notes that on earlier occasions his own department had expressed opposition to the creation of units composed of foreign nationals. It may be assumed that the writer of the memorandum said he had negotiated with representatives of an Austrian government in exile in order to justify the establishment of a new Austrian unit. This is all the more likely since the "negotiators" referred to the approval of the State Department and to the President's benevolent attitude.

Even though there was no Austrian government in exile—as the author of the memorandum must have known—he could have assumed that the State Department had approved in principle a provisional government in exile and that plans for the Austrian battalion were simply one step toward that end. Therefore, he may have used the memorandum to advocate immediate establishment of the battalion within the framework of the U.S. Army—though with reservations. In particular, he demanded that recruiting volunteers be delayed until a committee made up of Austrian nationals had determined, at least provisionally, that there would be a sufficient number of volunteers available for the battalion. Equally surprising was the stipulation that from the outset the officers of the unit be American citizens of Austrian descent who had mastered the "Austrian language." Further, "enlisted men" assigned to the unit would have to be familiar with the "Austrian language" and were to be replaced as quickly as possible with soldiers of Austrian nationality. Should the latter not be available in sufficient numbers, they would have to be supplemented with "Austrian-speaking soldiers" who were United States citizens. The oath, however, was to be taken to the United States and the uniform of the battalion was to be that of the U.S. Army.[7]

How could such a highly placed military man conceive that there might be such a thing as an "Austrian language," different from German? Surely in this case Austria was not, as in the familiar wartime joke, confused with Australia. Did he perhaps think of the Austrian vernacular, which differs somewhat from written German in vocabulary and intonation, or did he have in mind the colloquialisms, perhaps even the drill-ground slang, of the old Austrian army of the First World War? Were it not that on April 7, 1943, the very same Assistant Chief of Staff called for the dissolution of the battalion, having shown himself well-informed on Austria during the interim, the oddities in the memorandum might have been overlooked.

The writer of the memorandum apparently did not think that his proposal was altogether realistic, and his attitude during the short lifetime of the Austrian battalion confirms this view. This high-ranking officer had only reluctantly given in to the wishes of the President and the State Department. He had acted against his own convictions in implementing the military instructions, preparations, and arrangements for the formation of the battalion. Beginning with the memorandum of August 29, 1942, however, he seems to have taken advantage of every opportunity to characterize this unit—which had been imposed on him by the civilian authorities and which could not easily be coordinated with the style and regulations of the U.S. Army—as a peculiarity, unlike other troop units. But, in spite of his overt disapproval, the establishment of an independent Austrian battalion was approved by the Chief of Staff on September 4, 1942.[8] Another division of the War Department, G–2—Intelligence, however, had opposed with all its might the creation of the battalion, calling such a development not "prudent." In a memorandum of October 25, 1942, Brigadier General J. H. Edwards mentioned difficulties with the Norwegian battalion, which had been established as early as July 11, 1942, and he suggested that the Austrian battalion not be activated in spite of government approval.[9]

The brigadier who wrote the first memorandum took issue with the draft of a proclamation prepared by the recruiting committee. The draft had been submitted by Archduke Otto, the presiding officer of the Military Committee for the Liberation of Austria, which was supposed to take charge of recruiting volunteers. This body had obviously been set up without any formality and without public knowledge. The proclamation was intended to be issued simultaneously with the Secretary of War's announcement of the battalion.[10] Once again General Edwards noted that G–2 was opposed not only to the intended publication of the proclamation, but to the entire project. Otto's participation, he felt, would give the Axis powers propaganda material to be used in Italy, Romania, and Yugoslavia, where animosity to the Hapsburgs still ran high. At the very least, however, the officer demanded that the State Department give its formal approval to the proclamation, since the files of the War Department contained no other proof that it had been passed than Otto's statement. It is clear that the whole matter of the battalion ran counter to the military thinking of the officer in charge.[11]

As a consequence of all the confusion, on September 24, 1942, Secretary Stimson requested that the State Department state its official position concerning the intended proclamation of the recruiting committee. He explained diplomatically that the War Department would be willing to agree to the declaration, but, because of possible international complications, the State Department's approval was desirable.[12] Officers in the top echelons of the War Department, too, were aware that they were dealing with a delicate problem.

Even though all these documents presupposed that approval of the battalion would be forthcoming and that Otto von Hapsburg would be closely connected with it, the conflicts within the War Department did not subside. In General Edwards's memorandum of October 25, 1942, there was reference to the State Department's opposition to any connection between Otto's committee and the battalion, even though the committee had submitted the project to the War Department with full confidence that it already had the approval of the State Department.[13] Indeed the memorandum did not specify which person or section within the State Department objected to Otto's recruiting committee. But the document suggested that not everything the proponents of the battalion communicated to the War Department corresponded to the facts. Evidently the same people in the State Department rejected the Free Movements and most particularly the efforts toward restoring Austrian independence, while Otto and his associates could refer to the support of Undersecretary of State Welles.

On November 2, 1942, Secretary Stimson, in a short letter to Secretary of State Cordell Hull, referred once again to the adverse experiences with the Norwegian battalion and suggested abandoning the idea of an Austrian battalion. However, he allowed for a loophole the size of a barn door by noting that his own objection was of no importance if political reasons made further pursuit of the project desirable. Like other commentators, he objected to Otto's committee, saying that it would not be supported, and he emphasized the importance of a nonpartisan, effective recruiting committee. He urged that the War Department be assured of success before embarking on the project since failure could feed enemy propaganda.[14] The language is unambiguous: The issue reduces to the military versus the political government. The military is prepared to withdraw its objections only if a clear political line is laid down and there are political reasons for the creation of the battalion, which was regarded with hostility.

But a short two weeks later, on November 17, the War Department announced both the formation of the Austrian battalion and the State Department's approval of the Military Committee for the Liberation of Austria.[15] What had happened in the time between the two memoranda so to change the battalion's fortunes? The second memorandum clearly stated that Undersecretary Welles had imparted the State Department's approval to the Assistant Chief of Staff. But on earlier occasions, the authors of the State Department's objections had never been named. Obviously, on November 17 the War Department intended to place ultimate responsibility for the Austrian battalion with State Department personnel. One look at the documents solves the puzzle. The political situations of leading personalities, including Undersecretary Welles and, ultimately, the President himself, played the crucial role in determining the course of events.[16] We will let the documents speak for themselves in chronological order.

It is clear that the establishment of an Austrian battalion could not remain a secret, least of all to the allies of the United States. There already existed, since January, 1942, the "gentlemen's agreement" between the State Department and the British embassy in Washington, pledging reciprocal briefings on the national Free Movements.[17] On October 23, 1942, the battalion was the subject of a discussion between Assistant Secretary Berle and Sir R. I. Campbell, the British ambassador. Mr. Berle made it clear to the ambassador that American governmental agencies desired an Austrian legion but without the assistance of a political committee headed by Archduke Otto.[18] On November 2, 1942, Berle reported to the ambassador that the matter of the battalion was still under discussion in the War Department; indeed, on precisely the same day Stimson proposed abandoning the project altogether.[19]

On November 10, 1942, at the request of Undersecretary Welles, a conference was held with Brigadier General Edwards, the author of the first memorandum, and Berle. This time the Undersecretary set out the official policy for the still-reluctant Brigadier General and to Mr. Berle, who was hostile to the project: He told them that the President and the State Department wished the battalion to be organized.

The establishment of the battalion was to be announced at a press conference by Secretary of War Stimson, and this was to be followed by the Military Committee's offering to recruit volunteers and the Secretary's immediate acceptance.[20] At the same time the letters prepared by the State Department would be delivered to the War Department. Mr. Berle at least tried to minimize the Military Committee's participation by announcing that further offers of recruitment could be expected from other Austrian organizations. He had been informed by the Office of War Information that the Austrian Labor Committee and Austrian Action had put out feelers about the establishment of a Free Austrian legion, and that he would be hearing from them in a few weeks' time. Mr. Berle never made a secret of his opposition to the battalion. He stated as much in a correction he sent to the *Washington Post* concerning an article of December 6, 1942, by the columnist Drew Pearson, claiming that Berle was the intellect behind the battalion.[21]

It is clear that there were two opposing camps within the State Department—the group represented by Mr. Welles and the circle around Mr. Berle. In a letter of June 1, 1943, to President Roosevelt, Otto von Hapsburg commented that a faction in the State Department was opposed to any settlement, even a provisional one, of the Austrian question generally. In all these discussions the military also unreservedly showed their aversion to the Austrian battalion. When Mr. Welles told an Army officer that the President felt that Otto would best serve Austria if he and his brother Felix were to volunteer at once for the battalion, the officer assumed a negative stance. From the Army's point of view, Otto would have great difficulty adjusting to the routine of an American soldier; it would therefore be better if he and his brother were to serve only as members of the recruiting committee.

Here lies the core of all the difficulties. The military instinctively opposed the President's wish to see Archduke Otto as a soldier in the battalion, but they also opposed Undersecretary Welles's desire to have Otto removed from leadership of the recruiting committee and if possible have him separated from the committee altogether. Then again, the President and one faction in the State Department, with Welles at its center, did not want to eliminate or minimize Otto's participation in the battalion itself.

The War Department did not give up its opposition in spite of the wishes of the President and Welles. On November 13, 1942, Stimson delivered to President Roosevelt a new memorandum from the Organization and Training Division G–3, which was charged with establishing the battalion, outlining the difficulties of incorporating foreign units into the Army.[22] The President's resolution came in a memorandum to Stimson. This paper, declassified by the National Archives only at my request, is cited in the original wording of the document.

I have every sympathy with your note of November 13, in regard to the advisability of encouraging Americanization in the Army. Therefore I would go along with your objections were it not for two facts:

a) We already have a Norwegian Battalion, Filipino Units and a Japanese Battalion.

Therefore the creation of one or two small additional units would create no precedent.

b) The memo to you from Staff points out in the last paragraph that formation of such battalions should be strictly limited to cases where political advantages are to be gained. That is why I hope the matter will be kept open, and of course I must be the one to determine political advantages if any. It occurs to me there are distinct and definite political advantages in the case of a Polish or Czech or Danish Battalion. These cases should be reopened for further discussion with the State Department.

I have no desire for any large unit. Even if the numbers were small enough only for a company, the objective would be served. Most certainly I think there should be no German or Italian unit at this time.

F.D.R.[23]

The backstage battle had been resolved. By extension from the President's memorandum, we can say that it was he who was responsible for the creation of the Austrian battalion. To set up such a unit seemed so important to him that he would content himself with a single company to achieve his political aims. The symbolic significance of the unit was what was crucial to him. What other meaning could a small company have in a war where millions of soldiers confronted each other? Militarily the battalion had nothing to offer. The symbol was all.

Events unrolled in rapid succession, in the sequence that had been determined in the discussion of November 10, 1942. A press conference was called by Stimson, the formation of the battalion was announced, and a press release detailed its purpose: to show Austrians all over the world that the United States was determined to liberate Austria. The wish of many Austrians—to contribute to the liberation of their homeland by entering the conflict themselves—was granted. Service in the battalion was to be voluntary.[24] The long-standing Military Committee for the Liberation of Austria offered to help the Secretary of War with the recruiting; the Secretary, according to previous agreement, accepted this offer at once.[25]

Immediately a storm of protest boiled up. First to object were spokesmen of the Austrian Labor Committee; they sent a telegram to Secretary Hull[26] and immediately organized protest demonstrations. Julius Deutsch, their spokesman, addressed meetings and alerted newspaper reporters and most of all representatives of the other successor states. For him, the battalion was a "Hapsburg battalion," and anyone who was anxious to prevent its establishment was welcomed as an ally.[27] Deutsch also knew how great his own influence was with the faction of the State Department that included Assistant Secretary Berle. This group had always expressed its opposition to Otto, and it had adopted the viewpoint of the Austrian Labor Committee and Julius Deutsch, who had decided to stand aside on the Austrian question and remain at a remove from all the Free Movements, with the possible exception of the Italians'.[28]

Two days after Stimson's press conference, on November 19, 1942, the Austrian Labor Committee submitted a letter signed by the leaders Friedrich Adler, Julius Deutsch, and Wilhelm Ellenbogen. The document, addressed to the State Department, was accompanied by a memorandum entitled "The Service of Austrians in the US Army," which pointed to the Austrians' bad experiences in the English Pioneer Corps. Indeed, 90 percent of the Austrian "pioneers" in the British Army had voted for the British flag over the former Austrian flag.[29] But other Austrian organizations in Great Britain, such as the Free Austrian Movement, had called for a separate Austrian unit and had questioned that extraordinary verdict.[30]

Dorothy Thompson, the influential American newspaperwoman, also got into the controversy, approaching the War Department as early as December 21, 1942. Drawing on the observations of her husband, who was from Czechoslovakia, she reported that the Czechs and Yugoslavs were upset by

Otto's efforts to recruit an Austrian legion. The War Department referred Thompson to the State Department, whence she was sent back to the War Department—clear proof that the two departments were not of the same mind and wanted to avoid decision-making.[31]

Dorothy Thompson stuck to her guns. In an article occasioned by Otto von Hapsburg's thirtieth-birthday banquet, she described two other Austrian groups besides Otto's committee: the Austrian Labor Committee, which rejected an Austrian troop unit, and Austrian Action, which wanted a unit independent of Otto.[32] Thompson's citing the Austrian Labor Committee shows that opposition to the Austrian battalion was not merely a matter of anti-Hapsburg bias.

Through her widely read articles, Thompson both encouraged the Austrian socialists and made the battalion a national issue for Americans. Since a majority of the Austrian émigrés had leaned toward the socialists until the suppression of the Social Democratic party in February, 1934, her writings could not help but have a damaging effect on the battalion's fortunes, especially given the wide attention accorded Thompson's views.

The leaders of Austrian Action had written Secretary Stimson on November 27, 1942, to express displeasure that its earlier offers to establish an Austrian troop unit had not been accepted, and to call for an Austrian battalion established along nonpolitical lines.[33] The letter acknowledged Otto's influence, but on patriotic grounds the group wished to avoid a public confrontation with his followers.[34]

Two days later, on November 29, 1942, two other Austrian committees joined the issue. The Assembly for a Democratic Republic of Austria and Free Austrian Youth also demanded that an Austrian battalion be organized on an entirely nonpolitical basis. They rejected any form of collaboration with the Military Committee for the Liberation of Austria under Otto's presidency, since, as they claimed, the committee was dominated by monarchists who represented only a small minority of Austrians.[35]

The protests gained ground. As could have been foreseen, representatives of the successor states of the old Austrian monarchy stepped to the fore. These included spokesmen for immigrants from the successor states who had long before acquired American citizenship. On November 27, 1942, the Czechoslovak National Council of America in Chicago sent a telegram to Secretary Stimson, deploring the help being given to Austrian monarchists and expressing hope that the Austrian unit would be cleansed of monarchist contamination.[36] This attack was directed more against Otto than the battalion because the committee feared that the monarchists might someday raise new claims on Czechoslovakia.

On December 1, 1942, Vladimir Hurban, the Czechoslovak envoy in Washington, called on Secretary Hull and declared that the name of Archduke Otto was detrimental to his country. But he did not oppose a battalion as symbolic of Austria's independence.[37] For all the pressure brought to bear on him, Secretary Hull was not prejudiced on the battalion question. One could not say either that he had a special sympathy for Austria or that he particularly disliked the country and its efforts for independence. As an American states-man standing above the dispute, he noted that there was too little will to fight and too much discussion among the Austrians; everyone, both individuals and groups, were welcome to join the Allied struggle. Indeed, the American gov-ernment was eager to give Austrian volunteers an opportunity to help the United Nations by joining a national battalion. Hull rejected as unjust the ac-cusations that the United States bore sinister motives, such as the restoration of reactionary regimes in Spain and Austria.[38] As an American patriot, Cor-dell Hull was concerned only with winning the war.

But the opposition groups could not so easily abandon their opposition to the creation of an Austrian battalion. On December 1, 1942, they joined with the successor states in a common course of action. Thus the Austrian battalion became the focus of a dispute that was no longer only intra-Austrian. "No compromise with Hapsburg," was the slogan, and representatives of seven of the successor states signed the proclamation of December 1. For Austria, the signers were the Austrian Labor Committee—which was opposed to any Aus-trian troop unit—as well as Austrian Action, the Assembly for a Democratic Republic of Austria, and Free Austrian Youth, all now firmly allied against the projected Austrian battalion.

For the most part, only nonofficial individuals signed the proclamation for Czechoslovakia, Hungary, Italy, Poland, Romania, and Yugoslavia. One of these was the Hungarian historian Oskar Jaszi, who was in no way sympa-thetic to Austria.[39] Vojta Beneš, a former senator and member of the Czech State Council in London, joined the petition in a telegram of December 3, 1942; he acted as a sort of liaison to the Czech government in exile, thereby representing its interests without himself having to take part in official diplo-macy.[40]

Two official communications, however, deserve special mention, since they developed two points of attack that were to prove significant for the con-tinued controversy over the battalion. In a letter to Secretary Stimson dated December 6, 1942, a Yugoslav organization protested against the inclusion of citizens of the former monarchy in the projected battalion. They pointed out that there could not be as many as 10 million Austrians in the United States, as the Military Committee had claimed, since up to the First World War only 6.5 million former and current Austrian citizens had been resident in the United States.[41] The second communication, a letter to Hull from the Union and League of the Romanian Society of America, expressed the opinion that the United States would win the war more quickly without the participation of the Austrian battalion.[42] Representing the battalion as a military burden re-flected a point of view that soon gained greater currency.

Within the Austrian emigration, a newspaper campaign on the battalion question moved into high gear. The magazine *Freiheit für Österreich* [*Freedom for Austria*], frequently an outlet for Austrian Action, featured Dorothy Thompson's rejection of the battalion in its issue of December 15,

1942. The same number also contained articles entitled "Der Volkskrieg und das Haus Habsburg" ["The Popular War and the House of Hapsburg"] and "Für ein Österreichisches Bataillon ohne Habsburg" ["For an Austrian Battalion Without the Hapsburgs"]. The slogan "Hapsburg is a Liability, Hapsburg Must Step Down" became the focus of the newspaper attacks. Once this goal had been achieved, others could follow.[43] In barely two weeks a widespread protest action against the battalion was well under way.[44] The chorus of attacks against the battalion drowned out the uncoordinated voices of its supporters. Chicago's oldest Hungarian-language weekly, *Otthon,* called the battalion the symbol of an "Austro-Hungarian independence movement" with Archduke Otto at the head. The weekly assumed—not entirely incorrectly— that the Austrian battalion was intended to lay the cornerstone for Austrian and Hungarian independence.[45]

But the advocates of the Austrian battalion did not make an attempt to influence American public opinion; they did not even form committees to defend it. The total and conspicuous lack of coordination is incomprehensible to any retrospective observer. And yet there were voices even within the War Department that spoke in favor of the Austrian battalion, believing that the attacks on Otto were unjust.[46] These isolated voices were necessarily smothered by the attacks of the battalion's opponents. How did the American authorities react to the large-scale propaganda against the battalion?

The first to be heard from was Secretary Stimson. At a press conference on November 26, 1942, he defended himself against the accusation of having approved the battalion without consultation with the State Department. He declared that no Austrian group had been given an exclusive right to recruit volunteers and that help from all Austrian groups was welcome. He hoped that all loyal Austrians, without regard to partisan aims, would support the battalion.[47]

While Stimson, who had objected to the creation of the Austrian battalion, tried to defend it loyally once it had been created, the offices within the War Department, which had been extremely guarded about the battalion, did exactly what subordinate bodies always do when they are reluctant to carry out a set policy. They interpreted the decisions and guidelines on the formation of the battalion in a spirit that, while not going against the letter of the assigned instructions, nevertheless could in no way further the unit's establishment. The head of the organization division in the War Department rejected Archduke Otto as an officer of the battalion in spite of President Roosevelt's wishes that Otto act as a volunteer in the battalion. Also, when Otto's brother Karl Ludwig asked to recruit Austrian volunteers resident in Canada and Cuba, he was told that volunteers from these countries were undesirable because of immigration problems and that the Austrian battalion was an American troop unit.[48] The same reply was given to Father Odo von Württemberg: The Austrian battalion was to be an American troop unit.[49]

The military authorities stated that Otto's brothers could not become officers in the battalion, and when the younger Hapsburgs offered their services as liaison officers, they were told that this was impossible.[50] The authorities also emphasized that Otto's Military Committee was only a private group, without any exclusivity, and that every other group was entitled to the same privileges. Once again, the American leaders stressed that the battalion was to be a military unit, not the advance for a political faction.[51] The participation of other committees was hoped for, although the Americans' hostility suggests that the issue was not the freedom to recruit but the battalion's very existence.

The antagonism between military authorities and the highest levels of government was fundamental for the further history of the Austrian battalion. The government saw the battalion as a political symbol of Austria's future independence. It is a moot question whether President Roosevelt had his eye only on the restoration of Austrian independence or whether he envisaged the creation of a larger state or a federation of states including the Austria of 1938. The available documents cannot prove his ultimate objective, but a number of signs indicate that the President had plans that were more far-reaching than the restoration of the Republic of Austria, involving Hungary as well. In a letter of August 26, 1942, Otto von Hapsburg expresses gratitude to the President for his interest in Austria and Hungary and mentions plans for the future.[52] Though limited for the present only to the area of a military unit, the government saw the battalion as the first, provisional representation of Austria abroad.

President Roosevelt was much too knowledgeable in the history of the First World War—when he had been Undersecretary of the Navy—to underestimate the significance for political warfare of foreign troop units. He knew well how important the creation of Czech legions had been for the establishment of an independent Czechoslovak republic. He understood the role of symbolism, and, as noted in his important memorandum of November 17, 1942, he was willing to be content with an Austrian troop unit only one company strong.[53] Those members of the State Department who were familiar with President Roosevelt's plans tried to carry them out, as did Undersecretary Welles. (Cordell Hull was frequently neither informed nor consulted on the Austrian question.) They, too, saw the symbolic value of an Austrian unit to demonstrate to the Allies American interest in the restoration of Austria's independence.[54] But even in the discussions preceding the creation of the battalion it became clear that there was an opposition faction in the State Department. Its influence was obviously underestimated both by President Roosevelt and by Undersecretary Welles; its outstanding representative was Assistant Secretary Berle.

The War Department, the Army, and the subordinate military agencies were even more strongly opposed, looking on the battalion not as a symbol, but purely as a unit that should be of military value within the U.S. Army. The principal concern for the military authorities was to integrate these foreign-born volunteers into the Army with as few difficulties as possible.

From the first, they were aware of the difficulties inherent in such an operation and they stressed this viewpoint to the very last minute.[55]

The War Department itself remained formally loyal to the government in this connection. Yet, Undersecretary of State Robert D. Patterson, writing to Mrs. Eleanor Roosevelt on December 16, 1942, could not refrain from noting that the War Department had only reluctantly agreed to the establishment of national battalions in general and, more specifically, to Otto's participation in the formation of the Austrian battalion. The agreement, he added, had come only as the result of heavy pressure exerted by the State Department.[56] He also emphasized that the battalion was a purely military organization, not a political one, though he must surely have realized that the national battalions were to serve the political aims of the government. The War Department therefore loyally noted in its letter to the Austrian Labor Committee of December 2, 1942, that it would welcome the cooperation of other Austrian organizations in recruiting volunteers, just as in the preliminary discussion it had welcomed with obvious relief Mr. Berle's announcement that two additional Austrian groups would participate.[57] Undersecretary Welles, too, had previously mentioned these two committees in discussions with Sir R. I. Campbell.

The War Department, however, had still not realized that the opponents of the Austrian battalion, especially the Austrian Labor Committee, were concerned not only with eliminating Otto and his committee; *au fond,* target of their attacks was the battalion itself and with it the symbol of Austrian independence. In reply to the War Department, on December 5, 1942, the Austrian Labor Committee refused to participate in recruiting, even if a proposed battalion were independent of Otto's group. The Labor Committee expressed its dislike for the deliberately symbolic value of the battalion by mentioning neither the battalion nor the prospect of collaborating in its formation, choosing to attack Otto and the house of Hapsburg. As it had done since the outset of the war (in its January 16, 1942, letter to the State Department) the Labor Committee argued that it represented the largest Austrian political party and that therefore during wartime it was the custodian of the Austrian people's right to self-determination. This was tantamount to rejecting any anticipation of independence for Austria since the Austrian Labor Committee interpreted the right to self-determination as including the possibility of remaining a part of greater Germany.[58]

A parallel action, as proposed by the War Department, would have enabled the Austrian Labor Committee to recruit a larger number of volunteers and acquire supremacy for itself, pushing Otto von Hapsburg and his committee into the background. But this was not the issue. The Austrian Labor Committee had no desire to outdo Otto. It did not wish to push him into the background or fill the battalion with its own followers—for which the War Department's invitation would have afforded every opportunity. What they wanted was to prevent altogether the establishment of an Austrian battalion.

On December 9, 1942, Secretary Stimson declared once again that the War Department desired the collaboration of all Austrian public figures, that it was eager to attract all Austrians whatever their political orientations, and that Otto's committee was strictly private, not established by the American government.[59] Annoyed, Stimson refused to give any further explanations or to counter the protests against the battalion. It is not quite clear whether his silence was meant to convey that he excepted himself from the government's views. Even Senator Claude Pepper could not move Stimson to any further expression of his position when he noted in a letter of December 15, 1942, that bringing in Julius Deutsch could probably introduce harmony into the recruiting system.[60] Senator Pepper seems to have been familiar with the background of the political obstruction and urged the inclusion of Deutsch, perhaps because of the urgings from members of Otto's Military Committee. As is clear from the history of Austrian political emigration in France, Deutsch was, indeed, the only Austrian socialist abroad who seemed willing to collaborate with other Austrian groups. The Secretary of War, however, in his reply to the Senator, only mentioned that the Austrian Labor Committee had been invited to participate in the battalion and had rejected any collaboration. As far as the Department was concerned, therefore, that particular matter was closed.[61] He maintained this attitude in his reply of January 8, 1943, to Assistant Secretary Berle, who had asked him for a supplementary explanation; he referred to the President's summary statement delivered at a press conference on January 5, 1943. Unified participation in the battalion would be welcome, but intergroup rivalries among the Austrians must cease. In a prescient memorandum addressed to Prime Minister Churchill, Foreign Secretary Eden noted that any attempt to create an Austrian troop unit would have to fail unless there was prior unanimity among the political groups.[62]

During the January 5 press conference at the White House, President Roosevelt himself took a strong stand against the attacks on the Austrian battalion. In answer to a question, the President clarified the official position on Otto's role. The exchange is quoted herein its entirety.

> *Question.* Mr. President: There are reports that a committee headed by Archduke Otto of Hapsburg is controlling the organization of a Free Austrian battalion in our Army. I wonder if you could comment on it.
>
> *The President.* I think so. I would just as soon comment on it. I have read the reports. They are completely vicious and they are completely untrue. However, they have been copied in quite a number of papers around the country and that might just as well be exploded once and for all.
>
> I have a memo somewhere. I think you can put it down four ways, that the Army is organizing a number of Free Battalions, wholly a War Department matter. And as I understand it, there are several committees of Austrians in this country about it, so that it

will be thoroughly well known. One of these committees—I believe this young man [Otto] is on it and also that he has two brothers who have gone into it as privates. And the committee is to assist in informing reliable Austrian nationals in the United States as to how and where they can apply to the War Department just as any reputable committee of Austrians is given the same opportunity as those accorded to this committee that you were talking about. And any implication such as the one I have seen are just plain not true.[63]

President Roosevelt was annoyed at the attacks on the battalion, which came from all sides. When Ferdinand Czernin—speaking for Austrian Action, the Coordinated Assembly for a Democratic Republic of Austria, and Free Austrian Youth—proposed to the War Department that a nonpartisan committee, composed of all Austrian factions, be created for recruiting volunteers, he was told that this was not desirable and that the Department could fill the battalion from sources within its control.[64] When Czernin attempted to obtain a message of encouragement from President Roosevelt to be read at a mass meeting to commemorate the fifth anniversary of the occupation of Austria, his request was refused bluntly and not at all amiably.[65] The President was particularly annoyed by attacks on the battalion from these organizations, because he doubted their sincerity. A legal brief by Czernin's attorney, John W. Davis, in the Franklin D. Roosevelt Library, refers to the Austrian battalion as evidence for the émigrés' determination to liberate Austria. And yet Czernin was one of the battalion's most prominent opponents.[66] Clearly, Roosevelt noticed the discrepancy.

In spite of President Roosevelt's strong statement at the January press conference, the attacks did not die down. Otto von Hapsburg offered a highly visible as well as a stationary target; but there was still more at stake. The Austrian Labor Committee enlisted as many supporters as they could attract. David Dubinsky, the American labor leader, opposed the Austrian battalion in a letter to the State Department, and he enclosed a copy of *Austrian Labor Information* containing further attacks on the battalion.[67] There were statements in the United States Congress, and the matter even carried over into the formulation of American foreign policy. On March 12, 1943, Congressman Emmanuel Celler, arguing that Otto was not entitled to a diplomatic passport, requested that he dissolve his Military Committee on pain of losing the Belgian passport under which he had entered the United States. Assistant Secretary Berle, to whom the Belgian ambassor complained about pressure from Representative Celler, was successful in getting the Congressman to cease his attacks—but only after Celler told him that he had been acting on the basis of information from the Czech embassy. Mr. Berle replied that Celler knew very well about his own opposition to Otto's participation in the battalion.[68] The Czechoslovak National Council of Chicago also exerted pressure on the Belgian embassy.[69] A report from Undersecretary Welles to President Roosevelt further substantiates the successor states' opposition to the battalion.[70]

The subordinate sections of the War Department began to exploit the attacks on the battalion, at first cautiously and then later with increasing urgency. As early as January 1, 1943—four days before President Roosevelt's January 5 press-conference defense of Otto and the battalion—the War Department issued a memorandum, ''Political Aspects of the Austrian Battalion.'' The document notes that since the announcement of the battalion, the American government, and especially the War Department, had been heavily criticized by the press and by public figures and that the number of unfavorable comments was mounting daily; Otto and his association with the Austrian battalion through the Military Committee were cited as the objects of the attacks. It had been hoped, the document elaborated, that other Austrian political groups would help in the recruiting. But the opposition against Otto and his ''clique'' was likely to continue. The memorandum mentioned attacks by Dorothy Thompson, Drew Pearson, and Sava N. Kosanovich, as well as declarations from seven successor states and the United Council of Czechoslovak Legionnaires in Chicago.[71] Two countermeasures were suggested: either to let the protests run their course and state over and over again that Otto could not claim any more authority than any other honest Austrian, or to inform Otto that he was more of a hindrance than a help and plead with him to cease his recruiting efforts. In this memorandum the War Department essentially wrote off Otto von Hapsburg as sponsor of the battalion.

Opposition to the battalion from the Austrian Labor Committee and Austrian Action continued undiminished in their periodical *Freiheit für Österreich,* adding to the difficulties of Secretary Stimson, who, despite the resistance of subordinate agencies in his Department as well as his own aversion, endeavored to carry out the national policy indicated by the President, and to allay the Austrians' apprehensions. Finally, the War Department endeavored to end the debate by issuing a set of clear statements, published in *Freiheit für Österreich* on March 1, 1942: The Austrian battalion is an American military unit; soldiers in the battalion have the same rights as those serving in other units; they can acquire American citizenship and be transferred to officers' training schools: they wear American uniforms and take the same oath; the Austrian battalion is a fighting unit, not an occupation corps. Once again, the periodical declared that Otto's committee had no official or unofficial status and had no say in the conduct of the Austrian battalion.[72] Could anyone have asked for more? How then could the opposition groups continue to claim that the Austrian battalion was a Hapsburg structure?

All the controversy in the press was bound to have an influence on the composition of the battalion.[73] Originally the battalion was to have been an all-volunteer unit. But once induction got under way, subsequent directives from the military ordered soldiers of Austrian nationality to go directly from the induction center to the battalion.[74] The process of assigning recruits to the battalion involved numerous errors, and Poles, Czechs, Hungarians, and Slovaks were also assigned to it, along with Austrians. Actually, a War Department memorandum of February 5, 1943, noted that the Austrian battalion was

"Austrian" in name only; Poles, Czechs, and indeed all elements of the former Danube monarchy were serving in the unit. Another memorandum from the Assistant Secretary of War suggests that the mixture was not effective: "I have received intimations that the Austrian battalion is not doing so well."[75] The range of membership soon became even wider; a March 16 report mentions, besides members of the successor states, two Cubans, an Englishman, two Russians, and representatives of other nations, all included in a battalion intended to symbolize the Austrian nation. Some of the non-Austrian groups did not like the situation, and the Czech National Council in Chicago sent a telgram to Secretary Hull asking that all non-Austrian soldiers be immediately removed from the battalion.[76]

Once again, the War Department attempted to take remedial measures. *Freiheit für Österreich* carried an official announcement that all non-Austrians would be unconditionally withdrawn from the battalion and that those Austrians who did not wish to serve in the battalion would be transferred to other Army units. The Department hoped, once again, that this move would erase the impression that the battalion was a step toward restoring the Austro-Hungarian monarchy. Nevertheless, Otto's Military Committee was still the only authorized agency through which information about the battalion could be released, because all other Austrian emigration organizations had rejected or ignored the War Department's call to participate in the recruiting.[77]

The assignment of non-Austrians to the battalion was a real blunder, as might have been foreseen. The supporters of the battalion had said there were 10 million Austrian residents in the United States.[78] Of course, this number was a considerable exaggeration, but the 10-million figure persisted in the public mind even though many people were assigned to the battalion who could not speak the German language. The battalion commander even began a German-language course for officers and enlisted men.[79] But the mixed nature of the battalion was a major hindrance. Morale was low, and numerous members of the battalion asked to be transferred to other units.[80] There was no other choice, therefore, but to return to the original policy. According to a decree of March 8, 1943, Austrians were to be assigned to the battalion only if they so desired.[81] The battalion commander believed that much of the discontent could be traced to the large proportion (30 percent) of Jewish refugees in the unit. Old prejudices came to the fore for refugees who were in the Army against their will, who did not want to fight. The commander noted that most members of the battalion wished to give up their Austrian nationality in order to become American citizens.[82]

The War Department based its own conclusions on transfers from the battalion as well as the low morale. A memorandum of April 7, 1943, discussed the dissolution of the battalion. It was argued that Otto's recruiting efforts had been a total failure and had produced only twenty-five volunteers in three months, in spite of Otto's previous guarantee that a sufficient number of volunteers would be raised and that an adequate reservoir would be at his disposal. The memorandum also stated wryly that neither the President nor the

Secretary of War was in a position to fend off the storm of protest against the battalion. On April 2, 1943, the battalion was 199 men strong. There was no other choice but to dissolve it.[83]

Another document of the same date, "Implementation," mentions a strength of only 144 men, while on March 1, 1943, battalion strength had been listed as 528 men.[84] Even with a relatively good beginning, though, at the rate of recruiting twenty-five volunteers per month, it would have taken two and a half years before full battalion strength was achieved.[85] In the light of these discouraging figures, we must ask whether any volunteers at all had been recruited in the preceding months of December, January, and February. Clearly, the Army, which had only reluctantly acceded to the President's demands, was eager to get rid of the foreign body that had been forced upon it. A political aide also noted that the reaction of the American public to the Austrian battalion had been negative. It remained doubtful whether the battalion would ever have had real military or propaganda value.[86]

On April 12, 1943, the War Department was requested to dissolve the battalion.[87] The commander had already stated on March 16, 1943, that separate divisions had no place "in our Army."[88] Secretary Stimson handed his statement agreeing to the dissolution of the battalion to President Roosevelt on April 17, 1943.[89] The Department of Justice also concurred.[90] Finally President Roosevelt gave in.[91] On May 3, 1943, decrees were issued to dissolve the Austrian battalion—named the 101st Infantry Battalion—as soon as possible and without any public announcement. All volunteers were given the option of choosing their nearest troop unit. The others were simply transferred.[92]

Shortly thereafter, *Freiheit für Österreich* featured a front-page editorial titled "Das Österreichische Bataillon." It began with the words: "The Austrian battalion is dead. The unnatural product of joining a reactionary monarchist clique to the democratic army did not prove viable. The democratic army rejected this foreign body of a troop division under the patronage of Archduke Otto of Austria."[93] Indeed, the battalion had reached its end. Had it really been only the product of a reactionary monarchist clique? Was it really unnatural and not a viable undertaking? Or was it "unnatural" only because the Army did not want to incorporate the so-called foreign body? Among the diversified ranks of the émigrés, was it only a monarchist clique that wanted the battalion? Was its creation only the result of an "alliance," and was it not in the interests of American policy?

It is necessary to see these questions in the light of the larger efforts of the Austrian emigration. Could the creation of the Austrian battalion have helped restore the independence of Austria? In spite of its short life, the battalion is the only instance of an Austrian group's achieving a measure of official recognition.[94] In this study a positive value is assigned to the goal of restoring Austrian independence, and this is justified particularly since the Republic later did achieve independent status.

The creation of the Austrian battalion was not an unprecedented undertaking for the American Army. There already existed a Norwegian and a Japanese battalion, and a Greek one was organized at the same time. But these battalions were composed of citizens of existing states. The Austrian battalion, on the other hand, was intended to symbolize a nation that had actually disappeared. It was supposed to demonstrate that the strongest Allied power was interested in Austria's independence. That President Roosevelt would have been satisfied with a limited battalion, of only company strength—that is, 120 men—expresses this intent most clearly.[95] Was it necessarily unnatural to lay the symbolic basis for a government that had not yet been resurrected?

The creation of the battalion made the independence of Austria one of the goals of United States policy wihtout its having to be labeled a specific war aim. By combining the Austrian battalion with Otto von Hapsburg's Military Committee for the Liberation of Austria, as advocated by President Roosevelt and Undersecretary Welles, further possibilities for political development were left open—this in spite of Mr. Welles's emphasizing that the purpose of the battalion was "chiefly" a military one.[96] The symbolic significance was obvious and was so understood by those who opposed the restoration of Austria's independence. Even the recognition of Austrians as "nonenemy aliens," the introduction of "Austrian Days" in several American states, Secretary Hull's declaration of July 27, 1942, that the Anschluss had never been given *de jure* recognition, were all milestones in this direction. The solution to the Austrian question was thus brought up for public discussion and raised to the level of an international problem.

In sum, despite its ultimate failure, the battalion must be seen as a positive achievement of the Austrian political emigration. Barely half a year after it was dissolved, the Moscow Declaration of November 1, 1943, signed by all Allied powers, recognized the restoration of Austria's independence and liberty as an Allied war aim.[97]

These arguments are not intended to devalue the attempts of other emigration groups to make themselves available and to contribute to the war effort.[98] Other émigré figures, such as Dr. Ernst Karl Winter, also considered forming an Austrian battalion, immediately following the announcement of the Norwegian battalion.[99] But to have achieved the establishment of an Austrian unit at all remains the special achievement of Hans Rott's committee in conjunction with the efforts of Archduke Otto.

It must be added, though, that the stimulus, the preliminary work, and the actual formation of the battalion were undertaken in a manner that was secretive and not sufficiently thought through, abrupt and without adequately preparing the public. These omissions provided detractors from the very outset at every possible point of attack, whether or not such attacks were justified. As early as December 15, 1942, scarcely four weeks after the formation of the battalion was announced in Secretary Stimson's press conference, an American observer noted that Otto's fundamental mistake was not having carried out a major publicity campaign.[100] Otto and the people collaborating with him in the Military Committee, especially Hans Rott, were aware of the many obstacles in their way and had pinned all their hopes on President Roosevelt's authority. But in doing so, they totally forgot about the American public, which in the last analysis is the deciding factor in shaping American foreign policy. Even the President, if he is to carry out a foreign policy successfully, must have the support of the people.

Further, Otto and his associates must be blamed for inadequate preparation. They failed to inform themselves about the existing Norwegian battalion and about the difficulties arising, generally, from the establishment of national battalions in the framework of the U.S. Army. Nor did they bother to counter the objections of the American military or to make clear to the government the differences between a Norwegian and an Austrian battalion. Nowhere did they demonstrate that the Austrian battalion was intended to have much greater political significance than a national unit such as the Norwegian or the Greek, which did not have to symbolize a sovereignty in abeyance.

Among Hans Rott's posthumous papers there is a list of former officers of the old Austrian army—the Peter Paul group—which, functioning purely in their capacity as military experts, had proposed to take the place of the Military Committee in the establishment of the battalion. This group could easily have been put in touch with the Military Committee, or they could have been involved in establishing a second Austrian recruiting organization.

The only political figure who addressed himself to the model of the Norwegian battalion was Dr. Ernst Karl Winter, in a memorandum of July 18, 1942.[101] It was he who informed Hans Rott about the formation of a Norwegian battalion. However, the individuals close to the Military Committee failed to discuss this development with Dr. Winter, nor did they inquire why the military authorities were so strongly opposed to the creation of foreign national troop divisions.[102] It was not the last time that Dr. Winter's profound insights were ignored. And the military experts of the Peter Paul group did not fare any better.

An organization of experts could have removed the recruiting problem from politics and thus have won the participation of other organizations. Rott's posthumous papers contain a number of letters in which he inquires of close and devoted friends about their position on an Austrian battalion. Some of them raised objections to the project; some wondered what would happen if members of the battalion were to become prisoners of war. One raised the not insignificant question of where the unit's enlisted men were to come from, since he feared that the battalion might consist largely of people of an academic background and thus with some claim to be officers. Many doubted the possibility of recruiting volunteers at all, since a majority of the available men had already been inducted into the Army.[103] These were potential friends of the battalion; nowhere is there any evidence that Hans Rott invited people inclined to be critical of the project to evaluate it.[104] Most curiously, no attempt was made to determine precisely who were the volunteers to be included in the battalion. Long before discussions regarding the creation of the battalion were under way, Otto had already indicated to Assistant Secretary Berle that he hoped to be able to gather in 85 percent of the Austrian émigrés to the United States.[105] But Otto's hope was based on no real statistics.

Indeed, this estimate did not correspond to the real situation and was not considered realistic by Mr. Berle. Nevertheless, Otto must have given assurance to the War Department about the number of volunteers he could raise for the battalion. According to a letter from Undersecretary Welles to President Roosevelt in which he gives a detailed report of his discussions with Otto and with General McNarney, the War Department wanted eight hundred volunteers, preferably in the eighteen-to-thirty age range.[106] I am certain that the capability to enlist eight to nine hundred volunteers was guaranteed by Otto, since without such a guarantee the military authorities would have had sufficient reason to break off the negotiations at once.

Officials close to the Military Committee also failed to determine how many Austrian volunteers from Canada, Cuba, and the South American countries would be considered. Otto had requested access to the government files on Austrian aliens as the basis of his recruitment activity in the United States.[107] This request could hardly be granted; consequently the members of the recruiting Committee were dependent on their own lists of friends and acquaintances. Yet it would have been entirely possible to enlist systematically persons resident in the United States even without the help of the American authorities. Vague estimates should never have been allowed as a basis for enlisting a specific number of volunteers. Further, no agreement was reached with the military authorities as to when the battalion was to attain its full strength, since a recruiting organization, as yet unformed, would have had to precede the batallion.

Since the military authorities objected immediately to considering volunteers from countries other than the United States, a significant reservoir of potential volunteers had to be counted out at the outset. On the other hand, no indication can be found anywhere of how volunteers outside the United States might have been attracted. If we consider how many non-French volunteers could be recruited for the Foreign Legion in France, there is no doubt that in countries outside the United States many more volunteers could have been attracted to a fighting unit attached to the American Army. It would also have been possible to recruit Austrian volunteers from Europe and North Africa as soon as the Austrian unit, envisioned as a combat force, had been detailed to Europe or Africa. That no positive action was taken to overcome this significant obstacle was surely a serious omission.

The abrupt announcement of the battalion and the role of Otto's Military Committee in it could not help but arouse the embittered opposition of all other Austrian organizations, particularly since they were all taken by surprise. The files of the War and State Departments reveal that similar attempts by other organizations to establish an Austrian troop unit had not been granted the same reception as Otto's Military Committee. For example, in a letter of August 8, 1942, to Secretary Hull, Dr. Ernst Karl Winter outlined his ideas for an Austrian battalion and offered his services.[108] On August 20, 1942, the Secretary of War replied that, should an Austrian unit be established at some time in the future, Winter's offer would not be forgotten, and his detailed understanding of Austrian conditions would also be consulted. This was nine days before the first memorandum of August 29, 1942, concerning Otto's participation. No judicious historian of the Austrian battalion can ignore the fact that such a prominent figure as Dr. Winter was not only not consulted in the matter, but received an untruthful answer.[109]

Ferdinand Czernin also wrote the Secretary of War, on November 27, 1942, pointing out that his plea for a troop unit, expressed five months earlier, had been given no consideration.[110] Julius Deutsch had also inquired of the State Department about the possibility of forming volunteer troops as early as March, 1942.[111]

Undaunted, Dr. Winter still attempted to intervene as late as November 22, 1942, after the proclamation of the Austrian battalion. In vain he pointed out that had he been granted a hearing on his offer, the confusion, already quite conspicuous, could have been avoided. Nevertheless, he was not consulted.[112]

The lack of contact between Otto's Military Committee and the émigrés in general had a distinctly negative effect, even if representatives of the older generation of immigrants took a sympathetic view of Otto's efforts.[113] But these sympathies were not mobilized to serve the creation of the battalion.

The members of the recruiting Committee believed that they could not count on support from any individual or political group, and they pinned all their hopes on President Roosevelt, who alone could remove all stumbling blocks. Otto had even disregarded the opinion of Undersecretary Welles, who felt kindly toward the project but who urgently advised him to act as neither the chairman nor a member of the Military Committee but to remain in the background of his Committee's activities. When the Undersecretary learned that Otto intended to chair the Committee, he declared this development "highly unfortunate."[114]

If Welles's well-meant advice was not heeded and, further, Otto failed to comply with the President's wish and set an example by joining the battalion as a volunteer, it must be said that neither the policy of the Committee nor its composition were felicitous. Yet there is no doubt that the American government favored Otto's participation and set higher hopes on his collaboration than on that of any other Austrian group. Obviously the War Department was informed unofficially that it was to deal only with the Military Committee in handling battalion affairs. In accounting for the success of the Military Committee, Hellmut Andics goes so far as to claim that the original idea of a battalion came from President Roosevelt.[115] It is difficult to agree with this opinion; the first American initiative toward an Austrian foreign agency must be attributed to the U.S. ambassador in Paris, William C. Bullitt. In his letter to President Roosevelt of September 5, 1939, immediately after the outbreak of war in Europe, Bullitt quoted Otto as referring to him as the initiator of a government in exile. And, from the suggestion of an Austrian government in exile stem the notions of an Austrian troop unit and an Austrian legion in France. That the President saw in this group of ideas an instrument for his own foreign policy can be seen from his agreeing to the battalion. But the initiative for the battalion itself did not come from President Roosevelt.[116]

Why did the President favor Otto's offers and refuse to negotiate with other Austrian émigrés? President Roosevelt well knew both the history of Central Europe and current conditions there, and he was too shrewd a judge of personalities not to know that the name Hapsburg was a red flag, guaranteed to arouse opposition not only among Austrians, but also from the successor peoples. The only reasonable explanation is that the Austrian battalion under Otto was to serve not only as a symbol of Austria's independence, but also as an indication of more far-reaching goals—a Danube federation or a Central European confederation of nations. Given such goals, negotiation with Otto and his friends makes good sense. All the other Austrian organizations lacked the capacity to pursue aims beyond the borders of Austria.[117] The War and State Departments, however, caught at the straw offers of assistance from other groups of Austrian émigrés so as not to have to deal solely with Otto and his Committee. Only wide-ranging, multinational plans can explain President Roosevelt's almost passionate advocacy of Otto and his committee at the press conference of January 5, 1943.[118] He must later have come to realize that Otto could provide neither the support nor the recruits he had promised, but at the outset, Roosevelt accepted Otto's assurance that he could supply five thousand volunteers for an Austrian legion, as mentioned in a State Department note of June 6, 1942. Apparently, the President had greater confidence in Otto's reliability than the author of that document, who remarks wryly that he doubts if more than fifty volunteers could possibly be recruited.[119]

On essential points Archduke Otto and his Committee acted counter to the advice both of the President and of Undersecretary Welles, although Otto not only was dependent on both but also had based the whole plan for the battalion on the President's agreement and support. In the event, he did not assert himself with the military and preferred to remain a civilian, as he had in France.

But we must also ask whether the American authorities gave Otto and his allies the backing he believed he could count on, relying on Roosevelt's declared position.[120] In truth, the American military establishment had assumed an unhelpful attitude even before the creation of the battalion. Nor was political and administrative support forthcoming. Secretary Hull summed up the American misgivings: "There was not enough fighting and too much gossiping going on. . . ."[121] One could ask, however, why neither the American military nor Otto's Military Committee ever considered changing the American immigration laws so as to use Austrian nonresident volunteers to fill up the battalion.[122] The military had already begun to write off the battalion while President Roosevelt was still defending the unit at his press conference of January 5, 1943. But after this press conference, neither the President nor the State Department, and least of all the War Department, attempted any further public defense of the battalion. The question arises: Why?

At the time of the most intense press campaign against the Austrian battalion—the winter of 1943—there occurred the great turning point in the conduct of the war—the surrender of the German army at Stalingrad.[123] This landmark event was bound to influence the President's policy; in view of the decisive Russian victory, he no longer had any chance of success with his plans for the Austrian battalion. The President knew what was apparently not known to all the other officials concerned with the Austrian question: that the Soviet Union, even at the time of the steady retreat in 1941, had vehemently opposed a federation of small Central and Eastern European states. Roosevelt realized that a victorious Soviet Union would oppose any unification of the Danube states, especially in a federation including Austria. He must have concluded that the plans for Austria and Hungary involving Archduke Otto could not be realized unilaterally. Hellmut Andics believes that Austria was not important enough to "irritate an ally such as Russia."[124] Indeed, after Stalingrad, any American policy for Central Europe had to take Russia's aspirations into account.[125] If the Austrian battalion had already been functioning at the time of Stalingrad, then Roosevelt would have held a trump card in the confrontations with Russia over Central Europe that were sure to come. But since the opposite was the case, it was more expedient from the standpoint of American foreign policy to write off the battalion rather than to allow more time to overcome the resistance to it. Clearly, it is not possible to mount a troop unit in four months, particularly under difficult conditions—but that was all the time available to the Austrian battalion. After Stalingrad, however, the fortunes of the Austrian battalion had to take second place to the policy of the Soviet Union in Central and Eastern Europe. There was also the desire to prevent Russia from forming a communist Austrian troop unit, comparable to the communist units that had been created as a counterweight to the Polish armies fighting on the side of the Western Allies. After Stalingrad, any Austrian troop unit would have to be viewed as an expression of emigration organizations close in ideology to Western aims.

Thus, all the miscalculations that surrounded the establishment of the Austrian battalion had to be paid for: the abruptness of the announcement, the secret diplomacy, the misjudgment of actual conditions, and Archduke Otto's and his friends' excessive confidence in their good relations with President Roosevelt. Compounding his political errors, Otto did not bow to pressure from the opposition and resign as president of the Military Committee; then, countering the objections of the American military, he could have volunteered publicly to join the battalion. Undersecretary Welles had advised him well not to assume leadership of the Military Committee and his taking that position may be attributed to his inexperience, although in so doing he ignored the President's wish that he serve as a volunteer in the battalion. In a letter of March 30, 1945, to Julius Deutsch, Hans Rott reports that Otto had obligated himself—to whom he does not say—to resign at once from the Committee if his person were to present an obstacle for the socialists.[126] But he did not resign, and thus did not avert the attacks against the battalion and the recruiting Committee. Two years later the then Secretary of State, Edward H. Stettinius, clearly stated that the battalion had been a failure, principally as a result of Otto's efforts to take a leading position.[127] Until the battalion's demise, the Austrian Labor Committee had used Otto's perseverance at the head of the Military Committee as an excuse to reject any movements toward Austrian unity. Their justification was that Otto's position showed that the battalion was not a neutral instrument either of the American government or of Austria. During the negotiations Assistant Secretary Berle had reported that the Austrian Labor Committee and Austrian Action would participate in recruiting volunteers, and this announcement had been important for the War and State Departments in their discussions of whether to approve the battalion.[128] By publicly resigning from the chairmanship of the Military Committee, Otto would have presented the two rival Austrian groups with a new situation, and the Austrian Action in particular might have decided to support an Austrian army unit that had no connections with the Hapsburgs. But instead, as we have seen, Otto continued as president of the Military Committee, making himself the target of all attacks.[129]

No one understood how to overcome the resistance of the opposition groups. Rather, the Military Committee relied on the element of surprise. Nor was there any understanding how to approach the mass of nonpolitical émigrés. Also, the Committee did not realize that they were hardening the opposition of Austrian Action.[130]

The members of the Military Committee showed even less understanding for the Austrian émigrés who served in the American Army. The advocates of the battalion must have realized that, while Ferdinand Czernin, president of Austrian Action, was an implacable opponent of Otto, he was not so firmly opposed to an Austrian unit. As late as January 28, 1943, he had written to Secretary Stimson that he was ready to take part in a nonpolitical group recruiting for an Austrian battalion. He and the groups of émigrés allied with him, he said, had originally rejected, not the battalion itself, but its connection with Otto. Had Otto resigned, then the chief obstacle to collaboration with Austrian Action and the other emigrant groups united in a Federation of Austrian Democrats—the Assembly for a Democratic Republic of Austria and Austrian Youth—would have been removed. These groups had given evidence of a positive attitude; only the Austrian Labor Committee had kept its distance from this anti-Hapsburg federation, because it truly opposed any Austrian battalion, even an anti-Hapsburg one.[131]

But Austrian Action was the most important link with the nonpolitical émigrés in the United States, and the lack of genuine cohesion and understanding among the political émigrés and the general emigration once more took its toll. It was never made clear to the young Austrians that service in the battalion represented service in the best interests of their new country, the

United States, and not merely a symbol of the future independence of Austria—such public relations work was totally neglected.[132] Not even the favor of the President, so highly respected by all the émigrés, was emphasized by the Military Committee in public debate. In France the mass of interned émigrés had been bypassed without too much sensitivity; similarly, in the United States the émigré soldiers of Austrian nationality were seen only as material for an army unit about which decisions could be made without any consideration of their attitudes or motives. The Committee relied totally on the President's support, forgetting that special troop units also have a special mentality. If they had considered at least the difficulties with the Norwegian battalion they would have realized (and not been surprised) that the Austrian émigré soldiers in the battalion considered Americanization and the acquisition of American citizenship more important than the recovery of the independence of their native land, which was not always too fondly remembered. Nor did the Committee ever consider that members of the Austrian battalion who were taken prisoner might be accused of high treason by the Germans and dealt with accordingly. The Germans sometimes ignored the prisoner-of-war provisions of the Hague Convention, and after the invasion of June 6, 1944, even Allied prisoners were mistreated. Members of the Austrian battalion, of course, were exposed to a special risk.[133]

Even this problem could have been addressed, given proper preparation and encouragement by the American public, had the volunteers been told that they were to belong to an elite group formed specifically to pursue the President's aims. Such an explanation at the proper time would have effectively neutralized opposition to the battalion. Indeed, observers noticed as early as December 15, 1942, that Otto von Hapsburg was neglecting public opinion.[134]

After the unit had been established, the officers, who were directly concerned with the morale and motivation of the men serving under them, were not well informed about the battalion's aims. Possibly the military, who were not well disposed toward the battalion, merely neglected to explain why the President had specifically asked for an Austrian battalion. They were even less frank in failing to inform the officers that 30 percent of the men were Jewish; their presence presented problems both for the other men and/or the Jews themselves.[135] It was up to the Austrian emigrants, Archduke Otto, and his followers, to win over the 30 percent for the idea of the battalion. Their omission to do so resulted in a feeling of unease that contributed to the battalion's dissolution. And yet this group, whose fathers often were touchingly devoted to the old country, could have been made enthusiastic about the aims of the battalion.[136]

Thus the errors were compounded, omission followed upon omission. The failure in recruiting and the precipitate dissolution of the unit, however, must be blamed on the great proportion of the political emigration that strove for the restoration of Austria's independence and a foreign representation. If it was not possible to achieve the expression of Austria's independence that the President himself preferred, and if discord and personal animosity within the battalion obscured this goal, it is understandable that the American government acknowledged the failure and wanted to dissolve the battalion inconspicuously.

With the dissolution of the battalion in May, 1943, an important chapter in the history of the Austrian political emigration came to an end. The political potential of the entire emigration had been squandered. A political group that was unable to keep alive a symbol of Austria's restoration, as outlined to it by the President, was bound to lose all political significance. The hostile German authorities did not fail to exploit the failure for their own purposes. As late as January 15, 1945, the Gauleiter of Ober-Donau, Eigruber, addressing National Socialist functionaries in Linz, pointed out that since none of the Allied powers had recognized an Austrian government in exile, it was clear that the Allies would treat the Austrians just as they did so-called Reich-Germans.[137] Sadly, many captured Austrian Wehrmacht soldiers expressed the wish to volunteer for an Austrian legion in the Allied forces.[138]

Finally, without the battalion there was no official refuge where Austrian deserters and prisoners of war might have gathered in the recognition that independent Austria would be restored. Both the opposition in the State Department and the military authorities open only to tactical considerations were oblivious to the significance of troop units composed of émigrés and prisoners of war.[139]

Also from a political standpoint, the Allied powers, including the United States, failed to consider the symbols of Austrian independence, a foreign representation, or an independent military unit, once the battalion had been dissolved. Even after the release of the Moscow Declaration, a high official of the State Department wrote that no symbol was necessary to encourage the people in Austria.[140] From then on American policy dispensed with the Austrian political emigration altogether. A 1945 State Department communique reads:

> The Department has been following closely and with interest the efforts of individuals and groups both inside and outside of Austria to organize Austrian resistance. So far, however, it has not seen evidence of any coalition that would warrant or merit any support from this country that might be interpreted as constituting political recognition, or any formal recommendation from the Department of State to the military authorities that military aid may be granted. . . .
>
> For your background information, . . . the effort to form an Austrian battalion in the United States with War Department cooperation ended in failure largely as a result of the efforts of Archduke Otto to assume a position of leadership in the enterprise.

The Secretary of State who succeeded Cordell Hull and Edward A. Stettinius, Dean Acheson, had had occasion as Undersecretary to observe the work of the Department. In his memoirs he criticized the attitude disclosed above.[141] A more recent Austrian writer, A. Vodopivec, notes in *Die Bal-*

kanisierung Österreichs [*The Balkanization of Austria*] that the Austrians lost both any chance for an Austrian government in exile and the last opportunity to recover the South Tyrol on September 8, 1943, the day of the Italian armistice, when no other government could safeguard Austria's interests as a trustee—and, we may add, when there was no longer a battalion to be considered.[142] Otto von Hapsburg demanded the return of the South Tyrol in a letter to Secretary Cordell Hull of August 20, 1943, but only an Austrian government in exile could have had the demand stick, even if Otto had tried at the proper time to include this question in the Italian armistice negotiations.[143]

It must be asked whether the factions of Austrian émigrés who had so vehemently opposed the Austrian battalion were aware of what they were doing and what risk they were taking. Surely all shades of opinion among the Austrian emigrants share in the responsibility for the debacle. The Military Committee for the Liberation of Austria, in disregard of the other Austrian groups, heaped failure upon failure; Otto von Hapsburg assumed a leadership position that he should never have accepted and did not resign in time when opposition increased; Ferdinand Czernin and Austrian Action, out of hostility to Otto and out of hurt feelings, preferred to make a common front with the battalion's enemies rather than merely call for Otto's resignation; and the Austrian Labor Committee joined with the Austrian socialists in Great Britain in rejecting any Austrian military unit or foreign agency, regardless of whether a symbolic Austrian unit could have been created. Not least, also, the nonpolitical émigrés stood aside through indifference and ignorance of the reasons for the formation of an Austrian battalion.

The entire Austrian emigration must share the blame for the fact that Austria, after her liberation, had to wait ten years—until the State Treaty—for her independence and the departure of the occupation troops. Even then, only an unexpected sequence of lucky accidents came to the aid of the Austrian people, while her representatives in the political emigration, her natural trustees, had failed. With unity, not only the question of the South Tyrol could probably have been settled along lines more favorable to Austria. She could also have fared better on Trieste if a government in exile had existed, and she could have hastened the end of the Allied occupation. Austria could have started her reconstruction much sooner, and the eastern region of Austria would not have had to lag ten years behind the west.

VI
From the Dissolution of the Austrian Battalion
to the Moscow Declaration

On June 1, 1943, Otto von Hapsburg wrote to President Roosevelt that the dissolution of the Austrian battalion was producing tragic consequences for Austria. He asked the President to form a provisional Austrian National Council, not based on parties, emphasizing that such a body was not intended to anticipate the Austrians' eventual decision on their future.[1] Now that the battalion was part of the past, Otto had no wish to be a member of any Austrian government or national committee. The idea of waiting for the Austrians' final decision was also a bow to the Austrian Labor Committee's point of view: that the Austrian people (especially the Austrian workers) should exercise the right of self-determination. Otto's letter initiated renewed attempts of achieving political representation abroad. The letter stressed that the opposition within the State Department was working against even a provisional settlement of the Austrian question. Otto expressed his fear that, without Roosevelt's personal intervention, the whole of U.S. policy in the Austrian question was futile. If the President's reply—which cannot be located—was based on the memorandum prepared by the State Department and still available, it must have been noncommittal. Ever since the battalion was dissolved, and with it Roosevelt's policy in the Austrian question, the President seemed inclined to submit to the guidelines of passivity set down by the State Department. Never again, to the day of the President's death, was there a new initiative in the Austrian question. This omission affected all factions within the Austrian emigration, and Ferdinand Czernin, among others, also had cause to complain of the State Department's treatment of the Free Movements.

Archduke Otto's view is confirmed by an official note of August 28, 1943, to the Secretary of State from the British embassy in Washington, asserting that an absolute lack of direction marked the Austrian problem. But the British embassy passed on the draft of a joint declaration of the three Great Powers expressing the desire for the restoration of a free and independent Austria. The message emphasized that consultations on Austria with the Soviet Union were already under way.[2]

Otto clung to his cause. On August 20, 1943, he wrote to the Secretary of State demanding that the Quebec Conference issue a declaration to the effect that Austria was an occupied country that must be liberated.[3] He continued to urge that the South Tyrol be returned to Austria. In spite of the State Department's opposition, his pressure had some effect. On December 14, 1943, Otto criticized Assistant Secretary Berle, his chief State Department opponent, for failing to mention Austria as a nation in a speech. A number of commentators

urged that an Austrian representation be created at least for purposes of rehabilitation after the country's liberation.[4] Even from faraway Scotland a Mr.
James Clayton "informed" President Roosevelt on May 31, 1943, that he
desired to establish an Austrian government in Great Britain, based on
Schuschnigg's principles; for this he required American aid.[5] The failure of
the Austrian battalion left a political vacuum, and various forces were eager to
fill it.

But the State Department was still unwilling and unable to decide on guidelines and even less on a positive attitude on restoring an independent Austria.
A circular of June 1, 1943, to the U.S. diplomatic missions in Central and
South America referred to the first general guidelines of December 10, 1941,
concerning the Free Movements. It was noted that their participation in the
conduct of the war was desirable but that the policy of the State Department
had not changed—that is, the recipients of the circular were not to give official encouragement to the Free Movements. The circular continued, stating
that to this date no genuine leaders had emerged.

In his book of memoirs, Dean Acheson later remarked that during the war
years the State Department did not represent a functioning foreign office;
rather, it was working without any direction or planning for the future.[6] But
then came the crucial turning point of Stalingrad. The State Department noted
the pressure to create a united front of all opponents to Nazism, with the participation of communist émigré organizations. The June 1 circular mentioned
that, as a result of the Austrian battalion fiasco, the Austrian center groups—
such as Austrian Action, the Assembly for a Democratic Republic of Austria,
and Austrian Youth—had united in an American Federation of Austrian Democrats, but that it was vain to hope for the Austrian Labor Committee to join
the center groups. Therefore the new federation offered no new hope. This
view was entirely consistent with the thinking of leading figures in the State
Department, especially Assistant Secretary Berle.

Meanwhile, the efforts of the Department of Foreign Activity to achieve a
union of all European Free Movements remained unnoticed. Nor was the
State Department affected by other divisions' opinion that the power of the
Free Movements was not being utilized sufficiently and that the State Department's behavior in this area was merely contrary.[7] Nonetheless, the Department clung to its principle of speaking with the Free Movements but recognizing none of them. Mr. Berle explained this policy once more in a letter of
August 28, 1943, to the American Council for Public Affairs.[8] Ironically,
Berle's explanation was issued on precisely the same day that the British government urged a joint Allied declaration on the restoration of Austria.

The other figures who had been involved in the battalion controversy did
not abandon their efforts for an independent Austria in spite of the dissolution
of the battalion. Dr. Egon Ranshofen-Wertheimer became an increasingly
frequent guest of the State Department.[9] In a memorandum of October 13,
1943, he proposed circulating in both houses of Congress a declaration postu-

lating Austria's separation from Germany.[10] Then, on October 15, he called for an official statement from the President or the State Department that would declare the Austrian Anschluss as null and void, create a representative Austrian committee, and separate Austrian prisoners of war into anti-National Socialists and National Socialist party members and fellow travelers.[11] He succeeded in convincing Mr. Berle to the extent that in a memorandum of his own the Assistant Secretary suggested holding consultations on Austrian independence with Great Britain and Russia at the end of the Moscow Conference. He also recommended taking up relations with Austrian public figures of every persuasion, though without giving recognition to any Austrian committee. In Switzerland and elsewhere, leading Austrian figures, such as Ambassador Dr. Arthur Breycha-Vauthier, were consulted by the Allies on the independence question. In Sweden, Dr. Bruno Kreisky, the spokesman for the socialists, who was always well informed, must have had some knowledge of the pending discussions and inquiries. At the beginning of July, 1943, the trusted agents of the Austrian labor movement in Sweden sent a letter to the socialist foreign bureaus in London and New York requesting that these bodies take a position on the question of Austria's future.[12]

Mr. Berle's policy of keeping away from the Free Movements was coming to an end. Finally, two months after the British message of August 28, 1943, and shortly before the conclusion of the Moscow Conference, he too became convinced that discussions concerning the restoration of Austria would be desirable and that the other major powers were clearly in favor of Austrian independence. He composed a memorandum to this effect on October 19, 1943, barely two weeks before the Moscow Declaration concerning Austria's independence. Even at this late date he wanted first to consult the British, who had asked for such consultation long before. The memorandum states that he was not informed of the position of the Soviet Union. But why, one must ask, was he, an Assistant Secretary of State, ignorant of the Soviet position on the Austrian question? After all, the British aide-mémoire of August 28, 1943, mentioned Stalin's statement of December, 1941, that Austria should be restored as an independent country, along with Foreign Minister Molotov's discussion with the British ambassador of a federation of Central and Eastern European states. Mr. Berle must have known about the British proposals, since six weeks had passed between the British memorandum and his own.

Egon Ranshofen-Wertheimer's visits to the State Department provided Berle with a last-minute opportunity to become engaged in the Austrian question. He contributed a memorandum of his own on the issue, opposing the recognition of any particular Austrian group as dominant in the quest for independence, even in the future. This argument exactly corresponded to the viewpoint of Julius Deutsch, whom Berle had consulted as his principal informant. At last it had become clear even to Mr. Berle that at least the Soviet Union if not the Western powers had a clear conception of the necessity of restoring Austria's independence, regardless of the attitude of the Austrian political émigrés and the wishes of the American State Department and the British Foreign Office.[13]

The Russians were not concerned with the right to self-determination of the Austrian population at home, not to mention the Austrian workers. But the Soviet Union was certainly not guided by Otto Bauer's principle of expecting the liberation of Austria as the result of a revolution of all of Germany. If we consider that Stalin as early as December, 1941, on the occasion of a visit by British Foreign Minister Anthony Eden, declared that Austria was to be restored as an independent state and that he had never wavered in this view, the passive stance of the American State Department is difficult to explain. I am convinced that among the American leaders only President Roosevelt correctly assessed the early Russian attitude in the Austrian question and that he was eager to gain a head start by his attempt to form an Austrian battalion as a symbol of Austria's independence. Undersecretary Welles, in contrast to Assistant Secretary Berle, seems to have shared the President's point of view. But perhaps to prevent involving the Soviet Union prematurely, Roosevelt did not lead American public opinion on Austria after his press conference of January 5, 1943. Dean Acheson, at that time serving as Undersecretary of State, states correctly that during the first three-quarters of 1943 Russian attitudes were becoming increasingly clear. That the Austrian émigrés incorrectly evaluated the President's policy on the battalion, with its far-reaching expectations, may be excused by their not knowing the details of Molotov's discussions. Their parochial view never allowed them to realize that the leader of American foreign policy had access to information unavailable to the public.

But Molotov's communication to the British ambassador in Moscow, dated June 7, 1943, already contains the conclusions the Russians drew from their victory at Stalingrad and the Russian army's irresistible advance—exactly one month after the Austrian battalion was dissolved. In this note the Soviet Union expressly opposed any inclusion of Austria in a federation of the small states on the western border of the Soviet Union. The attentive reader will suspect some connection with the dissolution of the battalion, after the failure of the only positive position taken by America and the other Western powers in favor of Austrian independence. Molotov had carefully considered the political situation in Austria; his communication reflected his conclusion that public opinion in Austria lacked direction and that it required an assurance concerning the Allies' war aims.[14] The West's sole attempt to influence public opinion in Austria, that is, through the creation of an Austrian battalion, had failed. A renewed attempt was not even considered.

In its memorandum of August 28, 1943, Great Britain wanted to leave open the question of including Austria in a federation of Central or Eastern European states. This accorded with the policies of Winston Churchill, who had publicly proposed military intervention in Central Europe. The American State Department, on the other hand, opposed any mention of a possible federation in the declaration of Austria's independence.[15] The State Department memorandum postulates that the wish of the Austrian people to contribute to their own liberation was important and must be respected.[16]

Thus, in spite of the dissolution of the Austrian battalion, events followed in rapid succession, coming to a new climax in the Moscow Declaration.

VII
From the Moscow Declaration to the Armistice

At the conclusion of the Moscow Conference, the Three Power Declaration of the United States, Great Britain, and the Soviet Union was published. This document announced the restoration of Austria as one of the war aims, but at the same time it called for Austrians to participate in their own liberation.[1] The Moscow Declaration was made public on November 1, 1943.

Thenceforth, the Austrian emigration had no choice but to work within the framework of the Three Power Declaration, offering to serve as trustees for the Austrian people, who were still prevented from expressing their will. The Austrian émigrés tried to interpret the Declaration according to their points of view, stressing the provisions amenable to their interests and eliminating or minimizing the tenets that they felt were damaging to their political objectives. In any case, the question of Austria's independence was resolved once and for all by the Moscow Declaration. Even those émigrés who viewed the independence of Austria as an enforced policy, such as Dr. Friedrich Adler, were compelled to accept reality. From this time on, even more than for the earlier period, for both individuals and groups within the emigration, a history of activity in support of Austria's independence is to be considered a positive attribute, while opposition to Austria's independence or subordinating it to some future exercise of self-determination now must be viewed negatively.

The Allies—especially the Soviet Union, whose prestige was growing—also interpreted the Moscow Declaration according to their own interests. Russia's political objectives were expressed in her emphatic objection to including Austria in a federation, and she asserted energetically that Austria was well able to exist as a small independent nation. Soviet journalism attacked primarily the Austrian socialists, who still doubted, as they had for the twenty years of Austria's earlier independence, the country's economic and social viability.[2] Soviet interest in Austria swelled to a journalistic crescendo when the Russian armies came close to the borders of the former Republic. Like all Austrian Communists, the Austrian political émigrés in Russia had called for the restoration of Austria within the 1938 borders ever since the fall of the Republic; they now pursued a clearly nationalistic policy.[3] Russian propaganda stressed that only the Soviet Union had opposed the Anschluss in 1938; time and again the Russians declared that the majority of Austrians had been ready to defend Austria's independence. That Mexico also had taken this position on Austria was passed over. Russian attacks were directed with special sharpness at the Austrian socialists in London who had always advocated an Anschluss but now were rushing to distribute among themselves political positions in a new Austria. Thus one Soviet author hinted that the

Austrian Representative Committee, established in London under socialist leadership on November 9, 1943, immediately after the Moscow Declaration, had attempted to create a predominantly socialist foreign representation. While this Committee had reserved places for communists, the socialists' real purpose had been to prevent a united front of all Austrian parties. According to this writer, Dr. Friedrich Adler had approvingly admitted as much in *Austrian Labor Information*.[4]

The attitude of the other signatory states to the Moscow Declaration, the United States and Great Britain, was quite differfent. Even within the State Department there were several sections that raised the question of the recognition of an Austrian committee and suggested a positive attitude in the sense of the Moscow Declaration.[5] But whenever one State Department group attempted to deviate from the entrenched position of passivity, the opposing faction fought against such an attempt. A memorandum of December 1, 1943, from the Division of European Affairs weighed the possibility of a positive attitude, but it only produced an opposing memorandum on December 10.[6] The State Department's passivity on how Austrians abroad might contribute to the future independence of their native land was reinforced by the negative stance of the British government. No one among the Austrian émigrés in Great Britain, it was said, was fit to represent Austria, and no committee of émigrés could count on official recognition by the British government.[7] A further memorandum of January 4, 1944, reiterated the reasons for this negative attitude, quite as if nothing had changed and the Moscow Declaration had not been published.[8] The State Department followed the British lead in withholding recognition from any particular person or organization among existing groups or coalitions of these organizations. Ironically, in the past the Austrian groups' failure to unify had been given as the reason why the State Department had refused to recognize them. But now that the danger of a coalition of all émigré factions actually loomed on the horizon, recognition was refused all the more strongly.[9] Nothing had been done, except for President Roosevelt's attempt to create the essentially symbolic Austrian battalion. The State Department's opposition to the Free Movements in the United States lasted even after the end of the war. When the first provisional Austrian government under Dr. Karl Renner proposed to send the former Austrian minister Dr. Richard Schüller to Washington as the first postwar Austrian ambassador, the State Department cabled back that it wanted only an ambassador coming directly from Austria or at least a refugee who had never lived in the United States or been active in the Free Movements. The State Department even assumed, erroneously, that Dr. Schüller had been the chairman of the Military Committee for the Liberation of Austria. But of course that had been Otto von Hapsburg's position.[10]

The United States and Great Britain were content with safeguarding their political interests and objectives within the European Advisory Commission, founded in London by the Moscow Conference. This body was intended to form the basis for Allied occupation and administration of the occupied enemy territory, including the area of the Republic of Austria, and to facilitate the establishment of a separate Austrian administration.[11] After the Moscow Declaration, the Western Allies abandoned any efforts to call on the Austrian emigrants within their borders to make a contribution to Austrian independence. Instead, they counted on future military governments in Germany and Austria to maintain order. Further, they renounced any attempt to influence political developments in Austria, although it was obvious that the Soviet Union was intent on pursuing its own objectives in that country. From the standpoint of the military, this political position was certainly the simplest one, for a military government would comply with directives from Washington. The position of the military also corresponded with the views of the State Department that counseled passivity on the question of Austrian independence and saw salvation in the final decision of the Austrian people after the liberation of the country—even if the Soviet Union should occupy Austria's capital and eastern territories, as she had set out to do. As earlier, the State Department position corresponded to the principles of the Austrian Labor Committee under Julius Deutsch.

In spite of all difficulties, the Austrian emigrants in the Western countries attempted to present their views on the Three Power Declaration and to fulfill their own essential demand, Austria's own contribution to its liberation. Hans Rott worked untiringly in the cause of Austria's restoration. Immediately after the release of the Moscow Declaration, he wrote Secretary Hull, stating in detail his opinion on this contribution. Referring once again to the last Austrian federal constitution, he demanded to be recognized as temporary head of a legitimate Austrian government as well as leader of a committee to serve within this provisional Austrian government. Back in September, 1941, he had used the same reasoning to establish the Austrian National Council and had utilized every possible opportunity to advance his claim to represent his country.[12] Hans Rott argued that if Austria were recognized, 10 percent of the German Wehrmacht—the ratio of Austrians serving in the German forces—would become "unreliable" and would be a heavy burden on the German military machine.[13] Entire troop units would desert as soon as an internationally recognized Austrian government addressed an appeal to the Austrian soldiers in the Wehrmacht to lay down arms. The closer military operations came to Austrian territory, he argued, the greater the value of a provisional government including political emigrants.

Hans Rott had to note, however, that "it cannot be said that the three powers of the Moscow Declaration have up to this time drawn the logical conclusion of their own statement nor taken any steps to live up to it." Far less encouragement had been given to Austria and her people than to all the other victims of Germany's aggression. Rott was bitter as he emphasized the demands made on Austria to contribute to her own liberation, while she was denied the support granted to other nations and their resistance movements. This lack of logic and justice, he pointed out, could not but undermine the morale of Austrian patriots. Only the recognition of an Austrian government on the side of the Allies could put an end to this abnormal, paradoxical situation.[14]

In another telegram to Secretary Hull, sent at the time of the Quebec Conference (August, 1943), Rott made the same demand. At a press conference in Quebec, Hull had criticized Austria for doing too little for her own liberation, and had praised the Luxemburgers as a glowing example. But Luxemburg, Rott noted, had an acting government that could aid the underground; Austria had no government in exile and was prevented from achieving one by the same powers that kept demanding that she contribute to her liberation. Professor Robert Heine-Geldern, a man close to Rott, also sent a detailed memorandum to Secretary Hull on November 7, 1943, immediately after the release of the Moscow Declaration. He drew the legal and political conclusions for the Austrian point of view. What kind of contribution did the Allies desire? He too regarded recognition of a provisional government as the core of an Austrian resistance, and this government should be headed by Hans Rott, the last living member of Schuschnigg's pre-Anschluss regime. Heine-Geldern also suggested that Austrian prisoners of war be allowed to take part in the struggle for Austria's liberation.[15] Rott's efforts were also supported by Anton Retschek, the officially recognized chairman of the Austrian civil servants' committee in Brazil, as well as by the newly established Austrian Institute, which exists to this day.[16]

However, the State Department officials charged with Hans Rott's concerns immediately expressed objections to recognizing a government in exile. It was their feeling that the Moscow Declaration had promised the restoration of Austria only after liberation. Rott's efforts, therefore, were premature. But this reasoning was self-contradictory, if (as Rott maintained) the Austrians' own contribution to liberation could not be performed without a government in exile.[17] Rott wanted this contribution to be made at the proper time. How could the prisoners of war be won over if no Austrian representation abroad were allowed to approach them? How could an Austrian underground make any connection with the prisoners of war if no such representation were in existence?

The State Department's negative attitude showed even more clearly in a memorandum of December 30, 1943. The Department determined that the United States could not recognize Rott as representative of a provisional Austrian government unless the other signatories of the Moscow Declaration agreed. Admittedly, this alone was a weighty reason for refusal.

But the State Department went a step further. To make certain that no action could result from Rott's urgent memoranda, it cited the "nebulousness" of Rott's claim that he continued to represent the previous Austrian government.[18] Not unjustly did members of the Austrian underground movement, such as Felix Slavik, later mayor of Vienna, after the liberation of Austria reproach the Allies for their lack of support of the Austrian underground.[19] Nevertheless, Rott did not give in, even if he had to go far afield to find another opportunity to repeat his claim. One such was the attempt to reopen the Austrian embassy in Rome.[20] Rott later told me that all his various requests had also been submitted to President Roosevelt, but the President had declared he could do nothing more in the Austrian question. Roosevelt showed conclusively that he had abandoned any active policy for independent Austria at one of the last press conferences before his death. In answer to one journalist's question what the difference would be between the occupation government in Austria and in Germany, the President replied only that an Allied Council would be set up in Vienna. In other words, there would be practically the same occupation government for liberated Austria as for Germany.[21] This finally made it clear to the Austrians that they would have to expect occupation by the four major powers, unlike Czechoslovakia, Yugoslavia, or Poland.

Hans Rott tried in other ways to foster an Austrian contribution to independence. On March 16, 1944, he wrote Secretary Hull with photocopies of letters directed to him from sixteen Austrian prisoners of war in Camp Breckenridge, Kentucky, who had informed him of the suicide of one prisoner, Franz Kettner.[22] Referring to Article 9 of the Geneva Convention of 1929, which dealt with the separation of prisoners of war of different races and nations, Rott demanded that Austrian prisoners be separated from the German members of the Wehrmacht. Since the Anschluss had been declared null and void in Moscow, Austrians were again a separate nationality and should be treated accordingly. Professor Heine-Geldern also argued for the separation of prisoners. He had himself been a prisoner of war in Russia during the First World War, and he referred to methods used by the Russians, who separated Slavic-speaking prisoners of war from Germans and Hungarians, thus laying the cornerstone of the Czech legions who fought in the First World War. Like Rott, he was convinced that separation of prisoners of war and permission to fight on the side of the Allies would be crucial steps toward the Austrians' contribution to the war effort. Ferdinand Czernin's Austrian Action took an identical position: August 23, 1944, the group pointed out to the State Department that Great Britain and the Soviet Union had already undertaken the separation of their prisoners of war according to nationality.[23] Later, news reached the State Department from Stockholm that the Soviet Union had separated the Austrian prisoners of war.[24] But these requests were unsuccessful. In February, 1944, the War Department refused to effect a separation of prisoners. Secretary Hull merely directed a technical inquiry to the War Department, asking whether it might be possible to carry out some kind of separation later, without encountering administrative difficulties, should the occasion arise. But on September 5, 1944, it was ascertained that the Americans' treatment of Austrian prisoners of war had undergone no changes.[25]

Not surprisingly, the third faction among the émigrés, the Austrian Labor Committee, never asked the State and War Departments to separate prisoners of war according to nationality. (No documents to this effect have been turned up among the material available.) This faction always took a negative position whenever it was a matter of creating even a symbol for the restoration of Austrian independence. Attempting to remain consistent with its previous attitude, the Austrian Labor Committee made a cautious, step-by-step retreat from its original position of looking for the liberation of Austria through a Greater German revolution, and of course it had no choice but to accept the decision on the Allied powers in Moscow. Friedrich Adler, the leading theoretician of the Committee, was eager to continue pursuing the Anschluss idea even after the Moscow Declaration. But at the Committee's meeting of April 12, 1944, he was forced to resign the chairmanship. Julius Deutsch was content with preventing any chance that a provisional Austrian representation abroad would be created at the eleventh hour; he acted in pragmatic ways, without any theoretical foundations.[26] Since his objective coincided with the wishes of the American and British governments, little had to be done. At a gathering to commemorate the old Austrian national holiday on November 12, 1943, Deutsch was heard to say that the Social Democrats took a favorable view of the formation of an Austrian national committee. He added, however, that as a necessary condition such a committee's other members—by which he meant the other Austrian political organizations—must be prepared to give reassurance of their commitment to democratic institutions.[27] But he was surely aware that such a declaration on his part could not be considered a genuine call to political collaboration, since the Austrian Representative Committee in London, under socialist leadership and with the closest ties to his Austrian Labor Committee, had rejected any collaboration with the other emigrant organizations. The London Committee wanted to admit only such delegates as it selected itself; it reserved two seats for representatives of the Communist party. (In the event, however, these were never accepted, since the socialists finally refused any participation by communists.) The Austrian Labor Committee had gladly welcomed the successful formation of the London Committee, stating that it had gotten a start on "the reaction."[28] Deutsch's invitation to the other émigré organizations in the United States, therefore, was only made for show, and for all practical purposes such collaboration would have been prevented by his own Committee.

At the same time that Hans Rott and Austrian Action were eager to achieve the separation of the prisoners of war, the Austrian Labor Committee was much more deeply concerned that a representative of the Austrian trade unions be admitted as an observer at the International Labor Organization conference in Philadelphia. They were also occupied with the entry into the United States of Franz Novy, the chairman of the Austrian trade unions, who was coming over from London.[29]

Finally even Ferdinand Czernin and Austrian Action had to realize that it was impossible to persuade the Austrian Labor Committee to collaborate with other Austrian emigration organizations. Until this time the two groups had worked together in their common opposition to the Hapsburgs and their ambitions. After the Moscow Declaration, Czernin tried to organize an Austrian committee with semiofficial support from the State Department, but he later expressed apprehension that collaboration with the Austrian Labor Committee would not be achieved. He too had learned which were the insurmountable difficulties blocking the cooperation of all the emigrant forces, and he proposed that the State Department exert pressure on the Austrian Labor Committee to achieve the unification of all émigré factions. He said that an initiative from the ranks of the Austrian political émigrés would be in vain and unification could be achieved only under the aegis of the State Department.[30]

The State Department not only bluntly rejected his proposal but quite generally declared its opposition to any encouragement of individuals and groups. The Department made perfectly clear that singling out a group was not desirable, because this might lead to difficulties in the future. Czernin's proposal that the State Department bring about the unification was not taken up at all. The memorandum of December 7, 1943, a decisive rejection of his proposal, came to the astonishing conclusion that there was no need for any symbolic body to encourage the masses in Austria. This answer was wholly in line with the views of the Austrian Labor Committee, and indeed the Department appears to have consulted Julius Deutsch. This presumption is supported by a remark in another State Department document, in which Assistant Secretary Berle refers to "the return of Deutsch."[31]

At the same time the British Foreign Office noted once again that no Austrian émigré in Great Britain could be considered representative of his country and that no committee of émigrés would be recognized. Another memorandum which also pointed out that 90 percent of the refugees were Jewish, maintained that no outstanding personality was available.[32] Another State Department memorandum, dated January 20, 1944, again opposed recognizing any Austrian group or encouraging a coalition for fear of subsequent complications.[33] A final effort by Ferdinand Czernin to obtain an interview at the State Department also failed; Assistant Secretary Berle refused to receive him, saying he must not appear to support a particular group, as various émigrés claimed he had done in the past.[34]

We have seen that in the State Department there were not only two main policies on the question of Austria, but time and again the faction representing one policy contradicted the rival group. On January 20 and February 2, 1944, Department members mention the usefulness of an Austrian symbol in spite of its ultimate rejection, though barely six weeks earlier—on December 7, 1943—an Austrian symbol had been declared unnecessary. If a symbol was useful, why was the fear of complications so persuasive? The British, on the other hand, in rejecting any recognition of an emigration organization, justified their position in two ways: no outstanding personality was available among the émigrés in Great Britain, and also the 90 percent of the émigrés who were of Jewish descent could not be representative of the Austrian home country. Furthermore, there was no unity among the emigrants. In this memorandum, the Foreign Office ignored the two Austrian political organizations in Great Britain—the Free Austrian Movement and the London Bureau of the Austrian Socialists, which was succeeded by the Austrian Representative Committee. The British made no attempt to unify the two Austrian groups.

And Czernin's last-minute attempt to achieve a coalition in U.S.A. through State Department influence was disregarded in the United States.

The State Department and the Foreign Office had long held that recognition of an Austrian foreign representation could only follow unification of the Austrian emigration organizations. But when the possibility of coalition seemed to be at hand, it was pushed aside apparently as a demand whose time had passed. And yet some members of the American foreign service had misgivings about the passive policy of the State Department. A Department telegram to the American envoy in Berne, dated December 10, 1943, requests information about attitudes within Austria on the Moscow Declaration and on such personalities as Deutsch, Novy, and Rott; it asks whether these men still had any influence in Austria and whether Austrian leaders of the underground might not be brought out of the country to form a committee and guide the underground from outside.[35] The embassy in Switzerland reported that the majority of the Austrians were not impressed by the Moscow Declaration and that the prevailing opinion was that Austria would be punished in the same way as Germany. The correspondent discounted even efforts to establish an Austrian committee for "Relief and Rehabilitation," in a purely advisory capacity and without any claim to representation or symbolic importance.[36] And so the State Department faction sympathetic to a restoration of Austrian independence was influenced not to press their favored policy. Meanwhile, as throughout the controversy, diplomatic courtesy prevailed, since it did not obligate anyone to anything. A telegram of thanks of November 22, 1943, from the Austrian National Committee to President Roosevelt was answered in turn with thanks.[37]

We must assume that after the Moscow Declaration, the United States government no longer felt itself in a position to make unilateral decisions on Austria. In the reply to Rott's request for the recognition of an Austrian government, the State Department legal staff referred to this feeling as a compelling reason for its refusal.[38] The Austrian question thus became the first problem of the Cold War; even as the hot war was still being waged, the Austrian dispute showed that though the Allies had proclaimed Austrian independence as a war aim, the policy was interpreted in different ways when it came to its political execution. No agreement had been reached on how independence was to be achieved, what shape Austria's political structure was to be, and, most especially, how Austria's contribution to her own liberation was to be brought about. One American diplomat, queried by a reporter, replied sarcastically that it would be hard to assess a contribution to Austria's liberation in exact, precise tonnage.[39] Even though the Western Allies and Russia had agreed in principle on this first major political question, the sequel to the Moscow Declaration showed that, though they used the same wording, the parties to the contract were thinking of fundamentally different concepts and interpretations. And, of course, this pattern was to repeat itself in future agreements among the three Great Powers. Various examples might be cited:

the interpretation of the Geneva Convention on the question of the treatment of Austrian prisoners of war, or the various interpretations of Austria's role in its own liberation. In any case, there is no doubt that in interpreting the same conventions and contractual language the West and the Soviet Union developed different views. The United States and Great Britain thought in terms of containing Austria's political development in a vacuum and ruling through a military government. The Russians, on the other hand, pursued the course they initiated during the war—to appeal to the nationalism of the country's population and its émigrés, to aim for the unification of all Austrian parties and groups, and to exert an active influence on developments within the country.

The Western powers looked only to the Austrian home population for a contribution to their own liberation, as called for in the Moscow Declaration, without any influence or support from the political emigration. The Soviet Union, on the other hand, made efforts to increase its influence in Austria and to promote the participation of Austrians everywhere. The Western powers limited their thinking to an ideal postulate rarely possible in practice—the exercise of a people's right to self-determination. Russia's propagandists, on the other hand, were convinced that actual conditions were of much greater significance than future goals; the Russians believed they could best attain their goals by working with accomplished facts.[40] The State Department found it simplest to interpret the clause on the Austrian's contribution to independence to mean a military government in Austria, treating Austrian affairs from a military rather than a diplomatic viewpoint. Only in the long run would there be recourse to the Austrian people's right of self-determination.[41] But the State Department overlooked the Austrian underground movement, which was hampered by the lack of support from outside the country. In sharp contrast, the underground movements in France, Holland, Italy, and Norway were given help; but there was total inaction from outside in regard to Austria.[42] Cordell Hull had been, therefore, unjust in putting the blame on the Austrians that there was no Austrian underground organization. But though he was the head of the State Department, Secretary Hull had handed over decisions in Austrian matters to Assistant Secretary Berle, who in turn wanted to pass decisions on to the future Austrians' exercise of self-determination.[43]

When Czernin tried to unify all the émigré factions, he already assumed that pressure from the State Department would be required to influence the Austrian Labor Committee. Finally he realized with bitterness who was to blame for the failure of the unification efforts; in an interview in the New York *Aufbau,* he reached the following conclusion:

> Those Austrian groups, in particular the leaders of the Austrian Labor Committee, who for years have advocated passivity and to this day don't want to hear about a national struggle for liberation, must be blamed most for the suspicion the Allies harbor toward the Austrian liberation movement. Their behavior makes the world be-

lieve that a high percentage of Austrians really are "Anschlüsslers"; but they fail to point out that they were last elected by the Austrian people in 1932. In the past five years, however, in contrast to the social-democratic Austrian Labor Committee, the Austrians have learned a great deal.

Czernin forgot—or wanted to forget—that at one time he himself had been the Austrian Labor Committee's closest ally and for two years he had gone along with that group's policies. He had to adjust, in some discomfort, to the role of an abandoned ally. But late realization may be a characteristic of a politician whose failure can no longer be denied.[44] In the event, Czernin's Austrian Action, outmaneuvered in the United States, had no choice but to join with the Free Austrian World Movement in London, even though Austrian Action was still numerically the strongest association of political émigrés in the United States.[45]

It is not without interest, however, to trace the experience of the émigrés whom Czernin said caused the Allies' suspicions of the Austrian liberation movement. One week after the Czernin interview, the *Aufbau* published a "Call to Rising Up," addressed to the Austrian people; it was broadcast over the American and British foreign networks. "Austrian workers have never waited to be liberated by others"—as usual, the call addressed itself only to the Austrian workers and not to the people as a whole.[46] But when the group of émigrés who had demanded unification of all factions of émigrés suggested to the State Department that they turn their radio propaganda to the Catholic sector of the Austrian population—those in sympathy with the Christian Socialist party—they were turned down on the grounds that such broadcasts would be partisan.[47] The State Department employed a double standard when it suited its purposes to do so.

Those factions who favored a government in exile had lost out in the State Department, especially after Julius Deutsch became their decisive expert in Austrian matters.[48] Not only had he become the spokesman for the Austrian Labor Committee—preaching total passivity and trust in the Austrian people's right of self-determination—but through his interview with the *Aufbau*, he had also become the spokesman for the wider, apolitical circles of émigrés whom the *Aufbau* served. Nevertheless the *Aufbau*, with all its admiration for Deutsch, sometimes had to take a position against his remarks. On one occasion, the "proven and experienced" statesman was reproached for being unable to see any model for a liberated Austria other than the same old Austria he had left. Even his admirers and other believers in a policy of passivity finally realized that what had been valid in the years 1930 or 1932, that is, the time on which the Austrian socialists based their case, need not have validity for the year 1944.[49]

At last doubts arose about the Austrian Labor Committee's claim to speak as Austria's strongest political party. The State Department shared this concern. Perhaps out of a dawning self-criticism, and in order to be prepared for a different Austrian future, the *Aufbau* hailed as "perhaps the most important development in the camp of exiled Austrians" the formation in November, 1944, of a Christian Socialist party abroad. Hans Rott was its founder and provisional head.[50] At first the changed political climate affected only émigré circles; nothing changed in the official position of the American and British authorities. Neither the Western powers' nor the Soviet Union's attitudes, which were diametrically opposed, could be overlooked; the growing conflict between them gave grounds for apprehension for the future of Austria. Yet the United States could offer nothing more forceful than a press conference (on March 10, 1945), where Undersecretary of State Joseph C. Grew stressed his government's earnest desire to see a free and independent Austria restored, asking for the cooperation of the Austrians in the weeks to come. As it happens, there were then only three weeks before the Russian army reached the border of Austria.[51] Both Ferdinand Czernin[52] and Otto von Hapsburg[53] offered to coordinate the Austrian resistance movements, but neither received a response from the Allies. In a broadcast of April 2, 1945, the BBC asked of the Austrians nothing else than that they greet the advancing Russians as their liberators and in this way at last make a contribution to their own liberation.[54]

All this suggests persuasively that the American State Department and the British Foreign Office interpreted the Moscow Declaration as applying only to the political forces within Austria; any cooperation from Austrian political émigrés was rejected. On the other hand, Russia's policy toward Austria was entirely different. Long before Russian troops approached the borders of the Austrian Republic, the politically active Austrian émigrés in Russia, among them especially the radio commentator Ernst Fischer, had advocated a policy of restoring Austria's independence. Now, after the Moscow Declaration, official propaganda, too, was unequivocally of a nationalist Austrian taint.[55]

Writing in the Graz periodical *Die Abwehr* (*The Defense*) after the war, Ernst Karl Winter claimed with some justice that Ernst Fischer's ideas were romantic and universal—catholic. The ideas of this glib one-time editor of the *Wiener Arbeiter-Zeitung* (*Vienna Worker's Times*), who under the impact of the February, 1934, uprising had switched over to communism, could have originated with Richard Kralik, a well-known Catholic poet.[56]

On February 6, 1944, Foreign Minister Vyacheslav Molotov, in a conversation with the American ambassador to Moscow, W. Averell Harriman, stated the official policy of the Soviet Union, that recognition of an Austrian representation abroad was premature.[57] But immediately after the Moscow Declaration, the Austrian political émigrés in Moscow had told anyone willing to listen what Russia's program for Austria was to be: restoration of the Austrian national awareness and participation by all Austrian forces in the fight against Hitler. An essay published in the Russian periodical *War and the Working Class,* entitled "Austria's Fate", followed the same line.[58] The Austrian communists in Russia regarded the socialists abroad as the principal opponents of the policy of participation. The Russians wanted not only activity within Austria, but also an Austrian political center abroad. The Austrian communists in Great Britain, too, demanded a united front of all groups of émigrés, pointing to the establishment of an inter-Austrian liberation front and partisan groups in Carinthia and Styria.[59]

As Ernst Fischer admitted, policymakers in the East had their own doubts about a powerful Austrian national sentiment. These reservations derived from the correct conviction that, in spite of the common language, Austrians rejected much of the cluster of attitudes that made up Germanness; certainly they despised the characteristics they called "Prussian." The Austrians could easily be aroused against Reich Germans, whom they felt were strangers who lumped them with "the other Prussians." On February 16, 1945, the Moscow radio station called upon the Austrians to make Andreas Hofer (the Tyrolean hero in the Napoleonic Wars) their model in an uprising against the German-Prussian strangers.[60] The broadcast traced the history of Austrian nationalism back to Prince Eugene of Savoy in the seventeenth century, and stress was laid on the special course of Austrian might and culture in the past.

On April 7, 1945, *Pravda,* the official journalistic voice of Moscow, published a detailed account of how the Soviet Union wished to see the Moscow Declaration interpreted on the restoration of Austrian independence. This article expressed opposition not only to the idea of a federation but also to all current antiunification efforts of emigration groups. The Social-Democratic organization in London was the special target here. *Pravda* sharply assailed the socialists' assertion that a restored Austria would not be economically viable.[61] It is worth noting that Otto von Hapsburg and Schuschnigg were not mentioned—obviously, in the opinion of the American ambassador in Moscow, in order "not to prevent a later use of these men."

These intensive efforts on the part of the Soviet Union went unopposed in the West even though it was obvious that the Russians were pursuing their own aims in their Austrian policy. In the United States, it was not possible even to arrange the proclamation of an Austrian commemorative day on the seventh anniversary of Austria's occupation. The refusal was justified by noting that the Austrians were splintered—even though the State Department would not encourage a coalition of émigré factions.[62] President Roosevelt followed the passive line of the State Department without any objections.[63]

As the end of National Socialist rule in Europe came into view and the Russian armies moved closer to Austria's borders, it became clear that a passive policy was no longer possible. The West finally recognized that a form of *realpolitik* had become necessary. The armies of the Soviet Union, which had just brought Hungary to its knees, would soon set foot on Austrian soil and rid the land of German troops, long before the armies of the United States and Great Britain could approach.

Under a Russian occupation, there was no longer any possibility of either an all-German revolution or liberation by the Austrians themselves, rising up against the German occupation troops. The only thing left for the resistance within Austria to do was to help the advancing Russian forces or at least not to oppose them. Even if self-determination and antinationalism continued to be the guidelines of the Austrian socialists abroad, and also the British and American policy, the first glimmerings of the real situation began to dawn in the West, affecting even the most aloof groups of political émigrés.

Dr. Friedrich Adler, who supported a policy of Anschluss even after the Moscow Declaration, had to keep silent.[64] But while the Russians supported a resistance movement, in spite of the very limited enthusiasm for the Soviet Union in Austria,[65] the Western powers still were mired in inactivity. Although the Catholic population of Austria tried to establish contact with the Western powers, an offer from Hans Rott and Professor Heine-Geldern to address this segment of the population was turned down.[66] An American occupation officer was correct when he noted, after Austria's liberation, that the Austrian underground movement had suffered most from the lack of outside support.[67] Thus, some Americans recognized the missed opportunities in Central Europe, stemming from the State Department's general lack of attention to the national Free Movements.[68]

Many observers believed at the time and since that an Austrian government in exile would have solved many of Austria's postwar problems. Not unjustly, one Austrian writer stated that the question of the South Tyrol could have been unraveled if an Austrian foreign representation had existed at the time of the Italian armistice:

> Looking back, we realize today that the last real chance of regaining the South Tyrol for Austria was lost on September 8, 1943—the day of Italy's capitulation during the Second World War—because of the ideological and political prejudices of the Austrian emigration. An Austrian government in exile, recognized by the Allies, would probably have had a chance to obtain from the Western powers binding commitments concerning the reincorporation of the South Tyrol into Austria after the end of the war.[69]

After more than thirty years this assessment appears to be fully justified. The primary blame for this final loss belongs to the Austrian émigrés who insisted that the Austrian workers must decide the country's political system after the liberation. The blame is shared by the groups in the State Department and the Foreign Office who, advised by experts from the Austrian Labor Committee, maintained that until Austria's liberation nothing must be done to create a representation abroad.[70] This charge is borne out by a letter I received from Julius Deutsch:

> . . . . What I wanted was nothing more than to advocate the idea that the Austrian people themselves should decide the form of their independence. An independence whose form and content is determined from outside is not independence. . . . Once the Austrian workers have regained their freedom of action, they will and should make their decision. We émigrés have only the right (and the duty) to contribute as much as we can to securing the freedom of action of our people.

In defending this theory, the Austrian and American experts did not account for the period just before the actual liberation, when military events and new political alignments were certain to influence a subsequent decision by the Austrian population or prevent the freedom of such decision altogether. There is no standing still in the political life of a people, and the principle of passivity opened the way for unforeseeable forces to influence the future of Austria. Forces that develop in a political vacuum, under influences from the outside, seek to displace the old *status quo*. An example is the radical worsening of Austria's political situation in the period between the armistice with Italy of September 8, 1943, and the negotiations concerning the South Tyrol's autonomy after the end of the war. In 1944 and 1945, the Western powers looked upon Italy as a strong ally in the Cold War, which was already taking form, while the eastern part of Austria held by the Russians was an occupation zone. Austria's significance to Western powers and Austria's future role were obscure, and in any case Austria was less important than Italy. On September 8, 1943, the United States and Great Britain had had the upper hand in Italy, politically, militarily, and economically, and they did not require any agreement with the Soviet Union in determining the armistice conditions. Austria's interests in the South Tyrol were entrusted to the Western powers on this day, but there was no Austrian government in exile that could have brought its influence to bear. After the war had ended in Europe, Austria was occupied by the four powers with her government in the Russian zone; she had lost bargaining power *vis à vis* Italy. As a consequence, instead of possibly reincorporating the South Tyrol into Austria, autonomy for the region was the best solution available. Even this late, the political émigrés who had striven for an Austrian government in exile attempted to intervene in the dispute. Here the failure of the Austrian battalion looms most accusingly; that symbol of continuing Austrian nationalism might have played a considerable part at the armistice.[71]

During the final months of the war, portentous events followed one another in rapid succession, making clear, even to the hesitant West, the intentions of the East. On March 22, 1945, a Swiss cable reported that a Free Austrian Council was going to be formed in Debreczen, Hungary, by the Christian Socialists, the Socialists, and the Communists.[72] This development showed the direction of Soviet policy at this time: to establish abroad a representative Austrian committee rather than a military government. Earlier, when news of a Provisional Austrian National Committee (POEN) reached the West on December 14, 1944, the United States and Britain had begun to show a more active interest in Austrian politics and to think of the country in broader terms than as a territory to be administered in a military fashion. Although American agencies were told that the POEN owed its existence purely to the tolerance of the Gestapo, the British authorities decided to acknowledge Jean Lambert (pseudonym for Dr. Ernst Lemberger) as liaison to the Committee.[73] The POEN had itself expressed a desire to establish foreign agencies with the participation of émigré figures. Jean Lambert was scheduled to head the central office in Paris. Further, an American committee was to be formed, to be headed by Karl Hans Sailer and Ernst Karl Winter.[74] The American embassy in Paris met on March 15, 1945, with POEN representatives Jean Lambert and Wieser (pseudonym for Fritz Molden). These spokesmen reported that within Austria the POEN comprised forty members from every organization, including monarchists and Communists. Significantly, when the Austrian Labor Committee published "From the Underground POEN to the Renner Government," in *Austrian Labor News* in New York (June 1, 1945), this essay failed to mention that monarchists were part of the POEN. According to a telegram of March 30, 1945, the POEN consisted of roughly ten to fifteen thousand members and about sixty thousand reserves.[75] At the Paris discussions, the representatives insisted that the POEN was a resistance group and not yet an official government representation.[76] Yet these representatives had already met with the French and the Russians and had encountered a friendly reception.[77]

The POEN was viewed with hostility by the Austrian communists, probably because Jean Lambert, the representative assigned to France, was the head of the Austrian socialists abroad. The communist newspaper *Ce Soir* in Paris stated its doubts whether this committee could be counted on when it came to forming an Austrian government.[78] As events were to show during the month of liberation, April, 1945, the POEN had no decisive influence in the establishment of the first provisional Austrian government of April 27, 1945, even though some of its member came from the ranks of the POEN.[79] What was decisive was that the principles of the committee—the collaboration of all political parties—were applied rather than waiting for the Austrian people to exercise their right to self-determination.

The POEN was significant also in another respect. During the final months of the war, the political emigration had found, in the person of Dr. Ernst Lemberger, a man who, because of his energy and his courage, was capable of taking action when action was indicated. It does not detract from Dr. Lemberger's achievement to note that he seized an existing internal agency in the POEN, even though it did not represent the populations of Salzburg and Upper Austria.[80] Although he was a socialist, he had no hesitation in setting about to connect the émigré groups and the POEN, which represented all factions within the still-occupied Austria.

Dr. Lemberger reported in Paris that of the Committee's forty leading members, the ten socialists collaborated with the other factions, including monarchists and communists.[81] In proposing to establish representative committees in Paris and in the United States, Dr. Lemberger deserves credit for having brushed aside the objections of both the socialists in the United States and Great Britain and the American and British foreign ministries, all without deviating from his loyalty to the Socialist party. Before the end of the war he managed to introduce into the discussion the very thing rejected by the émigré factions in the United States, especially the Austrian Labor Committee—the unification of all political factions, the "Union Sacrée" for the liberation of

Austria that Ernst Karl Winter had called for. And *realpolitik,* as exemplified by Dr. Karl Renner within the country and Dr. Lemberger abroad, brought about what the socialist emigration in the United States, Great Britain, and earlier in France had refused to accomplish—collaboration with monarchists, semifascists, and communists.

Indeed, the Provisional Austrian National Committee included monarchists and communists. Dr. Ernst Lemberger was determined to work first for the liberation and restoration of Austria on the basis of unifying all non-National Socialist groups; the form of government for the new Austria could await a later decision. Finally, it was clear how unrepresentative the Austrian socialists abroad had been of the socialists who had remained in Austria and also how insignificant were the election results of 1930 and 1932 for political conditions during the occupation period. It was also evident that the claim to leadership of the Austrian socialists, based on numerical superiority in the emigration in no way corresponded to the situation within occupied Austria.

But the Austrian socialists abroad persisted in their refusal to work together with the monarchists and communists, who, they said, represented only "splinter groups." But the creation of POEN signified that the socialists remaining within Austria were pursuing a contrary policy. Thus it came about that the "splinter groups" of monarchists and communists, by participating in POEN, represented the true intent of the non-National Socialists in Austria better than did those socialists abroad who rejected any collaboration with other parties. Ernst Karl Winter, who was called an unrealistic dreamer and who had repeatedly called for a "holy union" of all non-National Socialist parties in Austria, was now seen to be far more realistic than the ideologues abroad. The émigré socialists' outstanding theoretician, Dr. Friedrich Adler, only reluctantly acceded that Anschluss with Germany was no longer a defensible position, once the Moscow Declaration had been issued.[82]

After the Russian troops marched into Austria in April, 1945, the Kremlin logically adopted the policy that had always been advocated by Ernst Fischer, speaking for the communist émigrés living in the Soviet Union: to support Austrian independence efforts and to create a representative political agency. In this effort the Soviet Union was aided by a happy accident that could not have been foreseen. The first Lower Austria county seat to be occupied by Russian troops, Gloggnitz, was the home of Dr. Karl Renner. Above all a practical politician, he at first refused to flee from the attacking Russians. But when the conquerors wrought unbearable havoc in Austria, he had the courage to turn to the Russian military authorities and demand that remedial measures be taken. The Russians soon realized what a fortunate solution this man presented to them. Dr. Renner understood that only a coalition could gain recognition from the occupation power, and he had the necessary intuitive feeling in politics to become for a second time a cofounder of an Austrian Republic. This realist realized that a unilateral decision by Austrian labor and the formation of a socialist government would have as little chance of recognition as would the demand for self-determination while the war was still in progress. He later supplied the American government with a detailed account of the steps he had to take toward his goal, in a memorandum of September, 1945.[83]

Thanks to Dr. Renner's efforts, the coalition of non-National Socialist Austrian parties was successfully achieved, and the first provisional Austrian government was formed in Vienna. The monarchists were not represented in it, though they had membership in the POEN, since first of all Renner needed recognition from the Russians, who would not countenance monarchist participation. On April 27, 1945, the independence of Austria was announced by a proclamation of her own provisional government, without the plebiscite that the socialists abroad had always demanded.[84]

The Western powers, who had counted on a military government, gave only a frosty recognition to the Provisional Austrian Government. The Soviet Union had omitted holding consultations with the other signatories to the Moscow Declaration before the formation of the provisional government;[85] and only through a cable sent by the American and British chargé d'affaires in Moscow did the West learn that an Austrian government was about to be formed.[86] Immediately, that is on May 1, 1945, Washington and London expressed concern at the unilateral actions of the Soviet Union but also consternation at the formation of a provisional government under Russian control in the Russian occupation zone.[87] Although the Western powers considered Renner acceptable, they felt that the provisional government was premature. And since the greater part of Austria had not yet been liberated, they did not see it as representative of the entire country.[88] The Russians had been in touch with Renner since April 3, 1945, and after the liberation of Vienna Renner himself had told the Russians of his intention to form a provisional Austrian government; but the American and British authorities had to admit that the Soviet Union, proceeding alone, had beat the Western powers to the punch. It is interesting to note that in justifying his claim to recognition, Renner referred to his position as president of the last Austrian National Council of 1933 rather than to his being among the socialist winners in the elections of 1930 and 1932. In this he was not unlike Hans Rott, who also derived his claim to seek recognition for a provisional government from being the only member of Schuschnigg's last government who was at large and available—a claim grounded in the old federal constitution.[89]

Official recognition of this first provisional government—established in one sector of Austria, while the rest of the country had still to be regarded as occupied territory—was the mirror image of a political representation abroad, which would also have had only limited jurisdiction. Considerable time had to pass until the United States and Great Britain also recognized Renner's provisional government—in October, 1945—thereby laying the foundation for free elections.[90] It must be emphasized that in spite of earlier disagreements, all factions of the Austrian emigration considered Renner's government representative.[91]

If we consider that only a chance of history brought the Russian armies to set foot first in the central area of Lower Austria near Gloggnitz instead of entering Austria at some other spot, and thus brought into new prominence one of the best known and most highly regarded Austrian statesmen, it becomes apparent that only an unforeseen stroke of luck rectified both the mistakes of the Austrian political emigration, especially the socialists', and the omissions of the Western political leadership. Had things turned out differently, it might have been the West and the Austrian socialists—at least in the eastern part of Austria—who would have undergone a different political development, not along democratic lines.

The formation of the Provisional Austrian Government on April 27, 1945, and the proclamation of Austria's independence signaled the end of the Austrian political emigration. The émigrés were given the chance to return to their native land, now liberated from the National Socialist occupation. Austria's independence was restored.

Thus the main goal of one large group among the emigrants, pursued for more than seven years, was a reality. The old controversies were concluded, and there was nothing left for the émigré organizations abroad but to criticize the political, social, or economic conditions within the country or, better, to help in Austria's reconstruction. Ferdinand Czernin's Austrian Action was the first émigré association in the United States to decide to disband—on October 19, 1945. Writing to the Secretary of State, Czernin asserted that Austria needed now nothing else but support and reconstruction. And this had better be left to special organizations.[92]

The Free Austrian Movement, headed by Hans Rott, continued to carry on a nominal existence in New York, but without attempting any political action. As we have seen, on November 27, 1944, Rott had formed an Austrian Christian Socialist party in New York, hoping that he could take an influential position as its head within Austria.[93]

The Austrian Labor Committee turned into an association of the Friends of Austrian Labor, and all the Austrian groups merged into an Associated Austrian Relief to provide help for the hard-pressed population of their homeland.[94] Some émigrés returned to Austria as soon as they could—for example, Dr. Oskar Pollak of the Austrian Representative Committee in London. Others, such as Hans Rott, believed that continuing their activities abroad would be more useful to the new Austrian government and their fellow countrymen than their return.

Most of the nonpolitical émigrés never returned to Austria. After the war's end the Jewish émigrés concentrated instead on obtaining restitution of the assets confiscated under National Socialist rule and reparation for damages suffered. But the Jewish émigrés transferred a considerable part of their resentment against the National Socialist system to the new Austrian Republic, which they viewed as a successor to the fallen Greater German Reich.[95]

VIII

Epilogue to the History of Political Emigration in the United States

Political emigration from Austria reached the climax of its effectiveness in the United States. The emigrants' experience in France was a preamble, and with the exception of Ferdinand Czernin, the same leading figures took the stage in France and in the United States. But the emigrants' efforts to attain an effective representation abroad also met their final defeat in the United States. Up to the fall of France, the emigrants then in the United States had striven for cultural goals only; it was not until the leading émigrés arrived from France that political goals became the objective.

For some of the émigrés, the formation of the Austrian battalion would be a tangible symbol of success. But for their opponents recognition of the battalion would mean the end of their opposition to the creation of an Austrian symbol. For a brief time the efforts of the two groups were equally balanced, because, in Julius Deutsch's opinion, "important people seemed to be doing their level best to maintain in a viable and effective form the symbolically granted Austrian independence." [1]

At least up to the Russian victory at Stalingrad, the turning point in the war, the United States was the most powerful country in the Allied coalition. A more than merely passing decision by the Americans favoring recognition of a provisional government abroad for Austria—or at least a symbolic representation—would have made the greatest impression on the Allies. The countries of South America and Great Britain as well as such neutrals as Sweden would have followed the example of the United States.

The Soviet Union was the only country where Austrian political émigrés played a significant role; true, this applied to only the communists, while the socialist *Schutzbündler* (workers' protective associations), who had fled to Russia after the February uprising in 1934, were unable to develop any political activity there. [2]

In the United States, as in France before, the Austrian political emigration was lacking in leading figures, such as Tomaš G. Masaryk or Edvard Beneš had been for the Czech emigration of the First World War. The refusal of Kurt von Schuschnigg, the last Austrian chancellor, to leave the country when Austria was occupied, robbed the political emigration of the representative of Austrian independence who was best known abroad.

Hans Rott and Guido Zernatto, members of his last government, had no international reputation; their voices lacked the psychological resonance of Schuschnigg's. They had an even harder time because they had been members of an authoritarian government and so were not considered to be democrats in the Western sense. True, Hans Rott came from the Christian labor movement and, as Julius Deutsch testified, among Austrians he was considered a democrat even by his socialist opponents—someone who had only halfheartedly gone along with the authoritarian course of the governments headed by Dollfuss and Schuschnigg.[3] He also received recognition for the goals he was pursuing during the 1930's: reconciling the former socialist labor movement with the authoritarian government and winning over neutrals to the defense of Austria's independence against National Socialism.

But for all his good intentions, Rott lacked almost every precondition for successful political activity abroad. In Austria he was a skilled speaker to labor groups and at labor conferences, he was knowledgeable about trade unions, he was a politician thoroughly familiar with the political forces acting within his own country, he was able to maintain good relations even with his party's opponents. But abroad he lacked the backing of a party organization. Thus, outside the country, he could not bring to bear his experience, knowledge, and relations, which were rooted entirely in his activities within Austria. His inadequate knowledge of foreign languages, his proletarian origin— once an asset in the Christian labor movement—now prevented him from using the weight of his own personality with the French and American leaders and influential political circles. Masaryk and Beneš came to the United States as to a second home, while Rott always had to look upon France and the United States as countries of exile. He was dependent on the help of associates who, with few exceptions, had neither political experience nor an understanding of how to attain political goals in the Western democracies. Hans Rott also failed to realize how important it was to have sympathetic experts in the French and American governmental agencies.

In these respects the Austrian Labor Committee was far ahead of him. Julius Deutsch was widely considered the authoritative spokesman in Austrian matters. In any case, the official American reports of the Office for Strategic Services (OSS) show an almost uniformly favorable attitude toward the socialist emigrants and their objectives. Because the American officials who dealt with the political emigrants of 1938–1945 generally came from Austrian immigrant families formerly affiliated with the Social Democratic party, they supported the socialists' principle of democracy above all, rather than the independence of a separate Austria, a policy from which Hans Rott never deviated. The investigators also relied heavily on socialist sources of information. An OSS report of October 5, 1944, noted with some justice that in the absence of prominent conservatives, the political emigration was dominated by the left. Rott also always had to cope with pressing financial needs so that he sometimes experienced difficulty paying his assistants. He could never keep up an adequate secretariat.

Further, the émigrés' varied political backgrounds made it impossible for Rott to organize even a small group of his own party followers, the Christian Socialist workers and trade unionists. His 1944 attempt to refound the Christian Socialist party in New York was of great consequence, but it came too late.[4] If he had acted earlier, the Austrian Labor Committee would not have been able to raise the objection that a Christian Socialist party abroad did not represent a corresponding Austrian party. Rott's opponents charged him with forming a coalition with monarchists and semifascists, and they rejected the rightwing participation out of hand. But if Rott had been able to refound the party earlier, he would have shown that the Christian Socialist party was still the organization that had emerged in second place from the last election in democratic Austria.

The relationship between Rott and Otto von Hapsburg is ambiguous. Otto possessed the advantages that Rott was lacking, but he was deficient in Rott's thorough familiarity with political conditions in Austria.[5] Since their meeting in Portugal, Rott and Otto had worked side by side, although they frequently also opposed one another. In any event, Rott's connection with Otto and his occasional dependence on Otto's aspirations, culminating in the Military Committee for the Liberation of Austria, meant that once the Austrian battalion was dissolved, Rott's personal effectiveness in the political emigration had come to an end. From then on he was considered Otto's follower. This situation changed only when Rott found his way back to his political home, with the formation of the Christian Socialist party abroad. Here there was a clear separation from Otto, since there was no way the Hapsburg heir could be connected with the Christian Socialist party.

Throughout the period of emigration, Otto von Hapsburg occupied a special position. Although he left Europe for weighty political reasons, he was not a political émigré from Austria in the sense the term is used in this book. Even though he had lived outside the Republic of Austria since 1919, for the Austrian monarchists he was the titular head of legitimism, and in this sense he represented an Austrian political movement. The socialists abroad had characterized the monarchists as a splinter group, but during the final months before the end of the war the Provisional Austrian National Committee (POEN) found it necessary nonetheless to include the monarchists. Yet in spite of Otto's historic connection with his homeland, he was not a citizen of the Republic. He was a *persona sui juris,* a citizen, as it were, of the Austro-Hungarian monarchy, or a stateless person. (The United States, incidentally, harbored many other immigrants who gave their nationality of "Austro-Hungarian.") Not until the conclusion of the Austrian State Treaty did Otto apply for Austrian citizenship; this request was granted him on May 8, 1956.[6] If Otto devoted to Austrian independence the considerable political capital he had in France and the United States, and if he intervened on the questions that arose among the Austrian emigrants, he did so as a figure who was outside of the émigré ranks. But his efforts could be useful only to one group of émigrés.

The confusion of the "Republic of Austria" with "Austria" as one of the two halves of the Austro-Hungarian monarchy had grave consequences.[7] The history of the Austrian battalion showed that the unspoken ambiguity furnished a point of attack, since Otto's participation suggested that the battalion was a monarchist, Austro-Hungarian stalking horse. Yet, in no monograph or newspaper article from the period have I been able to find the argument explaining why, because of his special position, Otto could not in truth represent the Austrian political emigration of 1938. Nor did his followers among the emigrants realize that historically and legally Otto had to be an outsider if the restoration of Austria's independence was the objective. When Otto assumed the presidency of the recruiting committee for the Austrian battalion, the action could have no other meaning than that the tacit objective of the battalion was an "Austria" extending beyond the borders of the Republic of Austria. As *persona sui juris* and an outsider, Otto could not be the true symbol of a restored Austrian Republic. Not without good reason did his political supporters advise him to keep in the background. To his own sorrow, Otto did not heed this advice.[8]

The Austrian socialists in Paris, London, and New York had no leaders comparable to Masaryk or Beneš. But they compounded their disadvantages by concentrating only on preventing both Austrian independence and the unification of other émigré factions. The socialists could have done much more. In Julius Deutsch they had a spokesman versed in the ways of the world, tirelessly active and a talented speaker. Deutsch possessed what Rott lacked: familiarity with foreign countries, flexibility, the gift of getting along well with foreign leaders. Time and again he succeeded in being named to official positions and securing other political favors. After 1942 he became the focus for the socialist point of view. And since the socialists abroad pursued an inactive policy, it was perhaps not necessary that he attain the stature of a Masaryk or Beneš.

In an exchange of lengthy letters between Rott and Deutsch, written during March, 1945, the attitude of the two groups of émigrés they represented was once more exemplified.[9] For his part, Rott wished to justify his political activity during the emigration.[10] This exchange of letters— reproduced in full in the Appendix—put an end to the confrontations between political émigrés in the United Nations. The issues that concerned them would never be resolved in exile. To cite a contemporary *Aufbau* headline: "No Unification Among Austrians in New York."[11]

IX
The Austrian Emigration in Great Britain

If we compare the activities of the political emigrants in France and the United States with the experience in Great Britain, the well-organized groups in the last-named country must seem like locomotives constantly kept under steam, ready to start, but shunted to a side track. Why do we have this impression of impotence? Why were the political émigrés in Britain never able to achieve the significant actions of their peers in France and America?

At the time work was being completed on the first edition of this study, the archives of the British Foreign Office were not available. When the records were opened in 1972, new leads emerged, as also happened when American data from the Office of Strategic Services (OSS) and the Office of War Information (OWI) became available. But there is no sufficient explanation in any of this new information for the immobility and failure of the Austrian émigrés in Great Britain.

The reasons can probably be found in the inner nature of politics in Great Britain and also in the conspicuous lack of leaders among the émigrés. As elsewhere, the Austrian émigrés in Britain were not particularly aware politically, and many of them were Jewish. For both reasons, the British authorities considered the refugees unrepresentative of the political spectrum within Austria.[1] Even when the émigrés organized in political groups, they were not seen by the British as representing political trends within Austria. Furthermore, the Austrian émigrés had to deal with British public opinion and a point of view on the Anschluss that was not dissimilar from that of the Austrian socialists abroad under the leadership of Otto Bauer. Neither the British nor the socialists could approve of Hitler's methods in incorporating Austria within the Reich. But the fact of the Anschluss itself was seen as a progressive development in the endeavor of maintaining peace in Europe.

The outrages that occurred in connection with the Anschluss were viewed as being unfortunate but predictable; they were in line with other violent political events of the period. Indeed, the consequences of the Anschluss were to be mitigated as much as possible, but the plight of the refugees was seen as a humanitarian problem rather than a political one. After Schuschnigg and Hitler met in Berchtesgaden in February, 1938, it was clear that Great Britain, under the leadership of Neville Chamberlain, would not take any measure to maintain Austria's independence.[2] When Anthony Eden resigned from Chamberlain's cabinet on February 20, the last obstacle to the policy of nonintervention was removed. Though formal protests were lodged against the Anschluss, Hitler's action was considered in Great Britain as the natural solution of the question whether or not Austria's independence from Germany should be maintained. During the less than two decades of the independent Republic, Great Britain had always doubted Austria's viability. These same doubts were shared by many Austrians, and they were surely not lessened by the likeness of the Austrian socialists to the Labour party; both socialist bodies justified the Anschluss by pointing to the small state's lack of economic viability. As late as February 9, 1940—after the war had begun—the Labour party demanded that Austria decide for herself whether she wished to remain within Hitler's Reich.[3] The doubts that Austria was viable and the idea that the Anschluss represented a natural solution of the Austrian problem remained alive during the entire war period. At the signing of the Austrian State Treaty in the Belvedere Palace in Vienna on May 15, 1955, a British diplomat allowed himself an unofficial comment: "So there you have it, your Austria— how long will it last?"[4] This skepticism reflects a basic and long-standing strain in British public opinion. Against such an ideological background, there could not be lively interest in the émigrés' plans to restore Austrian independence.

British doubts about Austria resulted in a policy that was not consistent. As an American commentator noted on June 25, 1942, "Great Britain's stand on the Austrian problem has been reserved and somewhat ambiguous" (OSS 181655). The Janus face of British policy did not change throughout the exile period. To an extent, the reserve and ambiguity can be explained by the inner insecurity of the leading British statesmen, most particularly the Foreign Secretary, Anthony Eden. First, Austria was regarded as subordinate to the Greater German problem that engaged British foreign policy. Alternatively, the Austrian problem was considered too complicated, too convoluted, and too difficult for the British to develop a consistent policy. On one hand, the Labour party branded the idea of an independent Austria "unnatural" and looked at the Anschluss as the natural solution of the Austrian problem. On the other hand, a detailed study performed at Balliol College, Oxford, characterized the annexation as the "least natural" solution of the Austrian problem. The study is dated April, 1941, long before Stalin described the independence of Austria as an essential element in Russian policy, in his discussions with Anthony Eden in December, 1941.

The British attitude toward Austria was supported in 1938 and 1939 by the deep-seated desire to preserve peace at any price and during the first years of the war by the hope for a peace treaty that would not conflict with Germany's position as a great power and would reverse only the occupation of non-German territories. Even after Winston Churchill took over the war cabinet in May, 1940, powerful pacifist groups still had not lost their influence. To this day the reasons for the former Deputy Führer Rudolf Hess's flight of May, 1941, to England are not clear, and the possibility of some sort of accommodation, which the flight suggests, may have included some provision concerning Austria. The Labour party maintained its anti-Hitler though pro-Anschluss policy, and not until the Moscow Declaration did they resolve whether the war was being waged against Hitlerism or against Greater Germany. Conservative groups in England were always interested in limiting Germany's power only to the extent it was desirable for a European balance of power. They were eager to fulfill German demands they considered justified, and thus would prevent an imbalance only by curtailing her expansion to non-German territories. Both left and right in Britain were concerned with supporting such allies as Czechoslovakia and Poland, whose national interests were the cause of the war, and Yugoslavia, which became an ally after the German invasion of April, 1941.

For an additional consideration was that after February, 1934, just as in the United States, public opinion was directed against the authoritarian regimes of Dollfuss and Schuschnigg. There was a tendency to go along with the socialist thesis of the unconditional primacy of democratic institutions, no matter what the circumstances, rather than seeing Austrian authoritarianism as an extreme but necessary measure to preserve the independence of a state whose viability had already been questioned. All these influences contributed to a general trend in British ruling circles that could not help but prove reserved and ambiguous in actual policy-making. If there was no clear concept of the aim to be achieved by the war, it is not surprising that when it came to dealing with the Austrian problem, British policy can be characterized as unsure or uninformed.

Of all the Austrian political groups, the numerically strongest one in Britain, the Free Austrian Movement, was headed by communist partisans, although the overwhelming majority of the members was anticommunist or nonpolitical. But the leadership's ideology made it impossible to recognize the Free Austrian Movement as representative of Austrian émigrés. Even though after June, 1941, the Soviet Union became a highly welcome Ally in the war against Hitler, in terms of domestic policy, adherents of communism were always regarded as inimical to the interests of Great Britain.

The only figure who could have gained immediate respect and access to British political circles for the proindependence émigrés was the former ambassador, Baron Georg Franckenstein, who was naturalized as quickly as possible after the Anschluss. The present Sir George Franckenstein had served as ambassador of the Republic of Austria in London for many years, and when he gave up Austrian nationality, the political emigration once and for all lost its naturally given leading personality. Franckenstein enjoyed the respect of every political circle; he was considered a friend of Winston Churchill. And his influence was considerable, even though his proposal to establish a trusteeship for Austria similar to the Danish Council did not meet with approval. Later, to be sure, he was seen as an "elderly monarchist" with little background in contemporary Austria. His letters of 1944 to the former Austrian ambassador to Turkey, Carl Buchberger, then resident in Stockholm, show that even Sir George was lacking in those leadership qualities which the British government continued to call for as a precondition for recognition of an

Austrian exile group. The problem of leadership among the émigrés is stressed repeatedly in the reports of the Office of Strategic Services.

In contrast to France, there was in Great Britain no Austrian political emigration before the outbreak of war with Germany. The London Austrian Center had been established on May 7, 1939, and there were also clubs and loose associations of former Austrian socialists and trade unionists and émigrés espousing other ideologies. But the aims of all these groups were cultural and social as in the United States. In contrast to the situation in France, the immigration of refugees was regulated, so that the authorities could at any time control them; and there was no illegal immigration. The government could deal with an immigration sifted beforehand. In Britain there was no mass immigration, such as threatened France, with her open borders. Refugees received work permits only when they were needed. A considerable part of the immigrants were women and young girls who entered the country as domestics. Before the outbreak of war, most of the men were forbidden to work. They were thus dependent on their own means or an aid from private supporters or organizations aiding refugees. The refugee committees performed very well and maintained useful connections with the authorities, which turned out to be very helpful to the refugees when the war broke out, since their economic bases and support possibilities were known to the authorities. With full confidence, the British could assume that the overwhelming majority of the émigrés was not a security risk for the country.

When the war came, almost all the émigrés in Great Britain escaped the hard lot of those in France—being put indiscriminately into internment camps. Emigrants were individually examined by special Alien Tribunals, and when the result of the generally benevolent tests was positive, the refugees were restored to a legally safeguarded life in liberty.[5] Only after the rapid progress of the German invasion of France in May, 1940, when the French Resistance collapsed within a few weeks and when a fifth column was feared, in Great Britain, too, enemy aliens were interned and deported to camps in Canada and Australia. But public opinion in Great Britain recovered quickly from the panic that had gripped the whole country, all the more quickly as the feared German invasion did not materialize.

On June 29, 1940, the House of Commons censured indiscriminate internment,[6] and Prime Minister Winston Churchill's assurance that Great Britain would not extradite any persecuted individuals also contributed to a feeling of relief.[7] At first only those refugees who had relatives in the English armed forces and those who employed a considerable number of workers were released,[8] but the Home Office reported that as many as 5,500 persons had been released by December, 1940.[9] The internment regulations had been the result of mass hysteria, and they were rectified as an admitted political error. The refugees were given a chance to serve in an English Pioneer Corps, and after the fall of France, the British government did all it could to bring back to Great Britain those members of the Pioneer Corps that had been sent to

France. Very soon these refugee battalions were recognized as effective units.[10] Generally, by comparison with France, the legal situation of the Austrian émigrés in Great Britain was favorable, both before and after the outbreak of war.

Forming political associations had to wait until the general restrictions for enemy aliens were relaxed and foreigners were included in the war economy, now coming into its stride. The British government, while not objecting to these organizations, did nothing to support them. At the end of 1940, Austrian émigrés tried to establish an Austria Office that would be above party lines. The most varied Austrian factions were members of this association, including the Association of Austrian Social Democrats, headed by Heinrich Allina.[11] But from the outset they were torn by political strife. The *Aufbau* printed a report of intrigue among the émigrés in London, maintaining that Heinrich Allina of the Austrian Office was attacked by the left, while the other leaders of the Association were attacked by the monarchists.[12]

A monthly, *Free Austria,* had begun publication in London. Heinrich Allina, Franz Klein, and Leopold von Adrian-Werburg were among the contributors. Of these, Allina, working for the restoration of Austria's independence, had split from the Austrian socialists abroad, who united in the London Bureau and looked favorably on the Anschluss. Klein was the former editor of the *Donauecho* (*Echo from the Danube*), a legitimist journal.

The Free Austrian Movement, established in London in the summer of 1940, became the largest Austrian organization in Great Britain. The only similarity to the *Frei-Österreicher Bewegung* (*Free Austrian Movement*) previously established in Toronto was the name, and the political objectives and the composition of its membership were different.[13] The group published its Declaration of the Austrian Society in Great Britain in December, 1941. If nothing else, the name of this Declaration made it clear that the Free Austrian Movement was intended to be an umbrella organization, independent of its member organizations. Like the Austrian Center, the Free Austrian Movement, which emerged from it, was also substantially controlled by émigrés of communist orientation, even though the large majority of the members were apolitical. But the urgent appeal for unification was so attractive to the apolitical émigrés that they did not consider the affiliation of the members of the executive board to be important.

With the exception of the Pollak Socialists and the Association of Austrian Christian Socialists, who considered themselves as representing the Christian Socialist party abroad, all the Austrian organizations were signatories to this declaration. The signers therefore considered themselves the representatives in Great Britain of the Austrian people. A detailed report of the American embassy in London to the State Department in Washington indicated that the groups united in the Free Austrian Movement had been called upon by the British to seek the unification of all Austrians as a precondition of recognition.[14] The report noted the absence of the Pollak Socialists, now styled the London Bureau of Austrian Socialists, who corresponded to the Adler

Group of the Austrian Labor Committee in New York. The Pollak Socialists developed a policy parallel to the line maintained previously in France and simultaneously in the United States: They proposed to avoid all collaboration with other Austrian organizations that envisioned the restoration of Austria's independence.[15] The justification was the same: There must be no involvement with Austrofascists and monarchists (OSS XL 1244).

In the report referred to in Chapter IV, the British set down their principles for dealing with émigré organizations. Recognition would presuppose, first, that a leading figure headed an organization, and, second, that the group represented a substantial political party or movement within the home country. Because Sir George had left his post, no political figure could be found either in the Free Austrian Movement or in the London Bureau of Austrian Socialists whom the British authorities considered a leader. Consequently Great Britain refused to recognize any Austrian political organization. Even if the socialists and trade unionists had been able to fulfill the second demand—representation of a significant political party within Austria—they were never able to measure up to the first demand. For its part, the Free Austrian Movement, which represented broad circles of the emigration, could point out that the socialist groups allied with it before the Anschluss had been in favor of Austria's independence. Since bourgeois groups as well as monarchists and communists found shelter under the same umbrella, the Free Austrian Movement could have stood for a wide spectrum of groups who had been suppressed in Austria—if only it had not been led by a predominantly communist group. This circumstance kept it from being acceptable. But the Free Austrian Movement needed to produce an outstanding leader in addition to being simply a functioning organization.

The Austrian Social Democrats were represented in the Free Austrian Movement by Heinrich Allina, a former member of parliament, and by Maria Köstler. They were not able to convince the British that the socialists who had opposed the Anschluss now represented the majority of the socialists within Austria. Thus, in the eyes of British public opinion, the true representatives of Austrian labor was the London Bureau. Indeed, from the outset the British Labour party supported the London Bureau of Austrian Socialists and the Group of Austrian Trade-Unionists; these groups were eventually recognized as bona fide representatives of the Revolutionary Socialists and trade unionists inside Austria—the recognition having been granted on the basis of the Inland Mandate. In these circumstances, the socialists abroad received favored treatment from English governmental agencies, especially the British Broadcasting Corporation. The Free Austrian Movement, even after the Moscow Declaration, missed no opportunity to try to draw the London Bureau of Austrian Socialists into a united front of all Austrian factions.[16] But their answer always remained the same: They wanted no collaboration with monarchists and unpolitical organizations belonging to the Free Austrian Movement. The Free Austrian leaders felt that the Bureau was evading the core problem, and they attempted to simplify discussions with the London Bureau by suggesting that the basic conditions for unification be limited to three requirements: unambiguous commitment to a free and independent Austria; abandonment of all ideas of a Greater Germany; and readiness to fight with all other Austrians for the victory of the Allies and a democratic, independent Austria. These preconditions made no mention of the possibility that the form of government for Austria might be a monarchy, and the socialists' claims that the Free Austrian Movement strongly favored a monarchist restoration were groundless. The Austrian League in Great Britain, a monarchist group signatory to the Declaration of the Austrian Society, subsequently withdrew from the Free Austrian Movement because it could no longer go along with its "Beneš-Stalinist policy."[17]

In actuality the Free Austrian Movement did not attempt to combine independence with the restoration of an Austrian monarchy extending beyond the borders of the Republic. If the London socialists had not opposed a united front, collaboration with them could have been possible, since the monarchists were not nearly as important in the British Free Austrian Movement as Otto von Hapsburg was in the United States. This was shown most clearly when, after the Moscow Declaration, the quick actions of the London Bureau of Austrian Socialists outmaneuvered the Free Austrian Movement.

On November 6, 1943, the Free Austrian Movement set about to organize an Austrian National Committee, as called for in the Moscow Declaration. At about the same time, on November 9, the socialists formed the Austrian Representative Committee, hoping to demonstrate that they, too, represented all Austrian factions. The London Bureau reserved two places on their committee for rank-and-file Christian Socialists and kept two places open for communists. In this connection, one may ask why the London Bureau did not get in touch with Dr. Josef Dobretsberger, a prominent Christian Socialist who could not be accused of Austrofascism. The Association of Christian Socialists had long considered him favorably.

Although the Representative Committee held two places open for communist representatives, the London Bureau accused the Free Austrian Movement—which had always included the Austrian communists—of harboring communist sympathizers.[18] After November, 1943, the London Bureau argued that the necessity of collaborating with Austrofascists and monarchists in order to unify all factions had been superseded by events. On the other hand, the Bureau were willing to collaborate with the communists only as a separate party, but they opposed any movement influenced by communists, such as they saw the Free Austrian Movement to be.

Dr. Friedrich Adler noted accurately that the Austrian Representative Committee had prevented the unification of all Austrian factions, and thus the London Bureau had thwarted the preliminary committee then developing an Austrian National Committee.[19] And thus the London Bureau and their Austrian Representative Committee achieved the same goal as was attained in France and the United States: preventing the unification of all emigrant factions. A telegram of November 18, 1943, from the American embassy in London to the Secretary of State, stated that there was little chance of unification. Stressing that the Free Austrian Movement commanded the allegiance of the majority of Austrians living in Great Britain, this report declared that the Austrian Representative Committee was "out of touch with Austria and Austrian opinion" but that the socialist group would never unite with the Free Austrian Movement. In effect, this report supported the parallel British conclusion: that the Austrian Representative Committee was not representative of Austria, and furthermore, that the émigrés could not represent the Austrian people.[20]

The British always maintained that in questions concerning the Free Movements, the United States had to take the lead. Yet, with the single exception of the Austrian battalion, American policy consistently assumed a staunchly passive posture. And the British did all they could to further this American position. The parallels between the opposing émigré factions in Great Britain and in the United States, as well as both powers' positions on the free associations, are striking.

There is still another context in which the Free Austrian Movement must be considered as an important phenomenon in the dispersion of Austrian émigrés throughout the world. The London organization not only stood as godfather to the Free Austrian World Movement, founded on March 11, 1944, that encompassed most of the countries of emigration during the last year of the war; it also functioned as the executive committee for the World Movement.[21] When problems arose in setting up an Austrian national committee, such as sabotage by the Greater Germany elements among the Austrian Social Democrats, the Free Austrian World Movement provided an ideological home for all patriotic Austrians.[22]

The Free Austrian Movement and the Free Austrian World Movement became the center and clearinghouse for most of the Austrian political organizations abroad, especially those in South America and parts of the British Empire. In South America the English organization became the model for the Austrian émigré organizations,[23] and the Austrian Central Committee for Latin America in Montevideo recognized the Free Austrian Movement in London as the policy-making émigré organization.[24] On October 30, 1943, a combination of thirteen Free Austrian committees in South America had formed the Central Committee for Latin America; and this organization offered full support to the World Movement. For example, the Latin American Committee backed up 1,250 Austrian trade unionists, who were protesting actions of Franz Novy, the president of the Austrian Representative Committee in London.[25] Indeed, the South American association took the same political line as the Free Austrian Movement, and they urged Novy to support the English group.[26]

The Free Austrian Movement, as the Executive Committee of the Free Austrian World Movement, encompassed the Free Austrian organizations in Argentina, Bolivia, Chile, Colombia, Ecuador, Mexico, Paraguay, Peru, Santo Domingo, Uruguay, and Venezuela, as well as the Austrian World Youth Movement, the Association of Free Austrians in South Africa, and the

Free Austrian organizations in Mauritius, Egypt, and Palestine. By July, 1944, the Free Austrian Movement had become the numerically largest emigrant organization—roughly seven thousand members in all countries, except the United States, France, and Sweden, which went their own ways.[27] Yet, in spite of its numerical strength, the organization remained ineffective because its host country, Great Britain, had never recognized the organization's representative character. The history of the Free Austrian Movement clearly shows that even the best and most active organization can fail if it is fated always to encounter political countercurrents.

The newly available documentation, especially in the archives of the British Foreign Office, confirm the need for the most detailed presentation of the history of the political émigrés also in France and in the United States. The history of emigration in Great Britain is revealed as the essentially futile efforts of a well-organized group who never succeeded in convincing Britain to recognize an Austrian foreign representation or government in exile. In France, the Bureau Autrichien might well have succeeded, had France not been eliminated from the war. In the United States, an Austrian battalion did come into being. But it is not possible to present as successful the political emigration from Austria in Great Britain.

X

The Austrian Emigration in Sweden

Neutral Sweden's geographical situation—to the south separated from Germany only by the Baltic Sea, to the east bordering on Finland, and to the west abutting Norway, since 1940 occupied by German troops—compelled her to take a cautious attitude to the problems of the Austrian emigration. When she admitted a considerable number of refugees from Austria, augmented later by others who came by way of Norway and Denmark, the northern kingdom was acting in accordance with her traditional neutrality and humanity. The situation for Sweden became progressively grimmer when, first, the Russo-Finnish war broke out in the winter of 1939, when Germany occupied Denmark in April, 1940, without encountering substantial armed resistance, and when Norway, occupied after a brief struggle, became the advance base of the German sea campaign against Great Britain. Shortly thereafter—in June, 1940—Russia also annexed the Baltic states, and Sweden for all practical purposes was bordered only by Germany and Russia, without direct overland access to any Western Allied nation.

The difficulties of Sweden's position mounted when, after the fall of France, Great Britain continued the war against Germany alone, by sea and air. The Norwegian coast represented a permanent flank menace to Great Britain, especially as sizable German units were kept on Norwegian soil. Sweden had to grant German demands to allow the passage of military units in transit to Norway to relieve troops there.[1] The situation became even more grave after the outbreak of war between Germany and Russia on July 22, 1941, after the German armies' victorious advance through the Baltic states, and after Finland's entry into the war on the side of Germany. Until the siege of Leningrad was raised in 1944, Sweden was completely surrounded and enclosed by Germany, the German-occupied territories, and Germany's ally, Finland.[2]

A report from the American embassy in Stockholm to the Secretary of State, dated July 13, 1942, describes the delicate position of the Austrian émigrés in Sweden, both political activists and other refugees. The refugees were unwilling to take political action. The embassy had not been able to establish even a single organized group of aliens that would lead to Free Movements for political objectives.[3] (The report from Stockholm coincided with the State Department's discussion concerning the usefulness of the Free Movements.)[4] As late as July, 1944, the Free Austrian World Movement noted that in Sweden political activity was "of course" impossible.[5]

Nonetheless, the situation changed after the victory at Stalingrad and the Moscow Declaration. Shortly after the release of the Moscow Declaration,

Carl Buchberger, the former Austrian envoy to Turkey and now a naturalized Swedish citizen, asked the American embassy how the Austrian refugees in Sweden could make their contribution to Austria's liberation, as demanded by the Moscow Declaration. The Club of Austrian Socialists and the communists had organized in order to plead for an Austrian committee, but Buchberger had so far opposed establishing a committee in neutral Sweden. In Buchberger's opinion, no Austrian in Sweden was prestigious enough to head an Austrian political group.[6] Ambassador Buchberger confirmed his opinion in a letter to me of July 16, 1973: "There was all the less reason to conceal this fact from my American friends as this lack was notorious."

But the issue did not rest there. Envoy Buchberger himself changed his line, and he later supported the socialist-communist group that he had called unrepresentative. Thus he took on the position of expert in matters Austrian. He advised four Austrian socialists and two communists in drafting a resolution composed by Dr. Bruno Kreisky that was to be sent by way of the American embassy to Dr. Otto Leichter, a leading socialist living in New York. In February, 1944, Buchberger told the American embassy that while no agreement was possible among the Austrian organizations in Great Britain, collaboration among the various factions in Sweden had come about through unification of the socialists and communists in his group. The Kreisky resolution also called for an Austrian national congress from all countries, to take place in London.[7]

Although on January 10, 1944, Carl Buchberger asserted that there were no significant Austrian leaders, he considered his own committee adequately representative. Dr. Kreisky's growing influence in the group can be clearly seen in the unusual request that his resolution be passed on to another socialist through official American agencies. Buchberger, the former Austrian diplomat, considered a conservative, transmitted the resolution to the American embassy, along with a request by the socialist Dr. Kreisky to send a copy to a prominent socialist in the United States. Simultaneously, a socialist member of the Swedish committee was sending the resolution to the British ambassador, and a communist member was handing it to the Soviet ambassador in Stockholm. We can assume that it was Dr. Kreisky who had thought up the elaborate routing.

Thus, in one of Dr. Kreisky's first appearances in the political arena, we already can sample the style of the man who was later to take the helm of government in Austria and whose policies often broke novel ground. Kreisky must have persuaded Buchberger that his Swedish committee had achieved unification, something never accomplished in Great Britain. In any event, the Austrian émigrés in Stockholm began to anticipate Germany's defeat and the sense that the war would end soon affected discussion of the Austrian problem in Sweden.[8]

An American diplomatic report of July 3, 1944, stated that an Österreichische Vereinigung in Schweden (Austrian Association in Sweden) had been established to serve as a nonpolitical body, with Dr. Bruno Kreisky as president and a Swedish national as honorary president. In spite of the association's nonpolitical nature, the correspondent pointed out that its objective had to be an independent Austrian republic.[9] Carl Buchberger also mentioned an Austrian exile group in Sweden, working to form a unification committee under his consultancy. Buchberger urged that a "representative committee" be formed in London; it was to include socialists, communists, bourgeois, and peasants, and also prisoners of war and delegates from Austria.

Carl Buchberger, too, had no qualms about requesting the American embassy to send copies of his committee memorandum also to the Austrian Labor Committee and to the Austrian Action, and probably the British and Russian embassies also received copies. However, he did not try to reach other Austrian political organizations in the United States or the Free Austrian Movement in London in this way.[10] Early in 1944, Buchberger also wrote to Sir George Franckenstein proposing that the Austrian émigré organizations be united under Franckenstein's leadership and that a unified national committee be created as a central organ of the Austrian resistance.

Under Dr. Bruno Kreisky's leadership, the Association of Austrians in Sweden became very active as the end of the war came into sight. In October, 1944, the Association informed the American ambassador that it represented two-thirds of all the Austrians living in Sweden. (In this connection it is worth noting that Arvid Fredborg noted in *Svensk Tidskrift* [*Swedish Times*] for April, 1944, that a majority of the Austrian emigrants were Jewish, which was expected to pose a special problem after the war.) But in representing two-thirds of the Austrians living in Sweden, Dr. Kreisky had of course to count some of the "unrepresentative" majority among the emigrants. As a broadly based body, his association was content with a simple commitment to an independent, democratic Austrian Republic. Probably he had been influenced in this by the Free Austrian Movement in London, which also claimed a large number of members.[11]

The search for a prominent leader became a theme throughout the period of emigration, and many Austrian exile groups involved themselves in the quest. A number of Austrians in Sweden attempted to persuade Sir George Franckenstein to participate in an Austrian foreign representation. As early as 1939 the Austrian émigrés in England had calculated that if they had been led by Franckenstein, they would have won recognition as friendly aliens and allies of Great Britain—if only he had not become an Englishman and a knight.[12] And Franckenstein wrote to Buchberger on August 14, 1944, of his continuing conviction that neither of the emigrant associations in Great Britain would ever gain recognition from the British government. He had been invited by the Free Austrian Movement in London to join an Austrian National Committee, but he had made it a condition of acceptance that the Austrian Association first be recognized by the British government.[13] Buchberger later wrote to me that Franckenstein's answer to the Free Austrian appeal was slow in coming—and a great disappointment when it arrived. He also learned much later that the invitation occasioned a lengthy interparty correspondence between Oscar Pollak and Bruno Kreisky. While Dr. Pollak continued to reject collaboration with other émigré groups, Kreisky said his procoalition position was "ephemeral"—that is, valid only under present conditions. As a seasoned politician, Dr. Kreisky had used "ephemeral" apparently only to pacify the irate head of the London Bureau. Buchberger still believes that this correspondence helped secure the establishment of the Austrian Association in Sweden. (Actually, he did not know about the letters until he learned about them in 1973 in K. H. Ritschel's biography, *Bruno Kreisky—An Austrian Statesman.*)

When Sir George made recognition by the British government a precondition for his participation in the Free Austrian Movement, he was really rejecting the Free Austrian request.

The ethnic makeup of the emigration was a bit of a red herring, obscuring the real issues in the Austrians' maneuvering toward their goals. Throughout the émigré records, one frequently finds the assertion that 90 percent of the Austrian emigrants in the United States were Jewish or half-Jewish. What mattered was action taken in the countries of refuge by the leaders of the political emigration. If the feuding émigré organizations in Great Britain and the United States could have agreed and have taken a common line, their efforts would have been much more fruitful. And it would have become clear that most of the politically active émigrés were not Jewish.

The large proportion of the émigrés who were Jewish were also, for the most part, nonpolitical. But they possessed an important political potential in that they had little interest in the restoration of Austria's independence. With the political instinct he had already demonstrated in Sweden, Dr. Kreisky had calculated very carefully the support he claimed from two-thirds of the Austrian émigrés in Sweden. As a seasoned pragmatist—like Julius Deutsch in France and the United States—Kreisky tried, whenever possible, to anticipate political developments, and he was prepared to pursue different courses of action. In France, Julius Deutsch had been eager to support an Austrian government in exile in spite of opposition from the doctrinaire leadership of the socialists abroad. He tried to collaborate with the Allied governments. But even when the war had entered its final phase, the Austrian socialists still refused to work together with other groups of émigrés. Kreisky had been involved from the first with the Austrian group in Sweden that began with four socialists and two communists; shortly thereafter, Kreisky's organization claimed as members two-thirds of the entire emigration in Sweden. But even this late the group rejected any cooperation with other organizations if they were not led exclusively by socialists.[14]

The first convention of the Austrian Association in Sweden in February, 1945, rejected affiliation with the Free Austrian Movement in London. But once again, the Association urged the Austrian organizations in London to unite, and they suggested that Buchberger be asked to get in touch with Sir George Franckenstein to expedite this.

Buchberger apparently tried to gain time and seek an agreement. But in

Sweden Franckenstein's position was already quite clear, if only from his detailed letter to Buchberger of August 14, 1944. The Austrian Association and its president, Dr. Kreisky, must have known where Franckenstein stood, and it appears that the waste of energy in this maneuver was clearly intentional. The Austrian organization in Sweden was only paying lip service to unification but did nothing to achieve it. Why should another intervention by Buchberger have been attempted? Why the constant reference to Franckenstein, who was sure to reject these appeals? Shortly thereafter, the Austrian Association in Sweden furnished proof that there was not the slightest desire for collaboration with other political organizations. When the Free Austrian World Movement established a branch in Stockholm with Dr. Karl Bittner as president, the Association immediately charged that the newly formed group was inspired by communists, and so increased the level of dissension among the Austrians in Sweden.[15]

On March 31, 1945, Dr. Kreisky pointed out in the Stockholm newspaper *Dagens Nyheter,* that various groups within Austria were active without a common leadership although all worked for the same objective—the liberation of Austria. Yet he failed to mention the striking development in Austria in those months. The Provisional Austrian National Committee (POEN) had been formed in Austria in December, 1944, serving as an umbrella organization for all the anti-National Socialist forces in Austria. POEN officials had approached the Western Allies in February and March, 1945, suggesting that similar committees be set up in the United States, Great Britain, and France. The familiar names of Karl Hans Sailer, a socialist, and Ernst Karl Winter, a nonsocialist who had held a leading position in the Dollfuss regime, were mentioned. Since Sweden, as a neutral country, could maintain much closer ties with Austria while she was still occupied by German troops than was possible to the POEN delegates in the warring countries of the West, events within Austria could be known in Sweden. In his article Dr. Kreisky did not mention that in Austria herself unification had been achieved with the establishment of the POEN, although it was still rejected by the socialists abroad. In neglecting to consider POEN, Kreisky missed the real reason why no Austrian provisional foreign agency was established. He merely lamented once again the absence of charismatic personalities who could assume leadership in a liberated Austria—there was for Austria no de Gaulle or Tito.

In all the countries of refuge, France, the United Kingdom, and the United States, recognition of a provisional foreign representation would have been possible if only the principal objectives of all parts of the political emigration had been in conformity with one another. Neither the French nor the American and British governments could have refused to recognize a politically unified Austrian emigration, as they had done with the Czechoslovak emigration during the First World War. Nor was there really a lack of outstanding personalities among the Austrian exiles. Dr. Bruno Kreisky in particular, as president of the Austrian Association in Sweden, must have known that Sir George Franckenstein, a man of great prestige in Great Britain, was willing to work with the Free Austrian Movement in London on the condition that this organization was recognized by the British government. And other outstanding personalities were available. Kreisky's article came to the same conclusion as Julius Deutsch, that only men with widely known and respected names could serve as rallying points. But conditions had radically changed, and younger men had taken the stage in every émigré group, as Dr. Kreisky's own example so strikingly demonstrates.[16]

If we compare the experience of the Austrian emigration in Sweden with that in England, a clear parallel emerges. The president of the Austrian Association in Sweden shaped it along the lines of the Austrian Representative Committee in London, but in the process showed more political acumen than the London group. Not only did the Austrians in Sweden cast Carl Buchberger as an expert vis à vis the Americans, but the Austrian Association in Sweden also made a point of calling on the support of the émigrés resident in the country—this was their second iron in the fire. But when it came to actual decisions—at the convention of February, 1945—the Austrian Association rejected any collaboration. When the Free Austrian Movement made its appearance in Stockholm, the Austrian Association attacked it for being communist-inspired, just as it had been attacked in Great Britain. The *Dagens Nyheter* article reported the final decision of the Austrians in Sweden: neither to collaborate with other groups of émigrés nor to form an Austrian foreign representation. The division between the Austrian Association and the Free Austrian Movement was so total that the two groups could not even hold a joint session to welcome Dr. Karl Renner's new government.

The history of political emigration in Sweden has been treated in considerable detail so that it can be demonstrated that even in a country offering far greater possibilities of maintaining contact with the population in the homeland and of being better informed about the position of the socialists at home, the same policies were pursued as in France, Great Britain, and the United States. A further reason is that one member of the Austrian political emigration in Sweden was destined to attain a leading position in the second Austrian Republic. Dr. Bruno Kreisky, acting within the restricting circumstances of the Swedish emigration, already exhibited a political awareness lacking in others. Finally, I am indebted to the diplomatic agencies of the United States in Stockholm, since their careful reports to the American central agencies gave me the opportunity to study the course of events in Sweden in spite of my ignorance of the Swedish language.

XI
The Austrian Emigration in the Soviet Union

The political emigration in the Soviet Union consisted in part of refugee Social Democrats, members of the Schutzbund (defense league) of the Austrian Social Democratic party that had been dissolved in February, 1934, and Austrian refugees who were members of the Communist party.[1]

Another not inconsiderable group of refugees, Jewish refugees, went to Russia after 1938. These had been deported from Poland by the German occupation officials, into those territories of the former Polish Republic that had been occupied by the Soviet Union after the partition of Poland. These refugees had sometimes been driven across the border by force and shared the fate of other Jewish refugees in the Soviet Union.[2]

Given the totalitarian system of the Soviet Union, associations of refugees were unthinkable. A history of the Austrian political emigration in the Soviet Union can be spoken of at all only insofar as the emigrants shared the objectives of the Soviet Union—that is, to the extent that the émigrés went along with the communists.[3]

XII
The Austrian Emigration in Latin America

As noted above, the Austrian emigration in Latin America looked for direction to the émigré institutions in London. Austrians in Latin America worked closely with the London Free Austrian Movement, which acted as executive organ of the Free Austrian World Movement. But Latin America was not simply a secondary arena. Matters developed differently there, at times in a very individual way. Despite the influence of London, the Austrian emigration in Latin America was not a hanger-on of the emigrant organization in Great Britain, nor of the Free Austrian Movement in Toronto and New York. Actually, the Latin American Austrians' tie with the Free Austrian World Movement was one result of their special evolution.

Immigration into the Spanish- and Portuguese-speaking countries of South America differed in several respects from immigration into the United States. First of all, in the United States the immigrant had the right to become a citizen after a residency of five years. This prospect was lacking over almost all of South America. Also, the unstable political conditions in South America did not instill the feelings of political and economic security that in North America encouraged the immigrant to put down roots. Further, several of the Latin American states were, if not exactly pro-German, nevertheless neutrally aligned, and the émigrés had to consider the political position of their countries of immigration vis-à-vis Germany. Public opinion in the United States was definitely not pro-German, but in several Latin American countries the German colonies were distinctly antipathetic to immigrants from National Socialist persecution. And the lack of democratic institutions and the presence of dictatorships in several countries did nothing to reinforce the feeling of security. Nor was security enhanced when various Latin American countries demanded that refugees make a profession of the Christian faith, since these governments were seeking to exclude practicing Jews. Actually it was not always the dictatorships that objected to the Austrian émigrés. The Dominican Republic, for instance, under the dictator Raphael Trujillo, allowed them a great deal of latitude, and it proved to be one of the most helpful countries. Even the socialist Julius Deutsch, who was opposed to any dictatorship, was assured of an unrestricted stay in Santo Domingo in his darkest hour, after the fall of France. The cable giving him this assurance was sent at Trujillo's direction; it further secured him a genuine Dominican passport.[1]

The immigrant groups from Austria sometimes found former compatriots in Latin America who, while they were not affected by German propaganda, were nevertheless indifferent to the newcomers. Hans Rott's posthumous papers contain a letter from the former Austrian general consul in Panama to the secretary of the Free Austrian Movement in Toronto which describes the emigrants' situation:

> Unfortunately there are very, very few genuinely patriotic Austrians. Then we have the majority of emigrants (Israelites), who surely and understandably harbor a deep hatred against Hitler and the Nazis and who would like to return to the comfortable life in Austria, especially Vienna—but that's all there is to their patriotism. The help that can be expected from these people is therefore limited. Next, we have the great majority of the simple, less well-educated people, such as waiters, cab drivers, etc. With these people patriotism is rather weak. That is not to say that they are favorably disposed to the Nazis but rather that they look only for their own advantage.

With all these disadvantages, Austrian organizations were established in all South American countries, including even pro-German Argentina. Without exception, the objective of these organizations was the independence of Austria.[2] These groups divided themselves into those that were in touch with the Free Austrian Movement headed by Hans Rott in Toronto and New York, and the far more numerous groups that modeled themselves on the Free Austrian Movement in Great Britain.[3]

Hans Rott's Free Austrian Movement first tried to gain a foothold in Mexico, Ecuador, Chile, Peru, Bolivia, and Argentina, as well as in the Central American states of Costa Rica and Panama. Thanks to the sympathetic attitude of the former Austrian ambassador, Anton Retschek, the organization was also influential on the course of events in Brazil, the largest South American country. But Rott's efforts were not successful in the end, and all these countries ended up members of the Austria Libre Movement and the Central Committee of Latin America, organizations that looked to the London émigrés for leadership.

There were several reasons for the decline of the North American Free Austrian Movement. Although the movement regarded itself as an alliance of republicans and monarchists, it came to be seen as exclusively monarchist. Also, since the dissolution of the Austrian battalion in the United States, its backers had suffered a conspicuous setback, and the leading figures, such as Otto von Hapsburg and Hans Rott, were considered to be implicated in the failure of the battalion.

The next step for the Austrians in Latin America was to turn toward Great Britain. "Living closer to home and experiencing all the brutalities of the war, our compatriots in England have forged the true Free Austrian Movement, to which all honestly antifascist forces belong." So read a circular of the Comité Austriaco in Buenos Aires, dated July 1, 1943. After the Moscow Declaration, the Free Austrian Movement in London, with its objective of uniting all Austrians, became the model.[4] Finally the failure in North America could be seen clearly; the Free Austrian Movement in Toronto and New York lost almost all its followers in Latin America because it was unable to achieve an Austrian government in exile, as had been expected of it.[5]

In spite of the differences between British and American adherents among the Austrians in Latin America, both groups shared the common objectives of Austrian independence and the unification of all Austrian émigré organizations. The foreign agencies of the Austrian socialists in France and Great Britain, as well as the Austrian Labor Committee in New York, were not emulated in Latin America. Perhaps it was the feeling of insecurity that suggested to the émigrés in the South American countries to summon all their energies to form an Austrian government in exile which might give them a new feeling of safety. They did not feel they had to wait for the people in Austria to exercise their right of self-determination after the liberation.

The Austrian organizations in Brazil were an interesting exception to the above generalizations. The laws of that country did not permit associations of foreigners with political objectives. In addition, there existed an intensive German propaganda which worked against any strivings for Austrian independence. But it was in Brazil where the Comité de Proteção dos Interesses Austriacos no Brasil was recognized by the government as the sole legal Austrian representation in Brazil.[6] It is interesting to account for this committee because the ban on new associations of foreigners was a law taken very seriously. The official pronouncements explained the official position. "The representation of Austrian interests in Brazil, its admission, composition, and jurisdiction were based on the conclusion of continuity [with prewar diplomacy] that the Brazilian government, in agreement with the Austrian colony, derived from the evolution of the Austrian question and subsequently from the Moscow Declaration." "Consequently, in this country, where organized association by foreigners is forbidden and most severely punishable, representation of Austrian interests rests exclusively with the Comité de Proteção dos Interesses Austriacos no Brasil, which is headed by me as the person authorized by the Brazilian foreign office to resume his functions and accredited here since 1925 as ambassador extraordinary and minister plenipotentiary."[7]

Thus the Brazilians interpreted the Moscow Declaration by recognizing the diplomatic agencies of the old Republic of Austria in the form of a committee for the protection of Austrian interests in Brazil. Because recognition in this peculiar case was given to an agency represented by officials of a former foreign state for a government that was not yet recognized, the committee was not considered a political association of foreigners. The Brazilian committee was authorized to issue certificates of Austrian citizenship as proof of Austrian nationality and as a basis for registration in Brazil. The former division of the country into consular districts was maintained except where reorganization had become necessary. The Brazilian committee later recognized the provisional government of Dr. Karl Renner in Vienna, after recognition had been extended by the United States and Great Britain.[8]

The committee in Brazil was actually an organization of former Austrian officials and, as Anton Retschek, its president, wrote in a letter to New York, it was "a semiofficial agency fighting Nazism and working on a democratic basis." It "maintains its nonpolitical and nonpartisan character, based essentially on the official character of its components and bound by the authorization of a friendly government, the only such act to date." If only to demonstrate its nonpolitical and nonpartisan orientation, the committee maintained friendly relations with other organizations of émigrés and with the Central Committee for Latin America in Montevideo.[9] It also tolerated a loose group of refugees, Austria Libre, established in São Paulo.[10]

Former Austrian officials' nonrecognition of the Anschluss always proved to be a significant enhancement for the émigré organizations that the officials belonged to. A case in point is the evolution of the Austrian association in Cuba. As early as 1940 the former honorary consul Edgar von Russ formed the Liga Austriaca in Havana. Its president was the former Social Democratic minister of justice, Dr. Arnold Eisler. Consul von Russ was a Dollfuss follower; at the time of the Anschluss he refused to turn the Austrian consulate in Havana over to the German officials. His collaboration with Eisler was an attempt to unite the most important political forces, Christian Socialists and Social Democrats.[11] But just as in Brazil, the formation of a foreign committee could be undertaken only after the United States had entered the war, because the Cuban authorities considered persons of Austrian nationality to be Germans and were very suspicious of a fifth column. In May, 1942, von Russ formed the Asociación Austria Libre to represent Austrian interests in Cuba and he became its first president. The association kept in close touch with the Free Austrian Movement in Toronto and New York.[12] Just like the Liga Austriaca, which had preceded the new organization and served cultural concerns, the position of Austria Libre was strictly above parties; its statement of objectives was clear on this point, and the executive board included socialists as well as nonsocialists. The association established the principle that the common goal of a free Austria must be placed above partisan considerations; and the association members believed that having had their committees deputized by all the Austrian organizations in the United States would lead to complete success.[13] Von Russ could not achieve this goal by himself but he made great progress in Cuba itself. A Free Austria radio transmitter was approved on Station COK, frequency 25, in Havana after the Moscow Declaration. It was on the air every Monday. Eventually von Russ, in line with what was done in other Latin American states, contented himself with joining up with the Free Austrian World Movement. As a practical politician, he made no further separate efforts to achieve recognition from the Allies.

A political organization in Venezuela was also successful in attaining partial recognition of Austria's independence. Here, recognition also of an Austrian nationality, separate from the German, was eventually obtained. According to the American embassy in Caracas, an Instituto Cultural

Venezolano-Austriaco flourished in Venezuela; it collaborated with the Free Austrian Movement in Toronto and New York as well as with the Austrian National Committee established in New York at the beginning of the war.[14] This cultural institute was subsequently followed by the Colonia de los Austriacos in Caracas. The latter organization became the leading Austrian organization in Venezuela; it contributed substantially to the recognition of a separate Austrian nationality. The efforts of this association extended over two years before the regulation was issued. The committee itself, however, was never recognized.[15]

A special position was also that of the Alianza Austriaca pro los Aliados in Asunción, Paraguay, which worked most vigorously for the restoration of Austria's independence. The letters of this organization, which tried to establish a legion of Austrian patriots with headquarters in Paraguay, represent perhaps the most glowing commitment of any Austrians abroad to fight for Austria's independence on an above-party basis and to reject any partisan activity until after the country's liberation.[16] The Austrian Association in Paraguay went so far as to consider itself the core of the entire political emigration pursuing the goal of creating an official Austrian foreign representation. The Alianza Austriaca therefore demanded that the New York Free Austrian Movement of Hans Rott join its central office in Paraguay. Rott rejected this proposal, arguing that "the good part of the decisions concerning Austria are made" in the United States.[17] The committee's position above parties was demonstrated by its refusal to send a congratulatory telegram on the occasion of Otto von Hapsburg's thirtieth birthday. The committee stated: "We therefore see Otto von Hapsburg only as a compatriot—an Austrian— who, like everyone else, has the right and the duty to contribute his part to the liberation of the Austrian homeland within this Austrian popular movement— but primarily as a son of our common homeland, not as a successor to the throne. . . ." This statement by an Austrian foreign organization accurately describes Otto von Hapsburg's position regarding the Austrian political emigration. The words are to the point and without resentment.[18]

But not even the glowing patriotism of the president of the Alianza Austriaca in Paraguay, Dr. H. M. von Schocher, could achieve the desired result—the uniting of all forces at a level above party strife. In November, 1943, he himself was murdered, allegedly at the instigation of opponents to Austria's independence.[19]

It can be argued that Brazil, Cuba, Venezuela, and Paraguay were special cases. Uruguay presented a more typical example of the evolution of Austrian organizations in Latin America. Attempts to establish an organization of Austrians were undertaken earlier in this state than in most other Latin American countries because the former Austrian consul in Montevideo, Anton von Babouczek, took an active part in organizing the former Austrians. At first a simple round table of like-minded people was organized, with himself as chairman. The Asociación Cultural Austro-Uruguayen, the name of this Montevideo organization, had as its honorary president Sir Eugene Millington-Drake, the British envoy in Montevideo. The American envoy also later accepted the organization's honorary presidency. In these early years any political activity was out of the question.

On April 23, 1942, however, the Asociación's leading personalities, president Anton von Babouczek and Professor Enrique Faltisek, resigned and established Austria Libre. This organization's objective was the restoration of Austria.[20] But subsequently this group became allied with the Asociación Cultural Austro-Uruguayen, which continued to exist under new leadership. The Montevideo association was also above party lines like most South American organizations, and here too a former Austrian consul was closely connected with it. Eventually the association made such progress that at the suggestion of the Austria Libre association of Chile, Österreichisches Zentralkomitee für Lateinamerika (Austrian Central Committee for Latin America) was founded in Montevideo. Its general secretary was Dr. Karl Stephan Grünberg.[21]

The Central Committee, composed of twelve Latin American Austria Libre associations, was established on October 30, 1943. Its newsletter, *Austria Libre,* was first issued at the end of April, 1944. With the exception of Brazil—which had a semiofficial Austrian Action agency—the other South American countries joined the Central Committee for Latin America, thus attaining a unification of foreign political associations that had never before been achieved. In a detailed report to the American embassy in Montevideo, the central committee's secretary related the history of the expansion of the Free Austrian World Movement and of the Central Committee in order to prove that Austrians in Latin America had been eager to comply with the demand for participation contained in the Moscow Declaration.[22]

In Argentina, the second-largest South American country, developments were similar. A Comité Austriaco under the chairmanship of Baron Ferdinand Erb was established in Buenos Aires on October 15, 1941. The former Austrian consul in this city, Guido Forsthuber, served as vice-president of the committee, which gave it semiofficial standing. The Free Austrian Movement in Toronto had tried to persuade Baron Ferdinand Erb to be its representative in Argentina, but in spite of all efforts this attempt failed. The executive of the long-established local Austrian organization in Buenos Aires later became regular delegates to the Central Committee for Latin America. Also in Argentina, as on the entire South American continent, the Austria Libre movement took over the leadership of the Austrian political emigration.[23]

Among the other states, the extremely active Austria Libre movement in Chile, established in 1940, distinguished itself. Its secretary, Hugo Moser, described to Hans Rott all the difficulties the organization faced in this still-neutral country. This situation changed after Chile broke with Germany in

January, 1943. It was only then that the Austria Libre organization achieved recognition of its Austrian nationality, just as had happened in Venezuela. Chilean identification papers were issued on the basis of documents issued by the organization; "Austrian nationality" was registered as citizenship in these papers.[24] It was also Austria Libre that initiated in Chile the formation of the Central Committee for Latin America.

The Federación de Austriacos Libres in Bolivia collaborated effectively with Austria Libre in Chile in the formation of the central committee in Montevideo, which for geographical reasons had been chosen as the most suitable location. An Austrian organization had existed in Bolivia since July, 1941. It carried on an active correspondence with the Free Austrian Movement in Toronto and established a connection with Austrian Action in New York but eventually went its own way. A report to the American Secretary of State notes approvingly that the association in Bolivia operated above party lines; 95 percent of the members were republicans, while two leading members of the executive were monarchists.[25] This association was especially eager to establish the Central Committee for Latin America.

With the exception of Brazil, the South American countries traveled a path from the Free Austrian Movement to the Austria Libre movement, avoiding much of the strife that plagued émigré organizations elsewhere. But in Mexico émigré efforts developed in ways not favorable for the overall interests of the Austrian emigration.

The case of Mexico proved again how important are the choice of participants and their personalities for any political activity in an exile situation. An official in an existing government does not need constantly to convince the individual citizen nor make any attempt to win over the wider public. He has ready recourse to the existing laws, from the constitution to the lowliest ordinance, whenever he has to communicate with either citizens or noncitizens. At most, he has only to justify his decisions when anyone who feels wronged appeals to a higher level of authority. Matters are different for the leaders or members of voluntary political associations who must seek, influence, and persuade members and coworkers to achieve their aims, without the psychological backing of constituted authority. They can refer only to a political program that is private and often created by themselves; they lack any official mandate. This applies all the more to a state whose existence is disputed, such as Austria, which had disappeared from the political map. Anyone pursuing political objectives within the Austrian emigration had to face serious problems. Personality and the power of persuasion were essential for even the smallest achievement.

The republic of Mexico should have been an ideal soil for a representative Austrian agency. She had been the only member of the League of Nations to raise her voice against recognition of the Anschluss, and she never recognized it.[26] A letter of February 19, 1943, to the former minister, Dr. Richard Schüller, stated: "Mexico is one of the few states that never acknowledged Austria's annexation. As a result the legal position of the Austrians in Mexico is quite good—though not quite as good as in the U.S. nor that of Czechoslovakia."[27]

Thus the fundamental ideological conditions for successful political activity existed in Mexico. But it was precisely here that the Free Austrian Movement in Toronto—which, as everywhere else in the Latin American countries, was the first organization to enter the political arena—failed to find a man who, by his powers of persuasion, might have been able to seek, influence, and win over members and coworkers to the association's objectives. The man chosen was Silvio Pizzarello von Helmsburg, who was later attacked even by adherents of the Free Austrian Movement itself; his reports to Toronto and New York were not considered adequate.[28] Pizzarello von Helmsburg had been appointed representative not only of Mexico but also of all of Central America. But his achievements were disappointing, and several months after his appointment an American report described the Mexican organization as being of minor importance.[29] As early as January 12, 1941, an action report of the Free Austrian Movement in Toronto expressed misgivings; a membership figure of thirty-one, in a city the size of Mexico City, suggested that little effective political activity had been performed in such fertile soil.

Interestingly enough, however, other factions of the Austrian political emigration in Mexico were not very successful either.[30] As the engineer Hans Altmann wrote to Minister Schüller: "In Mexico I regret to say the 'Austrian Movement' has gone completely into a blind alley." The American embassy in Mexico noted that both the Free Austrian Movement and Austria Libre, represented in all other South American states, were of little significance here. (Of course the United States paid more attention to the neighboring state of Mexico than to the other Latin American countries.) According to the State Department, Austrian Action in Mexico had only sixty-five members, few of whom took an active part.[31] Nevertheless, news from Mexico called up veritable tempests in teapots. An article entitled "Passports for Austrians" claimed that an Austrian organization had been attempting to issue passports. Although letters of the Free Austrian Movement in New York made it clear that the "passports" were only membership cards, this affair nevertheless harmed all factions of the Austrian emigration.[32] Then there was dissension because of a "government in exile" established by Pizzarello von Helmsburg—a piece of news that caused the Mexican foreign office to deny both the existence of an Austrian government in exile in Mexico and any connection with such a government.[33] In spite of all the hubbub, Pizarello von Helmsburg was not an unskilled politician. At least he knew how to maintain his position for a long time in spite of all attacks. And when, finally, Hans Rott attempted to dismiss him because of the accumulating opposition, he refused to accept his dismissal and persevered in his post.[34]

To report on the fate of every single Austrian association in Latin America would far exceed the limits of this study. Throughout Latin America Austrian political committees were established. They reflected the image of a political emigration that, far away from the decisive events, stood up for Austria's restoration in both the political and the cultural spheres. With the exception of those émigré committees that were established with the help of former Austrian consuls or officials, as in Brazil, or those that had had the support of former Austrian diplomatic agents, as in Cuba and Argentina, the émigré groups were organized by volunteers, and for the most part they encompassed nonpolitical émigrés. The committees in Latin America were guided by the principle of independence and freedom from party ties, each faction carefully avoiding any dissension with segments of the political emigration that held other views. In no European country—not in France, Great Britain, or Sweden—and even less in the United States was there even a fraction of the good will and lack of partisanship among the political émigrés that there was in Latin America. The Latin American committees were prepared at any time to collaborate with any recognized political leadership seriously striving for the restoration of Austria's independence. At first they followed the call of the Free Austrian Movement in Toronto and New York, which promised an association of all Austrian organizations for the purpose of Austria's independence. When the Free Austrian Movement was unable to achieve a foreign representation or government in exile, and recognition by the Allies, which all the Latin American organizations desired, they turned to the London Free Austrian Movement and the Free Austrian World Movement as part of a mass movement supporting Austria's freedom and the Austrian resistance. It is striking that there was no political dissension in Latin America, in contrast to France, Great Britain, and the United States.

Among some political émigrés the nonpolitical segment of the Austrian emigration in Latin America was a source of disappointment. Socialists in particular did not want to have relations with nonpolitical émigrés. In the words of the prominent socialist, Karl Hans Sailer: "This Jewish bourgeoisie, intellectuals and artists, which makes up the majority of this emigration has always turned toward progress. Could it be that they were progressive only because they were not allowed to be reactionary?"[35]

But it was these same intellectuals and artists who established the foreign committees in Latin America and in a spirit of keeping above party lines from the outset pursued the objective of Austria's restoration—an objective the socialists abroad considered "reactionary." These intellectuals favored Austrian independence long before the socialists, after the Moscow Declaration, had to accept a second Austrian Republic. For the overwhelming majority of the political emigrants in Latin America, Sailer's switching tracks was not an issue; they did not care whether they were seen as "reactionary," either from their own conviction or because "they were not allowed to be reactionary." All they cared about was to see their lost homeland restored and to gain a firm point of contact with the future and a new beginning. To achieve Austria's independence—that was and remained the first and last goal of the Austrian émigré associations in Latin America. In none of these countries did a committee support the socialists' insistence that the Austrian home population—or only its workers—should decide Austria's destiny as an independent country or as part of Germany.

A trenchant essay entitled "Suprapartisanship, an Exile Form of Democracy," published in a commemorative publication on the occasion of the third anniversary of the Federación de Austriacos Libres en Bolivia, thoroughly examines this principle, so universally upheld by the Austrian Latin American committees. The essay justly pointed out "that quite a number of Austrian groups in various countries began to work on the same basis—without having had even the slightest contact with each other before. Yet the party system was not thereby abandoned." There were two reasons why they elected to eliminate it, in effect, during the period of exile. One is the recognition that objectives were at stake that were of equal importance to all who cared for Austria, regardless of their party affiliation. The second is the awareness that the achievement of these objectives would be impeded, perhaps even thwarted, if partisans insisted on sticking to their exclusive principles. The article resolved that "laying down of the principle of suprapartisanship as the basis for pursuing common political goals was intended to eliminate mistakes," and that it should be made possible for these new associations to win followers. These should not be limited from the outset by a party program but should encompass all Austrians, "provided they were opponents of National Socialism and good democrats." The article sounded loud and clear:

> Though until today it has not been possible to solve all the problems of the emigration, as for example that of a national committee, this must by no means be attributed to the difficulties created by non-Austrians but rather mainly to the attitude of those Austrians who are unable or unwilling to recognize the needs of the hour and who are not prepared to place, at least temporarily, the common objective of liberating our homeland above their program.[36]

The success achieved in Latin America by the Austrian political emigration through the association of all emigrants without regard to party affiliation would have led to the recognition of an Austrian representation or a government in exile in France, Great Britain, or the United States, had this pattern been applied in those countries. Nowhere were the patriotism of the émigrés for the lost homeland and their efforts to restore Austria's independence so clear and free from partisan rancor as in the Latin American countries. The lesson is clear: Partisan attitudes and goals are not effective in a situation of exile. Thus, the Austrian experience in Latin America, far from being a remote backwater in the larger history of the Austrian emigration, is both essential and exemplary in furthering the overriding goal, the restoration of Austria's independence.

Appendix

[*Author's Note:* What follows is the entire text of the New York Free Austrian Movement's Newsletter for April, 1945. In addition to the editorial writer's opening comments, it comprises the fundamental correspondence between Hans Rott and Julius Deutsch on the failure of the Austrian emigration to achieve a government in exile—and the ramifications of that failure.]

FREE AUSTRIA REPORTS
Free Austrian Movement (Frei Österreicher Bewegung)

New York, April, 1945

The last attempt to save Austria has failed. Since the beginning of the struggle for the restoration of the liberty and independence of Austria, since spring of 1939, when Federal Minister Hans Rott and his coworkers in Paris began to organize the resistance of Austrians living in the free world against the Nazis and Greater Germany, it was their unremitting striving to establish a united Austrian front that told and kept on telling the free peoples about the terrible wrong done to Austria in March, 1938, and aroused the conscience of the world. The Austrian people were ravished, clapped into bloody fetters, and condemned to silence. It was all the more the sacred duty of all Austrians who had escaped the Nazi hell to raise their voices for Austria and to apply all their energies toward the liberation of their homeland.

The struggle for the restoration of Austria cannot and must not be the concern of one political party or a single group with a one-sided view. If it was to have any hope for understanding in the world, it had to be carried on by all non-Nazi Austrians. All Austrians abroad have the inalienable duty to take part in the struggle for liberation—all of them, whether Catholic, Protestant, or Jewish, whether they are Christian Socialists, Social Democrats, or Communists, whether they favor a republic or a monarchy. The struggle for Austrian freedom demands that all Austrians put aside party differences and dedicate themselves to the goal of liberating Austria from tyranny and restoring her independence.

All the peoples ravished by the Nazis have formed united fronts for the struggle against the enemy and to stand up for their interests. Poles, Czechs, Yugoslavs, Belgians, Frenchmen, Luxemburgians, Dutchmen, Norwegians— all of them formed governments in exile, which were joined into the United Nations after the United States entered the war, in order to be able to work not only for the liberation of their countries, but also to make all preparations for reconstruction in the postwar period. The Austrians, too, were duty bound to establish a united front for the liberation of their country. Imbued with this sense of duty, Federal Minister Hans Rott, immediately after the outbreak of war, entered into negotiations with Julius Deutsch, the leader of the socialists, in Paris. The bases for the negotiations were the establishment of an official Austrian representation and the mobilization of all Austrian forces available abroad for an Austrian legion. Julius Deutsch was ready to collaborate. A minimal program was worked out, which he submitted to the Representation of Austrian Socialists Abroad for their consideration. To the embarrassment and surprise of all Austrian patriots, the establishment of an official Austrian agency abroad for the purpose of safeguarding the interests of the Austrian people was rejected. The opposition to the formation of an Austrian legion of volunteers was particularly vehement. There was no willingness to fight voluntarily against Greater Germany. Although the socialist leaders were aware that thousands of Austrians had already volunteered to join in an Austrian legion in France, they unequivocally rejected participation; they even demanded of the Austrian patriots they cease recruiting for the legion.

The negotiations with the socialist leaders proved fruitless. It must be noted that it was Fritz Adler and Karl Hans Sailer in particular whose uncompromisingly negative attitude resulted in this outcome. Julius Deutsch was forced to retreat. The failure of the negotiations occasioned extreme displeasure in French ruling circles which—as could be noticed at the frequent conferences in the foreign ministry—had been very sympathetic to Austria. During 1934–1938 the Austrian socialist leaders had introduced themselves there as uncompromising Austrian freedom fighters. Not being aware of the Greater-Germany sympathies among the Austrian socialist leaders, high officials in the French foreign ministry thought that the socialists would be in the forefront of the struggle for the liberation of Austria from the German yoke. Their surprise was all the greater when it transpired that the Austrian socialist leaders were not prepared to take up the struggle against Greater Germany. Only at the expenditure of much distortion and evasion could Fritz Adler and his followers erase the bad impression evoked by their position.

In spite of this sabotage, the Austrians allied in France in the Ligue Autrichienne, around Hans Rott, continued their efforts for a free Austria. Both the French and the British governments were prepared to grant official recognition to an Austrian representation. But both governments made it a condition that this official representation present a united front and that its members belong to all the non-Nazi parties of Austria. This point of view was understandable. Both powers did not wish to expose themselves to the reproach of furthering a unilateral party rule for Austria—all the more so since all the countries overrun by Hitler had formed coalition regimes. The Austrian socialists were just as aware of these facts. They fully realized that their consent to the establishment of an Austrian representation constituted the condition for getting it officially recognized by the governments that mattered. But they also realized that recognition of an Austrian government in exile meant the restoration of Austria's independence after the war. And that was precisely what the Austrian socialist leaders wished to prevent.

On June 2, 1938, Dr. Otto Bauer published an article in Paris in *Der Sozialistische Kampf* [*The Socialist Struggle*]:

When the German troops had subjected Austria to the Third Reich, the proletarian parties in Austria were faced with this question: Should the Austrian socialists continue the struggle against Austria's subjugation to the Third Reich, the struggle for Austria's independence, which they had waged since 1933? Could and should their political objective be the detachment of Austria from Germany, the restoration of Austria's independence? . . . After the annexation . . . the communists . . . took up Schuschnigg's slogan of "Red-white-red until death" and did not hesitate to join the legitimists, the Patriotic Front, and the clericals in proclaiming the separation of Austria from the Reich and the restoration of an independent Austria as their objective. The socialists, on the other hand, noted at a conference that took place in Brussels in early April, 1938, that the Austrian people could be saved, not through separation from Germany, but only through a Greater German revolution against German fascism. They opposed the irredentist-separatist solution of the vanquished Patriotic Front in their support of the Greater German revolutionary solution. . . . Certainly, the annexation of Austria by Germany, carried out by Hitler, is quite another matter from the Anschluss of Austria to Germany for which Austrian Social Democrats were fighting at the end of the First World War. . . . The Anschluss we wanted was the incorporation of Austria into the Reich by the free will of the Austrian people. The annexation that was brought about is the violent subjugation of the Austrian people through superior armed force.

Bauer then deals with "the opposition of the Austrian people to the despots from the Reich placed above the Austrian people." But he does not draw the only possible conclusion from this, namely, that an act of imperialist arbitrariness carried out against the will of the people cannot under any circumstances be recognized, least of all by a party that calls itself "democratic." Instead, he arrived at the following paradoxical conclusion:

Engels' admonition to react critically rather than in a reactionary way to a historical event [defeat in the Austro-Prussian War, 1866] though it had occurred contrary to his desires, is valid also for us today. It applies to the accomplished fact of the forced foundation of the Greater German Reich as much as to the forced decision concerning the "kleindeutsch" solution of the German question in 1866. We must take a critical attitude to the accomplished fact of annexation, but we must not become reactionary. . . . The watchword we choose to set up against the alien rule of the satraps from the Third Reich over Austria must not be the reactionary slogan for the restoration of Austria's independence but simply the revolutionary watchword of the Greater German revolution, which alone can liberate the Austrian tribe of the nation, along with the other German tribes, from the despotism of the fascist tyrants.

This was the attitude that made the leaders of the Social Democrats sabotage all efforts to emphasize Austria's importance; they sabotaged the formation of an Austrian government in exile and the establishment of Austrian volunteer units to fight against Nazi Germany; they sabotaged all postwar plans and all preparations to combat the need, misery, and hunger that would without a doubt ravage Austria after the war.

In Belgium and France their organization was named "Auslandsvertretung österreichischer Sozialisten" ("Representation of Austrian Socialists Abroad"). It was headed by Dr. Fritz Adler; one of his most influential coworkers was Karl Hans Sailer. In the United States they called themselves the Austrian Labor Committee. This committee, too, was led by Adler, and Sailer collaborated in an important post. In England this organization dedicated to preventing the restoration of Austria's independence called itself London Bureau of Austrian Socialists; it was headed by Oskar Pollak.

These men claimed to be the only appointed and legitimate representatives of the Austrian socialists, nay, even of the entire Austrian working class. They succeeded so well in this maneuver because they appeared in the aura of freedom fighters. The fateful events of February, 1934, had created the impression abroad that the Austrian socialist leaders were the chosen defenders of Austrian independence. It seemed inconceivable that Austrian socialists might not take up the cudgels for the fatherland, since the socialists in every other country manifested an exemplary patriotism. It seemed inconceivable that the Austrian socialists would raise the concept of Greater Germany over that of Austria. And yet it was so.

The collapse of France put an end for the time being to all the strenuous efforts on behalf of Austria. They were continued in the United States. In November, 1940, Hans Rott and his followers established the Frei Österreicher Bewegung [Free Austrian Movement]. This organization proceeded at once to call on Austrians throughout the free world to take up the struggle against Greater Germany and for the liberation of Austria. Austrian movements dedicated to the restoration of Austrian independence sprang up in almost all the free countries.

The first approaches to the Department of State in Washington by the Free Austrian Movement were made in the summer of 1941. Although America had not yet entered the war, Washington showed great understanding for the efforts to achieve Austrian liberation. The American government had never recognized the annexation of Austria, and ways were sought to enable the formation of an Austrian agency abroad. These discussions provided the first occasion to point out the possibilities inherent in the Austrian federal constitution. The constitution of 1920 with the amendments of November, 1929, as well as the constitution of May, 1934, determines what is to be done if the federal president is prevented from carrying out his functions and if the federal chancellor and vice-chancellor are also incapacitated in some way.

High officials in the State Department argued that a provisional Austrian representation formed on the basis of these constitutional articles would be given official recognition abroad. But unauthorized persons who had somehow learned of these discussions published a notice in the *New York Times* to the effect that Hans Rott had named himself federal president and appointed Willibald Plöchl federal chancellor. There was not a true word in the entire report. On the contrary, the Free Austrian Movement based their arguments on the fact that both the federal president and the federal chancellor were alive but prevented from exercising their functions, and therefore, according to the constitution, a provisional deputation ought to be named. It hardly needs mentioning that the Austrian socialist leaders made every effort to prevent the formation of a provisional Austrian government in exile. And, unfortunately, they succeeded, so that new approaches had to be tried.

After the United States had entered the war, an Austrian National Committee was formed in New York. It was to include all Austrian groups prepared to fight. Time and again the Austrian socialist leaders were invited to join. They refused and established a countercommittee which they named Österreichisches Arbeiter-Komitee (the Austrian Labor Committee). All efforts over the years failed to persuade them to work together in the Austrian struggle for freedom.

When the deteriorating conditions in Austria could no longer remain concealed from even the blindest of the socialists, Hans Rott made a final attempt to save the day. Writing to Julius Deutsch in the most cordial tone, he proposed again and for the last time that they join in forming an Austrian representation. Deutsch often found himself in opposition to Adler, Sailer, and Pollak. He was still an Austrian patriot. Rott hoped that at the last moment Deutsch would overcome the negative attitude of his fellow party members. But in this he experienced a sad disappointment. Deutsch submitted Rott's letter to the Austrian Labor Committee in New York for a decision, and the committee decided on a reply that Deutsch had to sign. It was again a rejection.

In a letter of March 30, 1945, Rott replied in great detail to the socialists' rejection. In the final paragraphs he tried once more to persuade the socialists to work together in the interests of Austria:

> That is why I appeal to you once more. I appeal to your sense of responsibility and to your patriotism. Bring yourself to make a broadminded decision. If you and I and our friends in both camps stand together, we can create even at the last minute a public voice for Austria, we can take part in the coming decisions about our country, we can try through joint work to ameliorate the deprivations of our people in the postwar period. In this final hour I beg and implore you to review again the letter I sent you on March 9, 1945, and to appreciate the reasons that caused me to write you.

In view of the terrible situation in which our fatherland and our people find themselves, I beg you to set aside all petty considerations and to grasp the hand I am extending you.

This renewed request, this entreaty, was followed by no reply whatever. The answer was silence. But this silence already echoed with the sound of the Allies' guns at the borders of Austria. What fate was awaiting the abandoned, betrayed Austrian people?

On March 23, 1945, Julius Deutsch wrote to Hans Rott that he intended to publish in *Austrian Labor Information* both Rott's first letter and his answer to it. Rott agreed, provided that his detailed answer to the socialist rejection be published at the same time. This was too much of a risk for the Austrian Labor Committee. Rott's answer was suppressed, and only his first letter to Deutsch and the socialist reply were published. But Austrians are entitled to learn the contents of the entire exchange. Here it is:

HANS ROTT TO JULIUS DEUTSCH

Dr. Julius Deutsch   *New York, March 9, 1945*
243 Riverside Drive
(Apt. 504)
New York City

Dear Dr. Deutsch:

The speech delivered by the British Foreign Minister in the House of Commons on March 1 moves me to direct these lines to you.

Eden's remark about Austria illuminates like a searchlight the fate that awaits Austria after the defeat of Nazi Germany, unless at the eleventh hour the appointed spokesmen for Austria's working population gain a hearing from the statesmen of the United Nations. You, Dr. Deutsch, as the recognized representative of Austrian Social Democratic labor, and I, as representative of the Christian Socialist working population in urban and rural Austria, are morally and politically entitled and obligated to appear as spokesmen of the workers, farmers, small businessmen, and tradesmen of Austria, almost all of whom have been from the beginning one hundred percent bitter opponents of the Nazis. Both of us, dear Dr. Deutsch, have the right and the duty to appear before the representatives of the United Nations, to declare most solemnly that:

1. Since its military occupation by Germany Austria is de facto in a state of war with Germany, unable to make herself heard because of her total isolation and abandonment;

2. The "plebiscite" of April 10, 1938, which formally ratified the so-called Anschluss, is null and void because it was carried out in the presence of the enemy's military and police occupation troops and after Hitler's proclamation of Austria's incorporation. Hitler would never have canceled the plebiscite arranged for March 13 had he not been certain of his defeat;

3. Both of us assume the responsibility for the approval of our statements by the overwhelming majority of all Austrians, if only our fatherland is liberated and able to gain a hearing for herself;

4. That we Austrians abroad, living in the territory of the United Nations, demand that until that time comes, we have a voice and representation in all future negotiations of the United Nations and all of its organizations (UNRRA, etc.) in the name of our ravished fatherland, clearly the first victim of the Hitler-German aggression.

I am convinced that you, my dear Dr. Deutsch, are weighed down by the same concerns and the same feeling of responsibility for the future of the working people of Austria as I and my friends are. That is why I appeal to you and propose to you most urgently to sit down with me to work out a common program for provisional collaboration in order to achieve a voice for Austria at the United Nations.

All of us bear an immense responsibility, and neither the Austrian people nor the United Nations will ever forgive those Austrians living in freedom and also their party organizations unless at last that unity is brought about which is the indispensable precondition of any constructive work on behalf of Austria.

Finally, I should like to emphasize that the working collaboration I have proposed would be instantly taken over by a government elected by the liberated people of Austria and that the restoration of a free, politically and economically independent Austria on a democratic basis is the common goal of us all.

Eden's warning that "time is running short" calls for an immediate echo from Austria. For the time being this echo can only come from us. But I am certain that our joint action will create a favorable reaction on the part of the statesmen of the United Nations and will release all those physical and spiritual forces within Austria that have been fettered until now so as to contribute actively to the wrestling down of the oppressors, thus favorably influencing Austria's future.

Expecting a speedy affirmative answer, I remain most sincerely,

Hans Rott

JULIUS DEUTSCH TO HANS ROTT

Mr. Hans Rott　　　　　　　　　　　　　*New York City, March 13, 1945*
57 West 82nd Street
New York City

Dear Mr. Rott:

I have submitted your letter of March 9 to the Austrian Labor Committee, and I have been authorized to reply as follows:

The Austrian Social Democrats in exile were and are always prepared to collaborate with all truly democratic, antifascist forces to break the power of

Nazism. With this objective in mind, an Austrian representative committee was formed in London, for example, in which Social Democrats, Christian Socialists, and bourgeois democrats have been working together harmoniously. The fact that it was not possible to establish a similar body in the United States of America has its reason in certain personal relationships. To describe these openly would seem to be the best way to gain a clear picture of the situation.

Shortly after the Austrian political emigration had arrived in the United States, it found itself confronted with a peculiar situation. The *New York Times* of September 28, 1941, printed the surprising news that you, my dear Mr. Rott, considered yourself the successor of Schuschnigg's government and even felt yourself entitled to being addressed as "Federal President." After appointing yourself in this manner head of state, you designated a Mr. Willibald Plöchl to be "Federal Chancellor."

You will surely recall that this venture called forth a sharp protest by the officials and representatives of the Austrian labor movement who were in the United States at that time.

A second political action in which you were involved was no less unfortunate. Hapsburg's followers used the lack of information in American circles about conditions in Central Europe to undertake a vehement agitation for a monarchist restoration in Austria. The Hapsburg agitation reached its climax with the establishment of the Austrian Military Committee and the Austrian battalion connected with it.

You took a leading part in this campaign on behalf of Otto von Hapsburg. You share the responsibility for the fact that because of the Hapsburg agitation the Austrian emigration was torn asunder. It is indeed asking too much to expect the Austrian Social Democrats, whom you recently opposed as a protagonist of a Hapsburg restoration, to accept you now all of a sudden as a representative of democratic forces.

Anyone knowledgeable about political conditions in Central Europe is aware that, first, the great majority of the Austrian people energetically rejected the Hapsburgs and, second, the neighboring states would see a Hapsburg restoration as a hostile act.

That is why, both as regards internal and foreign policy, Hapsburg represents a danger for the peaceful democratic development of our country. Even if now and then Otto Hapsburg drops a few democratic phrases, this does not eliminate the fact that the system embodied in him would represent a return to the worst kind of reaction.

The Austrian Social Democrats refuse to form a working collaboration with "republicans until further notice." Rather, they continue to be prepared to work with all democratic groups within the population, whether they be peasants or members of the bourgeoisie. They ask for nothing more than that in such collaboration the democratic and republican basis be secured on which our nation was built and without which there can be no development in the direction of progress and lasting peace for Austria.

The Austrian Labor Committee is aware that the conditions that prevented the collaboration of all Austrian groups in America also impose on it a greater responsibility toward the homeland.

That is why for its part the Austrian Labor Committee has tried to serve the interests of the Austrian population to the best of its ability. In May, 1943, the Austrian Labor Committee submitted a detailed memorandum to the Food Conference of the United Nations in Hot Springs; the memo dealt with food-supply problems in Austria after the fall of Hitler.

Further, the committee published a description of Austria's overall economic problems as well as proposals in the area of schooling and education.

When America named its representatives to the administrative commission that was to be established in Austria after the expulsion of the Nazis, the Austrian Labor Committee got in touch with John G. Erhard, chief of the American delegation. The committee submitted to Mr. Erhard a memorandum containing concrete proposals concerning the political and economic reconstruction of Austria. This memorandum was discussed by a delegation of the Austrian Labor Committee with Mr. Erhard and some of his coworkers at a conference in the State Department in Washington.

In this context I may also refer to my personal proposal to make Vienna the seat of the future international organization of nations.

All this goes to prove that the Austrian Social Democrats living abroad at present have endeavored, and will continue to endeavor, to represent the interests of the working population of Austria and also to create an understanding for the special problems of the country. They deeply regret the fact that they must carry on this work alone until such time as unimpeachable representatives of the other democratic parties of Austria can join them.

Sincerely yours,
Julius Deutsch

JULIUS DEUTSCH TO HANS ROTT

March 23, 1945

Dear Mr. Rott:

The letter you wrote to me on March 9 and my answer to it have not remained unknown in Austrian emigration circles. To avoid any misinterpretation, we consider it proper to publish both documents in their original text in the forthcoming issue of *Austrian Labor Information.* We assume that you too will consider this proposal a loyal one; for your letter to me was not a private communication but a political one.

Respectfully yours,
Julius Deutsch

HANS ROTT TO JULIUS DEUTSCH

New York March 24, 1945

Dear Mr. Deutsch:

I have received your letter of March 23. You are mistaken. My words, which grew out of the agony of Austria, represent a purely personal message to you—just as our negotiations in Paris at one time were personal. The contents of the letter clearly mark this limit.

If—without consulting me first—you submitted this private communication to your committee and—to my considerable surprise—sent me the committee's statement instead of your personal reply, that is your business. But in choosing to do so, you have compelled me to answer in detail this communication, which is introduced with one sentence by you and ended with a formal conclusion. I would have to refuse, as wholly disloyal, any publication of the letters without the answer which, because of the pressure of work, I cannot let you have before next week.

I wish to observe briefly, that "Austrian emigration circles" could not have gained knowledge of the contents of my private communication from me, since I treated the matter in absolute confidence.

> Sincerely yours,
> Hans Rott

JULIUS DEUTSCH TO HANS ROTT

New York, March 26, 1945

Dear Mr. Rott:

Surely you could not assume that a letter with a political proposal, which you addressed to me, could be a private matter. It is a matter of course that within any democratic party its officers do not act as they see fit but solicit the opinion of their friends in the party. I adhered to this principle in Paris as I do here.

As far as we are concerned, my answer to your written proposal ends the matter. We continue to believe that we have proven our loyalty to the utmost by apprising you of the forthcoming publication of both letters.

> Sincerely yours,
> Julius Deutsch

HANS ROTT TO JULIUS DEUTSCH

New York, March 28, 1945

Dear Dr. Deutsch:

I am in receipt of your letter of March 26. Of course I understood that in the final analysis the representatives of both the Social Democratic and the Christian Socialist parties would have to decide about the proposal I made to you. But I thought that the matter would be better served if eventual official negotiations were preceded by a personal contact, as was the case in Paris at an earlier time. Surely, if you had not shared this view, you could easily have let me know that you were not in a position to agree to a personal meeting without first procuring party approval.

It goes without saying that I have not the slightest objection to the publication of our correspondence, provided that you include my answer to your letter of March 13, which will go out to you within a week. This course would not have been necessary if your letter had been of the same matter-of-fact character as mine. But you rejected not only the collaboration on behalf of Austria, in spite of the dreadful situation of our land and our people, but you raised in your letter a number of totally unjustified accusations against me, presumably with an eye to the intended publication. In a democracy it is a matter of course that the accused is given a chance to defend himself. Only fascism does not allow this. Since in your letter of March 26 you stress your intention of "proving your loyalty to the utmost," I have no doubt that you will comply with my wishes.

You say that your answer to my written proposal ends the matter for you and your fellow party members. I can assure you that for my and my fellow party members it will never be finished. We have the interests of the Austrian people far too much at heart for that.

> With best regards,
> Hans Rott

HANS ROTT TO JULIUS DEUTSCH

New York, March 30, 1945

Dear Dr. Deutsch:

I have received your letter of March 13, 1945, and I am taking the liberty of conveying to you the following remarks on the various sections of your communication.

In the first paragraph of your letter, you refer to the Austrian Representative Committee, established in London by Mr. Oskar Pollak, in which, as you note, Social Democrats, Christian Socialists, and bourgeois democrats work together. This committee was not entitled to the name it adopted. It is not "representative" in any respect, not even with regard to Social Democratic labor. This was clearly proven when a significant number of the Austrian Social Democrats living in England disassociated themselves from the Pollak group. This faction, led by Mrs. Marie Köstler, the former member of parliament, objected to the commitment to Greater Germany. Those members of the Representative Committee whom Mr. Pollak calls Christian Socialists were functionaries of the party and never were of any importance in it. Therefore they have no right whatsoever to speak in the name of the party.

The purpose pursued in the establishment of the London Representative Committee has already been expressed with commendable candor by Dr. Friedrich Adler in issue number 24 of *Austrian Labor Information* (March/April, 1944). He considered it to be to the "great credit" of his London friends that they prevented the formation of the Austrian National Committee planned by the Free Austrian Movement in Great Britain. "It is true," Dr. Adler admits, "the London Office of Austrian Socialists could blunt the initiative of the Free Austrian Movement only by beating it to the punch in establishing an Austrian representative committee." In other words: the London Representative Committee is a committee for the prevention of work to bring about an independent Austria. This is wholly in line with the policy Oskar Pollak has always pursued. He has always been a propagandist for Austria's Anschluss to Germany.

In the third paragraph of your letter you mention an item in the *New York Times* of September 28, 1941, according to which I regarded myself the successor to Schuschnigg's government, considering myself entitled to be called "Federal President," and having thus appointed myself head of state, named Mr. Willibald Plöchl to be "Federal Chancellor."

I must ask you to take note that I had nothing to do with this newspaper article; that I never considered myself entitled to be called "Federal President," that I never "appointed myself head of state," and that I never appointed Mr. Willibald Plöchl to be "Federal Chancellor." I reject any responsibility for newspaper canards.

Here, once and for all, these are the real facts of the case.

Article 77 (1) of the Austrian Constitution of May 1, 1934, reads:

"If the Federal President is incapacitated or the presidency permanently vacant, his obligations pass over to the Federal Chancellor."

Article 81 (2) reads: "The Federal Chancellor, if incapacitated, is to be replaced in his entire sphere of activity by the Vice Chancellor. If the Federal Chancellor and the Vice Chancellor are incapacitated simultaneously, the Federal President will appoint a member of the Federal government to represent the Federal Chancellor."

The constitution of 1920 with the amendments of 1929 contained provisions essentially to the same effect. The provision that states that, in case the Federal Chancellor and Vice Chancellor are simulanteously incapacitated, the Federal President is to delegate a member of the federal government to represent the Federal Chancellor was not added until 1929. This regulation makes it clear that it was the intention of the constitution—your party members had a substantial part in drawing it up—to make sure that the government would function under any circumstance. Because the Federal President has fallen into enemy hands, he is naturally unable to delegate a member of the Federal Government to represent the Federal Chancellor. The regulations of the constitution would therefore have to be applied analogously. This would be all the easier as the Federal President would have no choice but to appoint a member of the government who was at liberty to represent the Federal Chancellor.

These provisions of the Austrian constitution, and the conclusions to be drawn from them, were communicated to the Department of State. It should hardly be necessary to state that the temporary carrying on by proxy of state affairs (which in this case means representation of Austria's interests) does not mean appointing oneself to the Federal Presidency or appointing a Federal Chancellor.

I would like to take the occasion to add a few personal remarks. As you know, I come out of the trade-union movement and belong to the left wing of the Christian Socialist party. In November, 1936, Federal Chancellor Dr. Schuschnigg asked me to join the government and to restore relations with Social Democratic labor, which had been broken off as a result of the well-known unfortunate events. Should I have rejected this appeal? Would it have benefitted anyone except perhaps the Nazis if I had kept aloof? Was it not more important to try to heal the wounds of the year 1934 and to do my part in leading Austria back to normal conditions? I accepted the appointment because I considered it my duty to be available to my fatherland in its hour of need. My task was a difficult one. I encountered resistance from both sides, the left as well as the right. But in the end my work did bear fruit. A Social Democrat was once more a member of the last government. My negotiations with Social Democratic labor led to the result that this group declared its willingness to collaborate. There can be no quibbling with these facts, and the final result of my activity carried out in agreement with the Federal Chancellor would have been Austria's return to democracy. We had a good start on that road. Hitler's invasion prevented the attainment of this goal.

There has been no change whatever in my political attitude since then. My reference to the provisions in the Austrian constitutions of 1929 and 1934 was in no way intended to let the Schuschnigg government automatically be revived after the liberation of Austria or to create a prejudice in favor of retaining the constitution of May 1, 1934, which is surely in no one's mind. It was simply intended to provide a constitutional basis for creating an Austrian representation abroad. It is a matter of course that all Austrian parties would have to be asked to send representatives to it.

I do not regret having taken these steps. On the contrary, I would reproach myself most severely had I omitted doing so. When the time comes, I want to be able to face the Austrian people with a clear conscience and be accountable for having done *everything* in my power to try to create for Austria that international recognition to which she is both legally and morally entitled. I can assure you, however, dear Dr. Deutsch, that it is all the same to me on what basis an Austrian representation would be created. It does not matter whether theoretically it would be considered a continuation of the last government or an entirely new one. The only thing that matters is to create an agency that can explain that Austria is in a state of war with Germany, one that can call on the Austrian people and on the Austrians in the German Army to take up the struggle against Germany, one that can represent Austria's interests at all international conferences, and that can see to it that the misery of the Austrian people in the postwar period is mitigated. It goes without saying that such a representation must immediately relinquish its function as soon as the Austrian people are able to form a government they find acceptable.

Was it really a crime to try to create for the Austrian people a provisional representation of their interests? Would these interests not have been better served by the success of such an action than by a purely negative attitude and a sterile encapsulation in party doctrines?

In your letter you complain about a "vehement agitation for a monarchist restoration in Austria," and you claim that I "took a leading part in this campaign in favor of Otto von Hapsburg" and that I "share the responsibility for the fact that because of the Hapsburg agitation the Austrian emigration was torn asunder."

To this I want first of all to state that I have always opposed placing in the foreground the question of the form of government. I never left any doubt that at the present time I consider this question, as well as agitation for one or another form of government, as completely irrelevant. It is not up to the émigrés to make such decisions, but only to the Austrian people in a free, democratic election.

Of course, I have worked together with monarchists, just as I have with republicans and Social Democrats whose attitudes are not one-sidedly negative, and just as I was ready and continue to be ready to collaborate with communists. I consider it the absolute duty of every Austrian, in view of the predicament of the country and its people, to set aside all divisive matters and to dedicate ourselves—along with all our compatriots, no matter which faction they belong to—solely to the liberation and restoration of our homeland. I regret the fact that representatives of the Austrian Social Democratic emigration are unable to bring themselves to the same point of view, which transcends partisan concerns.

The reproach that I share the responsibility for the fact "that the Austrian emigration was torn asunder," is so grave that you will understand if in the following I shall state the true facts and remind you of certain circumstances.

In 1939, when war appeared to be inevitable, everyone who truly desired Austria's independence realized at once that Austrians would themselves have to fight for the freedom of their fatherland: Austrians within the country by creating uprisings and by sabotage, those abroad by fighting in the ranks of the Allied armies, whenever possible within the framework of a separate Austrian legion. The world expected this from Austrians abroad, since it would have given the necessary backing and encouragement to the true Austrians in their country. This idea was clearly expressed later in the Moscow Declaration. "Austria," it states, "is reminded that in the final settlement, account will inevitably be taken of her contribution to her liberation."

When I arrived in Paris in early January, 1939, and got in touch with the Austrian emigration, I found that this will to fight was present among the Austrians in the largest measure. It was to be translated into action after the outbreak of war. Preparations were indeed made to establish an Austrian legion within the framework of the French Army.

The execution of this plan presupposed the creation of a politically united front of Austrians. I was therefore delighted when General Consul Schnabel asked you, dear Dr. Deutsch, and me to meet at his home for an exchange of views. Its purpose, as far as I and my friends were concerned, was the establishment of an Austrian representation and the formation of an Austrian legion. Although you expressed certain reservations, we finally agreed on a minimal program, which you yourself had proposed. You did, however, call my attention to the fact that your collaboration was dependent on the agreement of the representation of Austrian Socialists Abroad, whose members were at that time held in French concentration camps. Their release was obtained on the grounds that they were urgently needed for the work in Austria's interest. When they had been freed, the Representation Abroad, however, rejected not only the program you had proposed but the creation of any Austrian representation whatsoever. It was willing to agree only to the formation of a welfare agency for émigrés—a completely superfluous gesture, since a welfare agency in the form of the Federation was already in existence. In addition, the Socialist Representation took a very strong position against the creation of an Austrian legion to fight against Germany. It even demanded of us that we cease any propaganda in favor of the formation of an Austrian legion.

The attitude of the Representation of Austrian Socialists Abroad was based on a resolution that had been taken in early April, 1938, at a conference of Austrian Social Democrats in Brussels. This resolution recognized Austria's Anschluss to Germany as an "accomplished fact" and explicitly rejected Austria's detachment from Greater Germany.

By this resolution, Dr. Deutsch, the Austrian emigration was indeed torn asunder, and this for the first time!

In an article which appeared on June 2, 1938, in Paris in *Der Sozialistische Kampf,* Dr. Otto Bauer pungently characterized the two camps: on the one side all those, whether they be republicans or monarchists, Christian Socialists or communists, who, as he put it, struggled for "the reactionary program of the restoration of Austria's independence" and on the other the "Foreign Representatives" of the Austrian Social Democrats, who took the part of Greater Germany and against the restoration of Austria's independence.

That is the incontestable state of affairs concerning the splitting of the Austrian emigration.

Since that fateful decision of the Social Democrats, by which they rejected the creation of an Austrian representation and an Austrian legion in the year 1939, time and again attempts have been made—in Paris as well as, later, in London and New York—to persuade the Social Democrats to change their attitude. As you are undoubtedly aware, these attempts were continued right up to the most recent months—unfortunately in vain.

After the United States entered the war, a number of outstanding Austrian scientists as well as men of the most varied political factions decided to form the Austrian National Committee in this country. The Social Democrats were asked to participate in it. The intention was to create a united front of all Austrians, and all factions were willing to collaborate. Only the Austrian Social Democrats living here refused to participate. As their response they formed the Austrian Labor Committee. Through this action at the beginning of 1942, the Austrian emigration was again torn asunder and this time for all the world to see. In the face of such a clear state of affairs, how can you claim that, by my participation in subsequent actions, it was I who split the emigration? To be sure, it had been split before.

Any impartial reader of your party organ, the *Austrian Labor Information,* will easily recognize where the blame for this split lies. My fellow party members and I, as well as our closer coworkers from other political camps, have imposed the greatest restraint on ourselves until recently—that is to say, as long as we could do so in good conscience—and we have published no attacks against the Austrian Labor Committee. We have not even reacted to attacks from your side. On the other hand, from the first day of its publication the *Austrian Labor Information* has cast aspersions on all the bourgeois individuals and organizations working for Austria's independence, calling them reactionary; it has made fun of the communists for defending Austria's independence, and it has derided as "fake organizations" and "pigmy groups" those Social Democratic groups that separated themselves from the New York Labor Committee and the London Bureau on the issue of Greater Germany. In short, all Austrians, without exception, were insulted, jeered at, and denounced, unless they unconditionally accepted the doctrine of the Austrian Labor Committee. Time and again it was stressed that collaboration with other groups was out of the question for the Austrian Labor Committee.

In view of this absolutely negative attitude, can you be surprised, can you complain if Austrians who truly cared about the liberation of Austria and the restoration of her independence went their own way? Under these circumstances, can it be held against me that I tried to create a basis for the formation of an Austrian representation? Can Otto von Hapsburg be blamed because, once the War Department had decided in November, 1942, to establish an Austrian battalion in the framework of the American Army, he acted with the knowledge and consent of the American authorities, taking the direction of the Military Committee for the Liberation of Austria, whose task it was to recruit for the battalion? You accuse me of having worked with this committee. Of course I did so; I considered it my duty as an Austrian to do so. I would have participated in the same way if someone else, no matter which party camp he came from, had headed the committee. The question of who headed the committee was secondary, as far as I was concerned. What mattered was that, after all the disappointments, the establishment of the battalion finally represented a real achievement on behalf of Austria—that here, at last, Austrians were given an opportunity to fight for the liberation of their country, that here a first step was taken to open the way to Austria's admission to the United Nations. Faced with these considerations, all my other concerns had to recede into the background.

I wish to state that the Social Democrats were also invited to join the Military Committee. They refused to participate, not only because Otto von Hapsburg headed the committee but also because they were not willing under any circumstances to participate in promoting an Austrian battalion. If at the time you had made it a condition of your participation that Otto von Hapsburg step down from the chairmanship of the committee, this demand would have been complied with without any argument. Otto von Hapsburg had explicitly obligated himself to step down at once, should he prove to be an obstacle to the participation of the Social Democrats.

You write that "Hapsburg agitation reached its climax with the establishment of the Austrian Military Committee and the Austrian battalion connected with it"—as if the Military Committee were the main thing and the battalion only an appendage. This is nothing short of standing facts on their head. Furthermore, you blame "the lack of information in American circles about conditions in Central Europe," for the establishment of the Austrian battalion. This statement is a grave and wholly unfounded reproach against the highest authorities of the United States government. Those authorities are very well informed about conditions in Central Europe and Austria. They are mistaken only in their assumption that all Austrians without exception—regardless of whether we are dealing with Archdukes or socialist labor leaders—would be prepared to fight for the restoration of Austria's independence, as is actually the case with any other people. They could not anticipate that a segment of the socialist emigration, in spite of all the terrible things the Austrian people had to endure from Germany, would still frown upon Austria's independence.

The intense agitation that the Social Democrats and other groups close to them undertook at that time did actually succeed in bringing about the abolition of the Austrian battalion. When the responsible American government agencies saw that their friendly intention to further the interests of Austria was misinterpreted and seen as propaganda for a particular form of government, they dissolved the battalion. As true democrats, they did not want to expose themselves to charges that they had tried to interfere in the shaping of Austria's internal politics. This was a perfectly proper attitude and as such, completely understandable. Thus it is left to the Austrian people to settle the account with those who, in the hour of greatest need, were not prepared to place themselves alongside the fighters for Austria's freedom.

In your letter you call me a "republican until further notice." No, Dr.

Deutsch, you are mistaken, I am neither a "republican until further notice" nor a "monarchist until further notice," since as a genuine democrat I am quite content to leave the decision concerning the form of government to the liberated Austrian people. I am just an Austrian democrat but not one until further notice. I was always an opponent of the Anschluss idea. Nor did I declare in April, 1933, as your party convention did, that I was willing to put aside the desire for Anschluss for as long as Hitler ruled in Germany; thus I did not make a declaration of renunciation of Anschluss "until further notice." My fellow party members and I were not among those who in April, 1938, recognized the Anschluss as "an accomplished fact," calling the desire for the restoration of Austria's independence "reactionary." Nor have we ever complained that because of the Moscow Declaration which promised the restoration of an independent Austria, the Austrian people's right to self-determination had been infringed upon, as you and your friends did so often in *Austrian Labor Information.*

You mention the memoranda that the Austrian Labor Committee submitted to Mr. John G. Erhard and the Food Conference in Hot Springs, as well as the various published proposals concerning economic problems and education. Do you really believe that with these you have done enough? You must know yourself how little effect such memoranda have. Several hundred memoranda concerning Austria are in the files of the various departments in Washington, and most of them were submitted by private persons. This is quite understandable, since a private person has no other way of working for his country, which is occupied by the enemy, except through the press or the submission of memoranda. But that the representatives of a large political party in the hour of greatest need, instead of themselves taking a hand in shaping the fate of their country, as would be their duty, content themselves with addressing memoranda to foreign powers, leaving it to the latter to do the work which, as responsible representatives of their people, they should be doing themselves—that will not easily be forgiven by the liberated Austrian people. To create the impression of doing something but in reality to prevent any positive work on behalf of Austria—for this attitude, there will be little understanding in Austria.

I beg you, my dear Dr. Deutsch and your fellow party members, just once to draw the balance sheet on your activities since 1938.

Many countries have declared war on Germany and were admitted to the United Nations, although they have never fired a single shot. Former enemy countries—such as Italy, Romania, Bulgaria, Hungary, and Finland—have been recognized as cobelligerents—that is, practically as allies. But Austria, though in the years 1933 to 1938 she was the first of all the countries of Europe to offer armed resistance to Nazism and to its craving for world domination—Austria, which was the first of all the countries to have made bloody sacrifices in this struggle, Austria whose freedom fighters have had to bemoan thousands of casualties since the annexation (among them many of your fellow party members): Austria is the only country that has found neither admission to the United Nations nor recognition as an ally. Austria is the only country that possesses no officially recognized representation.

Have you ever given yourself an accounting of the terrible consequences of this situation, that Austria has no government, or national committee, or whatever you want to call it? Do you understand what this state of affairs has done to our country and our people and will still do?

Here you are:

Austria is the object of decisions by other powers without being able to raise her own voice and to share in decisions about her fate.

Austria will be administered by foreign military authorities. She is the only country that has no government of her own, which could take over the administration and initiate the transition to democracy after the liberation.

Austria is the only one among the countries ravished by the Axis that was not given a chance to organize the struggle for freedom according to plan and to provide the fighters within the country with that moral and material support that the governments in exile of other countries were able to provide to their fellow citizens.

It was not possible to influence effectively those Austrian soldiers and officers forced to serve in the German Army in such a way as only a government or recognized national representation can do, but never mere political parties, however sonorous the proclamations they may announce. Because of this, heavy damage was done, not only to Austria's moral prestige but also to the Allied conduct of the war.

Although thousands of Austrians fought in the ranks of the Allies, it was impossible to set up a separate Austrian unit, thus securing for Austria all those advantages that would have been granted to an Allied country. Austria is the only country whose liberation is not shared by its own national army.

Austria is the only country that could not participate in any international conferences—neither the Food Conference, nor the Currency Conference, nor the Conference of the International Labor Organization. Nor will she be able to take part in the San Francisco Conference. She cannot raise her voice to make her interests heard. She must watch in silence as the most important decisions are made; she has no part in them but must nevertheless submit to them.

And Austria is the only one of the countries occupied by the enemy that has no possibility whatsoever to make preparations toward alleviating the needs of the people in the postwar period. The little that various private committees have been able to accomplish in this regard deserves the highest praise but it cannot replace the kind of systematic activity that can, after all, be performed only by a recognized official authority.

Austria is the only one among the occupied countries that is unable to make any systematic preparations for the reconstruction of her administration, industry, agriculture, banking and credit institutions, currency, and school system. Not even the most beautiful memoranda can change that.

Austria is the only one among all the countries occupied by Germany that is unable to take any steps in preparing the restoration of law and order, punishment of political and military crimes, restitution of expropriated property, and indemnification for the victims of National Socialism.

Austria is the only country unable to make preparations for the repatriation of those of its citizens who have gone into exile.

Throughout all these years Austrian citizens were unprotected, living at the discretion of the governments of those countries to which they had fled. Not every government showed such a high degree of humanity and understanding as that of the United States. In a number of countries the Austrians were viewed as enemy aliens and treated accordingly. Thousands of refugees from Nazism, among them women and children, were put into concentration camps in the countries of refuge, for shorter or longer periods, some of them even for a very long time, and there they lived under the most primitive conditions, only too frequently having to suffer cold and hunger. Some of them found their health impaired, some succumbed to the rigors of this incarceration, all this because there was no Austrian government or recognized national representation to look after them.

All this could have been avoided if you, Dr. Deutsch, and your fellow party members could have brought yourself to espouse a more broad-minded, more productive policy, if you had put the welfare of the Austrian people above rigid party doctrine and the desire to serve the Greater German ideal. How very different Austria's fate would have been if the Representation of Austrian Socialists Abroad had accepted our proposal, made in Paris in 1939, to create an Austrian representation and form an Austrian legion! Even later it would still have been possible to salvage a great deal in the interest of Austria if you and your friends had given a favorable hearing to our repeated attempts to pave the way for collaboration. But you wanted it otherwise: You rejected all our attempts with derision. You and your fellow party members must therefore bear the moral responsibility for all the consequences which your negative policy has already caused and will still cause.

I regret that the accusations contained in your letter of March 13 have forced me against my will to engage in polemics. As the tone of my first letter of March 9, 1945, can prove to you, nothing was further from my mind than raising recriminations. We should direct our gaze less to the past than to the future. And after all, in the future Christian Socialists and Social Democrats will somehow have to get along again.

The Social Democrats have repeatedly stressed the necessity of working together with Christian Socialists in the Austria of the future. But how can such an understanding come about unless the way is paved for it here, if we cannot reach an agreement here at least about the fundamental problem of our attitude toward Austria?

The policy of Anschluss has foundered most terribly. It has brought unspeakable misery to Austria, it has taken tens of thousands, probably even hundreds of thousands, of victims, it has crippled innumerable Austrians, it has destroyed our cities and our industries, it has destroyed our currency, it has made beggars of our people. Indescribable hatred will be directed against all those who preached Anschluss, against all those who came to terms with it. And in April, 1938, your party was the only non-National Socialist group of Austrians who accepted the annexation as an accomplished fact. Your party has called reactionary all striving for the restoration of an independent Austria and has fought it most bitterly. Your party, or at least a considerable number of its members, has clung to the idea of a Greater Germany until most recent months. These facts are supported by innumerable proofs, and by printed statements at hand that cannot be denied. Nor can these facts be done away with by belated and weak attempts at embellishment such as those in the latest issue of *Austrian Labor Information*.

Viewed from a purely partisan standpoint, nothing could please the Christian Socialists more than the policies advanced by you and your friends since 1938. But right now it is not a matter of partisan advantage. Party politics must fall silent when the existence, the future of our people is at stake.

That is why I appeal to you once more. I appeal to your sense of responsibility and to your patriotism. Bring yourself to a generous decision. If you and I and our friends in both camps stand together, we can perhaps create even at the last minute a public platform for Austria, we can be involved in the coming decisions about our country, we can try through joint work to mitigate the deprivations of our people in the postwar period.

In this final hour I entreat and implore you to review again the letter I sent you on March 9, 1945, and to appreciate the reasons that occasioned my writing to you.

In view of the terrible position in which our fatherland and our people find themselves, I beg you to ignore all petty considerations and to grasp the hand I am holding out to you.

Sincerely yours,
Hans Rott

Bibliography

Books, dissertations, and articles

Acheson, Dean. *Present at the Creation: My Years in the State Department.* New York: W. W. Norton and Company, 1969.

Andics, Hellmut. *Der Staat, den keiner wollte.* Vienna: Verlag Herder, 1962.

——. *Der Fall Otto Habsburg.* Vienna: Verlag Fritz Molden, 1965.

Arbeitsgemeinschaft zur Wahrung Sudetendeutscher Interessen, eds. *Dokumente zur Austreibung der Sudetendeutschen.* Munich: 1951.

Bärnthaler, Irmgard. *Die Vaterländische Front: Geschichte und Organisation.* Vienna: Europa-Verlag, 1971.

Bauer, Otto. "Nach der Annexion," in *Der sozialistische Kampf.* Paris: 1938.

Beneš, Vaclav L. "The Slovaks in the Hapsburg Empire: A Struggle for Existence," *Austrian History Yearbook, 1967.* Houston: Rice University, 1967.

Breycha-Vauthier, Arthur. *Die Zeitschriften der österreichischen Emigration, 1934–1946.* Vienna: Österreichische Nationalbibliothek, Biblos-Schriften No. 26, 1960.

Brook-Shepherd, Gordon. *Dollfuss.* New York: St. Martin's Press, 1961.

Buttinger, Joseph. *Am Beispiel Österreichs.* Cologne: Verlag für Politik und Wirtschaft, 1953.

Coing, Helmut. *Grundzüge der Rechtsphilosophie.* Third edition. Berlin-New York: Walter de Gruyter (de Gruyter Lehrbuch), 1976.

Deutsch, Julius. *Ein weiter Weg.* Vienna: Amalthea-Verlag, 1960.

Federación Austriacos Libros en Bolivia, eds. *Festschrift.* La Paz, Bolivia: 1944.

Fischer, Ernst. *Erinnerungen und Reflexionen.* Reinbeck b. Hamburg: Rowohlt Verlag, 1969.

Free Austrian World Movement. "Survey of Austrian Organizations Abroad." Mimeographed. London: 1944.

Frei, Bruno. "Einige Bemerkungen zum Mexiko-Exil." Paper read at the Internationales Symposion zur Erforschung des österreichischen Exils von 1933 bis 1945. Mimeographed. Vienna: 1975.

Frick, Bruno. *Umdenken hinter Stacheldraht: Österreicher in der USSR.* Monographien zur Zeitgeschichte. Vienna: Europa-Verlag, 1967.

Fuchs, Martin. *Showdown in Vienna.* New York: G. P. Putnam's Sons, 1939.

Gazda, Antonin. Articles in *The Providence Journal* and *Providence Bulletin.* Providence, Rhode Island: 1942.

Gulick, Charles A. *Austria from Hapsburg to Hitler.* 2 vols. Berkeley: University of California Press, 1948. (*Österreich von Habsburg zu Hitler.* Vienna: Forum-Verlag, 1976.)

Jedlicka, Ludwig. *Vom alten zum neuen Österreich: Fallstudien zur österreichischen Zeitgeschichte, 1900–1975.* St. Pölten: Niederösterreichisches Pressehaus, 1975.

Karbach, Oskar. "Die politischen Grundlagen des deutsch-österreichischen Antisemitismus," in *Zeitschrift für die Geschichte der Juden,* edited by Hugo Gold. Tel Aviv: Olamenu Publishers, 1964.

Kelsen, Hans. *Österreichisches Staatsrecht.* Tübingen: 1923.

"K. V." "The Fate of Austria," in *War and the Working Class.* Moscow: 1943.

Lendvai, Paul, and Ritschel, K. H. *Kreisky: Porträt eines Staatsmannes.* Vienna: Paul Zsolnay Verlag, 1972.

Maderegger, Sylvia. *Die Juden im österreichischen Standestaat, 1934–1938.* Veröffentlichungen des Historischen Instituts Salzburg. Vienna: Geyer-Edition, 1973.

Maiman, Helene. *Politik im Wartesaal: Österreichische Exilpolitik in Grossbritannien, 1938 bis 1945.* Vienna: Hermann Boehlaus Nachfg., 1975.

Mattern, Karl-Heinz. *Die Exilregierung.* Tübingen: Verlag J. C. B. Mohr, 1953.

Meisels, Lucian Otto. "Die politischen Beziehungen zwischen den Vereinigten Staaten von

Amerika und Österreich, 1933–1938.'' Ph. D. dissertation, University of Vienna, 1960.

Molden, Otto. *Der Ruf des Gewissens: Der österreichische Freiheitskampf, 1938–1945.* Third edition. Das Einsame Gewissen. Vienna: Verlag Herold, 1975.

Muessener, Helmut. *Exil in Schweden: Politische und kulturelle Emigration nach 1933.* Munich: Carl Hanser Verlag, 1974.

Pelinka, Anton. *Stand oder Klasse? Die Christliche Arbeiterbewegung Österreichs, 1933 bis 1938.* Vienna: Europa-Verlag, 1972.

Reichhold, Ludwig. *Geschichte der OEVP.* Graz: Verlag Styria, 1975.

Reimann, Victor. *Bruno Kreisky: Das Porträt eines Staatsmannes.* Vienna: Verlag Fritz Molden, 1972.

Rie, Robert. *Die Entwicklung der Anerkennungspolitik der Vereinigten Staaten von Amerika im 18. und 19. Jahrhundert.* Archiv für Völkerrecht, edited by Hans Jürgen Schlochauer, Tübingen: Verlag J. C. B. Mohr, 1964.

Schärf, Adolf. *Österreichs Erneuerung.* Vienna: 1955.

Scheu, Friedrich. *Die Emigrationspresse der Sozialisten, 1933–1945.* Monographien zur Zeitgeschichte. Vienna: Europa-Verlag, 1968.

Schwedische-Österreichische Vereinigung, eds. *Festschrift: 20 Jahre Schwedische-Österreichische Vereinigung, 1944–1964.* Stockholm: 1964.

Shell, Karl L. *Jenseits der Klassen? Österreichische Sozialdemokratie seit 1934.* Vienna: Europa-Verlag, 1969.

Shirer, William L. *The Rise and Fall of the Third Reich.* New York: Simon and Schuster, 1960.

Spaulding, Wilder E. *The Quiet Invaders.* Vienna: Österreichischer Bundesverlag für Unterricht, Wissenschaft und Kunst, 1963.

Stadler, Karl R. ''Das London Bureau der Österreichischen Sozialisten.'' Paper read at the Internationales Symposion zur Erforschung des österreichischen Exils von 1933 bis 1945. Mimeographed. Vienna: 1975.

———. *Opfer verlorener Zeiten: Geschichte der Schutzbund-Emigration, 1934.* With a Foreword by Bruno Kreisky. Vienna: Europa-Verlag, 1974.

U.S. Department of State. *Foreign Relations of the United States: Diplomatic Papers* for 1938 and 1943–1945. Washington, D.C.: U.S. Government Printing Office, 1956–1969.

Vasari, Emilio. *Dr. Otto Habsburg oder die Leidenschaft für Politik.* Vienna: Verlag Herold, 1972.

Vodopivec, Alexander. *Die Balkanisierung Österreichs.* Vienna: Verlag Fritz Molden, 1966.

Vogelmann, Karl. ''Die Propaganda der österreichischen Emigration in der Sowjetunion für einen selbstandigen österreichischen Nationalstaat, 1938–1945. Mimeographed. Ph.D. dissertation, University of Vienna, 1973.

Wandycz, Piotr S. Contribution to *Austrian History Yearbook, 1967.* Houston: Rice University, 1967.

Weinzierl, Erika. *Zu wenig Gerechte: Österreicher und Judenverfolgung, 1938–1945.* Graz: Verlag Styria, 1969.

Wereszyki, Henry. Contribution to *Austrian History Yearbook, 1967.* Houston: Rice University, 1967.

Werth, Alexander. *Russia at War, 1941–1945.* New York: E. P. Dutton and Co., 1964.

Whiteside, Andrew J. Contribution to *Austrian History Yearbook, 1967.* Houston: Rice University, 1967.

Willars, Christian. *Die böhmische Zitadelle.* Vienna: Verlag Fritz Molden, 1965.

Wissenschaftliche Kommission des Theodor-Korner Stiftungsfonds und des Leopold Kunschak-Preises zur Erforschung der österreichischen Geschichte der Jahre 1927 bis 1938. ''Festgabe anlässlich des dreissigjährigen Bestandes der Zweiten Republik Österreich und der zwanzigsten Wiederkehr des Jahrestages des österreichischen Staatsvertrages,'' edited by Ludwig Jedlicka and Rudolf Neck. (Educational Commission on the Exploration of Austrian History from 1927 to 1938. ''Proceedings,'' etc.) Vienna: Österreichische Staatsdruckerei, 1975.

Periodicals

Die Abwehr. Graz. 1950.

Aufbau. New York. Vols. V–XI, 1939–1945.

Austria Libre. Buenos Aires. 1943.

Austria Libre. Havana. 1944.

Austria Libre. Montevideo. 1944. (Newsletter of the Austrian Central Committee for Latin America.)

Austria Libre. Santiago, Chile. 1943.

Austrian Labor Information. New York. 1942–1945.

Austrian News. London. 1944.

Austro-American Tribune. New York. 1947.

Dagens Nyheter. Stockholm. 1945.

Freiheit für Österreich. New York. 1942–1943.

Frei Österreich. New York. 1942–1945. (Newsletter of the Free Austrian Movement.)

Journal Officiel. Paris. 1938–1940.

Mitteilungsblatt. New York. 1942. (Newsletter of Austrian Action.)

The New York Times. New York. 1938–1945.

Österreichische Post. Paris. 1938–1939.

Österreichische Rundschau. New York. 1942.

The Providence Journal. Providence, Rhode Island. 1942. (Source of articles by Antonin Gazda.)

Providence Bulletin. Providence, Rhode Island. 1942. (Source of articles by Antonin Gazda.)

The Rubicon, Criscuolo Newsletter. Washington, D.C. 1942.

Svensk Tidscrift. Stockholm. 1944.

Zeitspiegel. London. 1944–1945.

Archives

Bruno Kreisky Archive. Vienna.

Franklin Delano Roosevelt Library (abbreviated FDR Library). Hyde Park, New York. The Morgenthau Diaries and other collections.

Republic of Austria. Dokumentationsarchiv des Österreichischen Widerstandes, Katalog No. 9, Periodica 1939–1945. Underground Exil-Alliierte. Vienna, 1975.

Rott, Hans. The unpublished papers of Hans Rott. New York.

U.K. Public Records Office (abbreviated PRO). London.

U.S. Department of Justice records. Department of Justice. Washington, D.C.

U.S. Department of State records. Department of State. Washington, D.C.

U.S. Department of State records. National Archives. Washington, D.C.

U.S. Department of War records. Department of War. Washington, D.C.

U.S. Office of Strategic Services (abbreviated OSS). National Archives. Washington, D.C.

U.S. Office of War Information, Overseas Branch (abbreviated OWI). National Archives. Suitland, Maryland.

West German Federal Republic. Auswärtiges Amt. Akten zur deutschen auswärtigen Politik, 1933–1945. Politisches Archiv des Auswärtigen Amtes. Bonn.

NOTES

Chapter I The Concept of Political Emigration
from Austria, 1938–1945

1. "Refugees," U.S. State Dept. File 840.48. Franklin D. Roosevelt, "Political Refugees"—Telegram (Hyde Park, New York: Franklin Delano Roosevelt Library), OF 3186. French law of May 2, 1938, Preamble, in *Journal Officiel*, 4967.

2. Julius Weigert, "Soziologie der Emigration," *Aufbau* (New York), Vol. VI, No. 18 (Nov. 10, 1940).

3. Walter Tritsch, "Österreichs burgundische Erbschaft," *Österreichische Post* (Paris), Nos. 17–18 (Sept. 1, 1939). U.S. State Dept. File 863.01/809.

4. U.S. State Dept. File 863.01/809. See also "Austrian Politics in Great Britain," May 30, 1944, OSS 88818: "The bulk of the Austrians in this country did not come for reasons of political conviction, but rather they suffered racial persecution."

5. *Österreichische Post* (Paris), No. 1 (Christmas, 1938). Walter Tritsch, *loc. cit.*

6. Paul Kris, "Zur Rechtsstellung der österreichischen Flüchtlinge in Frankreich," *Österreichische Post* (Paris), No. 1 (Christmas, 1938).

7. *Ibid.* Article also continued in subsequent issues.

8. Address by the French Minister of the Interior, Albert Sarraut, at a police convention, reported in *Österreichische Post* (Paris), No. 5 (Feb. 15, 1939). The minister pointed out that the government had been forced to "dam up the rushing tide of immigrants and in addition to increase domestic security services in order to have better control over undesirable elements." But, he continued, in spite of the severity of some measures, care had always been taken to preserve the validity of France's traditional ideals of humanitarianism.

9. Armistice agreement between Germany and France (June 22, 1940) (Bonn: Auswärtiges Amt, Akten zur deutschen aüswärtigen Politik, 1941–1945), Series D. Vol. II, p. 554.

10. Joseph Buttinger, *Am Beispiel Österreichs* (Cologne: Verlag fur Politik und Wirtschaft, 1953), pp. 536, 541. Kurt L. Shell, *Jenseits der Klassen? Österreichische Sozialdemokratie seit 1934* (Vienna: Europa-Verlag, 1969), p. 36. Julius Deutsch, "Zwei Emigrationen" (Interview), *Aufbau* (New York), Vol. VIII, No. 9 (Feb. 27, 1942).

11. Hans Rott, "Free Austria," *Free Austrian Movement* (folder) and "Communications of the Free Austrian Movement, New York" (New York: The unpublished papers of Hans Rott). Buttinger, *op. cit.,* p. 535.

12. Buttinger, *op. cit.,* pp. 526 ff. U.S. State Dept. File 863.00/8–745. "W.T.," "Einheit," *Freiheit für Österreich* (New York), Vol. 1, No. 5 (Oct. 5, 1942). A report from the British embassy in Vienna to the Foreign Office in London of March 9, 1938, notes that Rott and Watzek had been delegated to negotiate with the workers (PRO FO 371 22318 8218, No. 76, 179/1/38). An American report, "The Moscow Declaration on Austria" (1944) includes a detailed discussion of the problem of the Anschluss. Four principal groups (15 percent Schuschnigg followers, 30 percent workers, 25 percent National Socialists, and 30 percent undecided voters) were involved in the plebiscite planned by the Federal Chancellor, Dr. Schuschnigg, so that he could count on the votes of his followers, the workers, and those among the undecided who usually vote for the government—that is, 75 percent of the total. But there were always Austrians who, without regard to regular party affiliation, rejected the Anschluss. "A Survey of the Austrian Emigration," April 11, 1945, OSS 2853, points out that Karl Hans Sailer, referred to repeatedly later on as a leader of the underground, was supposed to become head of the socialist trade unions in the socialists' planned compromise of the workers with Schuschnigg. He was to have appealed to the workers to vote for Schuschnigg. Sailer left Austria on March 11, 1938, the day the Schuschnigg referendum was canceled.

13. Joseph Buttinger, *op. cit.,* p. 537. "The Austrian Underground: Strength, Tactics, and Prospects," OSS XL 2101 (1944).

14. Otto Bauer, "Nach der Annexion," in *Der Sozialistische Kampf* (Paris), No. 1 (June 2, 1938). Joseph Pratter, "Der Österreichische Arbeiter, Arbeiterschaft und Grossdeutschland," *Österreichische Post* (Paris), No. 3 (January 15, 1939). Joseph Buttinger, *op. cit.,* p. 545. Kurt L. Shell, *op. cit.,* p. 36.

15. *Ibid.* "Austrian Communist Party," March, 1943, OSS 33855: "The Communist Party of Austria has, since 1935, advocated the independence of the Republic of Austria in contrast to the earlier policy which was identical with the Socialist-Democratic objective of Anschluss to the German Reich."

16. Joseph Buttinger, *op. cit.,* p. 534: "The political persecution mania of the National Socialists was at first primarily directed against the rulers of yesterday, the spokesmen of the authoritarian regime." See also Hans Rott, folders "Free Austrian Movement," "Free Austria," and "Communications of the Free Austrian Movement," No. 1, p. 6. "The Hapsburg Problem," The Royal Institute of International Affairs, Balliol College, Oxford, PRO FO 371 24409 6054 C 2953 (January 30, 1940), pp. 15 ff.

17. Kurt L. Shell, *op. cit.,* p. 36. Joseph Buttinger, *op. cit.,* pp. 487, 548, 549.

18. Werner Thorman, "Die katholische Emigration," *Aufbau* (New York), Vol. VII, No. 20 (May 16, 1941). The article notes: "Except for the so-called non-Aryan Christians, the numerical strength of the Catholic emigration is not sizable, even after the occupation of Austria and Czechoslovakia. Catholic emigrants—politicians, journalists, writers, scientists—were insignificant in numbers, people forced to flee not because of their Catholic faith, but because of their past opposition to National Socialism or because of their resistance to Kulturkampf measures after the establishment of the Third Reich. This Catholic emigration gives evidence of many political shadings—from religious socialists to Austrian Heimwehr men. It included absolutely nonpolitical emigrants who had simply fled religious persecution—that is, members of the priesthood."

19. Kurt Blumenfeld, "Überwindung des Antisemitismus," *Aufbau* (New York), Vol. VII, No. 43 (Oct. 24, 1941). The article posits three statements as political axioms: (1) the fact of anti-Semitism; (2) the error of assimilation; and (3) the truth of Zionism. Blumenfeld, a leader of German Zionism, therefore designates the assimilation of German as well as Austrian Jews and their commitment to Germany or Austria as an error that can only be corrected by the "truth of Zionism," that is, overcoming assimilation. See also John C. Wiley to Secretary of State, July 26, 1938, FDR Library, File 760 F 62/67/1. Also Circular, "Die Judenfrage als Faktor der Aussenpolitik im Jahre 1938" (Jan. 25, 1939): "The greater the poverty of the immigrating Jew, the greater a burden he places on the country of immigration, the stronger the reaction in the host country, and the more desirable the effect in the interest of German propaganda," Auswärtiges Amt, Akten zur deutschen auswärtigen Politik, 1941–1945, Series D, Vol. V, p. 780.

20. Thomas Mann, for example.

21. Joseph Buttinger, *op. cit.,* p. 63.

22. Oskar Karbach has shown that the so-called race principle in Austria was used, from its inception by Georg Ritter von Schönerer in the year 1882, in the political life of the Austrian Germans as the explosive to undermine first the monarchy of the Hapsburgs and especially the Austrian Army, and later the independent Republic of Austria. Karbach, "Die politischen Grundlagen des deutsch-österreichischen Antisemitismus," in *Zeitschrift für die Geschichte der Juden,* ed. Hugo Gold (Tel-Aviv: Olamenu Publishers, 1964), No. 1, p. 1., and No. 4, pp. 173–178. See also Sylvia Maderegger, *Die Juden im österreichischen Standestaat, 1934–1938,* Veröffentlichungen des Historischen Instituts Salzburg (Vienna: Geyer-Edition, 1973), pp. 115 ff.

23. "In retrospect we must therefore conclude that in the political and legal fields the corporative state left the situation of the Jews unaltered (this is doubtless not so, if we examine the economic sphere)"—Oskar Karbach, *loc. cit.,* p. 177. See also Sylvia Maderegger, *op. cit.,* pp. 215 ff.

24. Karbach points out that the appointment of representatives of Jewry to the corporative organizations was made without regard to any particular commitment of these Jews as Austrians or Germans of the Jewish faith. (*Loc. cit.,* pp. 173–178.)

25. "The integration of the emigrants into American society has priority," in "Allen Leuten recht getan . . . ," *Aufbau* (New York), Vol. V, No. 24 (Dec. 15, 1939). See also "Vergangenheit bleibt Vergangenheit," *Aufbau* (New York), Vol. VI, No. 43 (Oct. 25, 1940): "The *Aufbau* is an anti-Nazi publication that concerns itself . . . exclusively with Jewish and American matters."

26. "Is the history of the Jews in Germany and Austria, which covers a period of 2,000 years, finished and historically completed, as is the history of the Spanish Jews in the year 1492? We do not know. . . ." W. C. Hulse, "Zur Geschichte der Juden in Deutschland und Österreich," *Aufbau* (New York), Vol. VI, No. 48 (Nov. 29, 1940). See also Arthur Greenwood, "The Future of the European Jews," *Aufbau* (New York), Vol. VII, No. 41 (Oct. 11, 1940).

27. In an unsigned article entitled "Heimweh," *Aufbau* (New York), Vol. V, No. 23 (Dec. 8, 1939), the complaint is made that the emigrants are glorifying the past. See also "Allen Leuten recht getan. . . ," in *Aufbau* (New York), Vol. V, No. 24 (Dec. 15, 1939), and "Österreicher im Exil," *Aufbau* (New York), Vol. VI, No. 5 (Feb. 2, 1940), where the difference between the emigrants from Austria and those from Germany is pointed out: "As compared to the Reich Germans, the emigrants from Austria occupy a kind of separate position which is often obscured by the sameness of the language, and this incorrectly."

28. The meritorious publisher of the weekly *Aufbau* compiled a history of Jewish writing in its transformation under National Socialism, "Eine jüdische Zeitung," *Aufbau* (New York), Vol. VII, No. 29 (July 18, 1941).

29. Ferdinand Kuhn, in *The New York Times,* Feb. 16, 1938. Also Otto Bauer, *loc. cit.*

30. According to a report in the *Aufbau,* Vol. VI, No. 20 (May 17, 1940), when the Germans marched into Belgium and Holland on May 10, 1940, there were roughly 23,000 refugees in Belgium, 21,000 in Holland, 500 in Luxemburg, and about 18,000 in Switzerland. I am adding here that among them a significant number must have been from Austria. See also Hans Oberwalden, "Schwyzer Trost und Trotz," *Aufbau* (New York), Vol. VIII, No. 1 (Jan. 2, 1942).

31. Ambassador von Plessen, "Bemerkungen zu den deutsch-italienischen Beziehungen aus Anlass des Jahreswechsels 1939/1940," Jan. 3, 1940, Auswärtiges Amt, Akten zur deutschen auswärtigen Politik, 1941–1945, Series D. Vol. VIII, p. 478. See also "Jüdisches Schicksal in Skandinavien," *Aufbau* (New York), Vol. VI, No. 15 (April 12, 1940): In April 1940 there were 1,572 refugees in Denmark, around 1,000 in Norway, and roughly 3,000 in Sweden, among them certainly also refugees from Austria. See further "Right of Political Refugees to Asylum in Non-belligerent Countries," June 15, 1945, OSS R&A Branch No. 2465, 097.3 Z 1042 according to which about 50,000 refugees sought sanctuary in Sweden during the course of the war. Anthony Eden to Lord Halifax, Washington, March 12, 1942, PRO FO 30942 8374 C 2281/1364/18.

32. Ernst Fischer, *Erinnerungen und Reflexionen* (Reinbeck b. Hamburg: Rowohlt-Verlag, 1969). Fischer deals extensively with the life of the members of the Schutzbund (Workers' Defensive Alliance) who emigrated to Russia at the time of Schuschnigg's government. See p. 364. Karl R. Stadler, *Opfer verlorener Zeiten: Die Geschichte der Schutzbund-Emigration 1934* (Vienna: Europa-Verlag, 1974).

33. Ernst Fischer, *op. cit.,* pp. 350 ff.

Chapter II   Austrian Political Emigration in France

1. French law of May 2, 1938, Preamble, *Journal Officiel,* 4967: "Le nombre sans cesse croissant d'étrangers résident en France impose au Gouvernement investi, du pouvoir législatif dans une domaine nettement définie, d'édicter certaines mesures que commandent impérieusement le souci de la sécurité nationale, de l'économie générale du pays at de la protection de l'ordre public."

2. *Ibid.*

3. *Österreichische Post* (Paris), No. 5 (Feb. 15, 1939).

4. *Ibid.,* No. 3 (Jan. 15, 1939).

5. "Refugees," U.S. State Dept. File 840.48. U.S. Department of State, *Foreign Relations of the United States,* 1938–1945 (Washington, D.C.: Government Printing Office, 1956–1969),

Vol. I, *Diplomatic Papers, 1938,* p. 740. Franklin D. Roosevelt, Press conference, March 25, 1938, Presidential Press Conferences of Franklin D. Roosevelt, FDR Library. German Secretary of State, Letter, July 8, 1938, Auswärtiges Amt, Akten zur deutschen auswärtigen Politik, Series D, 1937–1945, Vol. V, pp. 753–754: "Germany immediately rejected all participation."

6. Ferdinand Kuhn, "British Write off Austrian Question!" "London now regards it only a matter of months before the swastika clasps Czechoslovakia in its arms just as it has gripped Austria. Not a shot will be fired according to expectations here"—*The New York Times,* Feb. 16, 1938. *The Österreichische Post* (Paris) Nos. 17/18 (September 1, 1939) quotes Ernest Pezet's address in Paris of Aug. 2, 1938. Joseph Buttinger reports in *Am Beispiel Österreichs,* p. 525, that one of his collaborators, "little Otto Bauer," said on March 7, 1938, "that this meant packing one's bags." A Report of the Chairman of the American Joint Jewish Committee, *Aufbau* (New York), Vol. V, No. 23 (Dec. 8, 1939), states that not only people coming from Germany were in danger, but also people coming from German-occupied countries and Italy, Hungary, and Rumania. Report of Nov. 14, 1938, Auswärtiges Amt, Akten zur deutschen auswärtigen Politik, Series D, Vol. IV, pp. 561 ff., the "Kristallnacht."

7. French law of May 2, 1938, *Journal Officiel,* 4968.

8. *Ibid.,* Preamble, 4967.

9. Karl-Heinz Mattern, *Die Exilregierung* (Tübingen: Verlag J. C. B. Mohr, 1953).

10. U.S. State Department File 863.00/1731. Dr. Paul Kris, "Zur Rechtstellung der österreichischen Flüchtlinge in Frankreich," *Österreichische Post* (Paris), No. 1 (Christmas, 1938).

11. Saltus, in "Zur Frage des Status des Ex-Autrichien," *Österreichische Post* (Paris), No. 3 (Jan. 15, 1939), wants to regard all former citizens as "Ex-Autrichiens," whether they are emigrants or residents of France. In a narrower interpretation, however, he feels the name Ex-Autrichien to be justified only in the case of those Austrians who do not claim allegiance to the German state and who give up the protection of the German Reich or have not sought it.

12. French law of May 2, 1938, *Journal Officiel,* 4967. "Décret réglementant les conditions du séjour des étrangers in France," *Journal Officiel,* 5492, May 14, 1938. "Décret précisant le sens et la portée de l'article II du décret du 2 mai 1938 sur la police des étrangers," *Journal Officiel,* 7614, June 17, 1938. This last law, in conformity with the law of May 2, 1938, defines the refugee as a "foreigner not in a position to leave French territory." It is decreed that such foreigners can be prescribed places of residence and the duty to report their domiciles to the police. Actually, a number of Austrian refugees were officially sent to Chelles, Département Seine-et-Marne.

13. "Décret relatif à la création d'un Centre Spécial de Rassemblement," *Journal Officiel,* 1644, Jan. 21, 1939.

14. French law of May 2, 1938, Preamble, *Journal Officiel,* 4967: "Elle reste toujours aussi largement ouverte à la pensée, a l'idéal persécuté qui lui demandaient asile." At the same time the measure expresses anxiety that the asylum could be misused: ". . . à la condition toutefois qu'il ne soit pas fait du titre respectable du réfugié politique un usage illégitime qui serait un abus de confiance. . . ."

15. Joseph Buttinger, *op. cit.,* p. 578.

16. *Österreichische Post* (Paris), No. 1 (Christmas, 1938). U.S. State Department File 863.00/1731. U.S. State Department File 863.00/1724. U.S. State Department File 701/625/5. (Composition of the Conseil National Autrichien) PRO FO 371 23104 8395.

17. *Ibid.,* No. 1 (Christmas, 1938).

18. Joseph Buttinger, *op. cit.,* pp. 550 ff.

19. *Österreichische Post* (Paris), No. 10, May 1, 1939.

20. Otto Bauer, *loc. cit.* A memorandum of July 7, 1944, "The Austrian Emigration in Great Britain," OSS XL 1615, states: "The Socialists still maintain Austria's inability to function, although the years 1936/37 had proven the opposite to be true. Besides, Otto Bauer underestimated the terror of the Gestapo." "Free Germany," Nov. 26, 1943, OSS 1593, states that it is improbable, because of Himmler's terror, that Hitler could be toppled by a workers' revolution.

21. Hans Rott, "Free Austria," *Free Austrian Movement* (folder), Oct. 10, 1943, p. 7. OSS XL 2101.

22. Hans Rott to Julius Deutsch, March 9, 1945 (reprinted in full in the Appendix), folder

"Free Austrian Movement." British Postal and Telegraph Censorship, "Free Austrians," Dec. 9, 1942, PRO FO 371 30911 8273 C 12767: "There is a noticeable division between those who place the independence of Austria first on their programme and those for whom democracy comes before anything else. This is the main issue separating the monarchists from most of the socialists." "The Austrian Emigration in London," Oct. 5, 1944, OSS XL 1824.

23. Joseph Buttinger, *op. cit.,* pp. 594, 595.

24. Address of the Ligue Autrichienne (Paris), "A Fatal Hour for Humanity," *Österreichische Post* (Paris), No. 17/18, Sept. 1, 1939, p. 3. Hans Rott, "Free Austria," *Free Austrian Movement* (folder), (April, 1945). PRO FO 371 22318 8218, R 2964 No. 76 (179/1/38): British Embassy in Vienna to Viscount Halifax, March 9, 1938, concerns the activities of Hans Rott in March, 1938.

25. Karl-Heinz Mattern, *op. cit.,* mentions the establishment of the Czechoslovak government in exile. In this book Mattern examines various types of governments in exile and contrasts the Czech organization with the Belgian, Dutch, Luxemburger, or Norwegian representations, which had assumed government functions after each country's occupation.

26. Hans Rott, "Free Austria," *Free Austrian Movement* (folder), (April, 1945).

27. Martin Fuchs, *Showdown in Vienna* (New York: G. P. Putnam's Sons, 1939), quotes letters from Otto von Hapsburg (Feb. 17, 1938) and Schuschnigg (March 2, 1938). "Otto von Hapsburg," March 14, 1943, Foreign Nationalities Branch, OSS 34484S, states that Hapsburg's name carried great weight and that Otto's influence might have prevented the Anschluss.

28. U.S. State Department File 762.63/484. John C. Wiley, "Report," Feb. 19, 1938, FDR Library. "The Hapsburg Problem," Jan. 30, 1940, PRO FO 371 24409 6054 C 2953. British Embassy, Paris, to Foreign Office, Oct. 21, 1939, PRO FO 371 23104 8395 C 17025. British Embassy, Paris, to Foreign Office, Dec. 11, 1939, PRO FO 371 23104 8395 C 20168. British Embassy, Paris, to Foreign Office, Dec. 12, 1939, PRO FO 371 23104 8395 C 20210. OSS 34484S, pp. 1 ff.

29. "The Hapsburg Problem," Jan. 30, 1940, PRO FO 371 24409 6054 C 2953. William C. Bullitt to President Roosevelt, Sept. 5, 1939, PPF Bullitt, France; White House memorandum, March 6, 1940, OF 166, FDR Library.

30. State Department File 863.01/631. British Embassy, Paris, to Foreign Office, Oct. 20, 1939, PRO FO 371 23104 8395 C 17025: Otto von Hapsburg did not follow this precept and demanded the establishment of a monarchy as a war aim; this press conference was judged to have been futile. Note from A. Cadogan, Oct. 30, 1939, PRO FO 371 23104 8395 C 17466/G: As a result, Otto's brother, the Archduke Robert, was not received by the King of England.

31. Paul Hertz, "Frankreich und die deutschen Flüchtlinge," *Aufbau* (New York), Vol. VI, No. 1 (Jan. 5, 1940). *Ibid.,* Vol. VI, No. 7 (Feb. 16, 1940), regarding erosion of French law of asylum. K. K. Gilbert, "Flüchtlinge—wichtiges Kampfpotential," *Aufbau* (New York), Vol. VII, No. 15 (April 11, 1941).

32. "W.C.H.," "Emigranten in Frankreich," *Aufbau* (New York), Vol. VI, No. 2 (Jan. 12, 1940). Dr. Robert W. Hutchins, University of Chicago, to Franklin D. Roosevelt, Jan., 1940, FDR Library, File OF 166a.

33. Joseph Buttinger, *op. cit.,* p. 578.

34. *Ibid.,* p. 583, connecting the release with negotiations concerning an Austrian foreign representation. British Embassy, Paris, to the Foreign Office, Telegram, Nov. 23, 1939, PRO FO 371 22940 8235 C 19067.

35. *Aufbau* (New York), Vol. VI, No. 4. (Jan. 26, 1940). According to French Minister of the Interior, Albert Sarraut, only 15,000 interned persons had been released.

36. *Aufbau* (New York), Vol. IX, No. 7. (Feb. 12, 1943). Emil Ludwig, in "Versuch einer Täuschung," mentions a meeting of Otto von Hapsburg with Edouard Herriot, even though he blames Otto for failing to serve in the Austrian battalion.

37. Joseph Buttinger, *op. cit.,* p. 579, quotes the statement by Starhemberg: "He would not have thought it possible that he would ever become the leader of Jewish gangs." British Embassy, Paris, to Foreign Office, Nov. 6, 1939, PRO FO 371 22940 8235 C 17995, concerns the visit of the former Austrian Ambassador to the Hague, Georg M. V. Alexich, who turned against Martin Fuchs, a Jew, remarking that Austrians deplore the treatment of Jews by the Germans but

are also glad to be rid of them. Victor Reimann, in *Bruno Kreisky: Das Porträt eines Staatsmannes* (Vienna: Verlag Fritz Molden, 1972), p. 124, notes: "The fact that some of the emigrants were arrested, and others were not, created a mood of mistrust and hate." A Foreign Office memorandum about Robert von Hapsburg's visit to the Foreign Office on August 30, 1944 (PRO FO 371 38830 8416 C 11492), shows that even at this late date Robert von Hapsburg did find it necessary to mention that 98 percent of all Austrian refugees were non-Aryan and 75 percent were communists.

38. Arbeitsgemeinschaft zur Wahrung Sudetendeutscher Interessen, eds., *Dokumente zur Austreibung der Sudetendeutschen* (Munich: 1951) p. 517: Jan Masaryk to Max Weinreich, Director of the Jewish Scientific Institute (IVO), (New York), May 5, 1942. Edvard Beneš, "In the footsteps of Masaryk," *Aufbau* (New York), Vol. VII, No. 41 (Oct. 10, 1931).

39. Joseph Buttinger, *op. cit.*, p. 554.

40. *Österreichische Post* (Paris), No. 15/16 (Aug. 1, 1939). William C. Bullitt to President Roosevelt, Sept. 5, 1939, FDR Library, File PSF France, Bullitt, describes the French ministry official, Rochat, as being favorably disposed to these efforts.

41. Joseph Buttinger, *op. cit.*, p. 557. Immediately after the outbreak of the war, on September 4, 1939, a Conseil National Autrichien was founded in Paris, with Hans Rott as president, Karl Hartl as secretary, and Martin Fuchs as secretary of foreign affairs and press. Viscount Halifax was notified of the founding by Count Kurt Strachewitz, the representative of the Conseil in England, by letter of September 13, 1939. The Conseil National Autrichien demanded to be recognized by the British government as the sole legitimate representative of Austria (PRO FO 371 23104 8395). Foreign Office to British Embassy, Paris, September 18, 1939, PRO FO 371 23104 8395, takes a cautious point of view, although it was announced that French Premier Daladier favored the organization. Robert Boothby to Lord Halifax, October 12, 1939, PRO FO 371 22940 8235 C 16545. Memorandum from I. Kilpatrick, October 18, 1939, PRO FO 371 22940 8235 C 17029. British Foreign Office, "The Austrian National Council," October 23, 1939, PRO FO 371 22940 8235 C 17235. British Embassy, Paris, to British Foreign Office, December 11, 1939, PRO FO 371 23104 8395 C 20168, mentions the lasting interest of Daladier in the reestablishment of Austria; Daladier had convinced French President Lebrun to name Austria as one of the countries subjugated by Germany in his message of November 15, 1939, to Queen Wilhelmina of the Netherlands and King Leopold of Belgium. British Foreign Office to Major-General Beaumont-Nesbitt, C.V.Q., M.C., PRO FO 371 22940 8235 C 15717/C. British Foreign Office, "Austria and a Habsburg Restoration," Dec. 16, 1939, PRO FO 371 23104 6059 C 20660.

42. Kurt L. Shell, *op. cit.*, p. 16, n. 3, reports that the postwar Party of Austria tried to forget Joseph Buttinger.

43. Joseph Buttinger, *op. cit.*, p. 596.

44. Hans Rott to Julius Deutsch, March 9, 1945 (reprinted in full in the Appendix), folder "Free Austrian Movement." Joseph Buttinger, *op. cit.*, p. 578.

45. Julius Deutsch, *Ein weiter Weg* (Vienna: Amalthea-Verlag, 1960), p. 315: "My task to speak on behalf of the Socialists was not easy, as we were as little united as the bourgeois." Joseph Buttinger, *op. cit.*, pp. 578, 583.

46. Joseph Buttinger, *op. cit.*, p. 551.

47. *Ibid.*, p. 555. U.S. State Department File 863.01/689. PRO FO 371 30943 8378. "Great Britain and the Austrian Problem," June 25, 1942, Foreign Nationalities Branch, OSS 181655: The Revolutionary Socialists turned out even later to be "noncooperative," especially as after the fall of France their connection with the homeland was almost completely broken off.

48. Julius Deutsch, *op. cit.*, p. 313.

49. Joseph Buttinger, *op. cit.*, p. 555. Julius Deutsch, *op. cit.*, p. 315.

50. Joseph Buttinger, *op. cit.*, pp. 554, 578.

51. (Hans Rott), "Free Austria," *Free Austrian Movement* (folder). Rott provided a retrospective view of the Free Austrian Movement in April, 1945, covering all the contradictory relations from the beginning of the political emigration to the approaching end of the war. Karl Hans Sailer, "Aufgaben der Emigration," *Austrian Labor Information* (New York), No. 1 (April 20, 1942). Karl Hans Sailer, "Einigung der Österreicher—auf welches Zeil?" *Austrian Labor In-*

formation (New York), No. 6 (Sept. 20, 1942). Otto Bauer, *loc. cit. Austrian Labor Information* (New York), No. 15, (June 20, 1943). Friedrich Adler, "Die Legende vom glücklichen Österreich," *Austrian Labor Information* (New York), No. 20/21 (Nov./Dec., 1943). Friedrich Adler, "Zwei Jahre österreichische Labor-Information," *Austrian Labor Information* (New York), No. 24 (March/April, 1944).

52. U.S. State Department File 863.01/631. British Embassy, Paris, to Foreign Office, November 6, 1939, PRO FO 371 22940 8235 C 17995, reported that negotiations with Austrian exile groups were "absolutely nil."

53. Hans Rott, "Free Austria," *Free Austrian Movement* (folder). Karl Hans Sailer, *loc. cit.* Otto Bauer, *loc. cit.* Friedrich Adler, *loc. cit.*

54. Julius Deutsch, *op. cit.*, pp. 314, 315. "The Austrian Emigration and its Activities," May 7, 1942, OSS 16588 S, p. 3, reports that the Ligue Autrichienne was collaborating in Paris with the Social Democrats in the Service National Autrichien.

55. Julius Deutsch, *op. cit.*, p. 315. British Embassy, Paris, to Foreign Office, November 13, 1939, PRO FO 371 22940 8235 C 18527. British Embassy, Paris, to Foreign Office, December 19, 1939, PRO FO 371 22940 8235 C 20861. Telegram from British Embassy, Paris, December 23, 1939, PRO FO 371 24409 6054 No. 1686 (306/36/39). British Embassy, Paris, to Foreign Office, December 27, 1939, PRO FO 371 23104 8395 C 20929. British Embassy, Paris, to Foreign Office, January 3, 1940, PRO FO 371 24409 6054 C 210. British Embassy, Paris, to Foreign Office, December 19, 1939, PRO FO 371 23104 8395 C 20705. "The Hapsburg Problem," Jan. 30, 1940, PRO FO 371 24409 6054 C 2953. British Embassy, Paris, to Foreign Office, Dec. 11, 1939, PRO FO 371 23104 8395 C 20168. British Embassy, Paris, to Foreign Office, Dec. 12, 1939, PRO FO 371 23104 8395 C 20210.

56. Letter of recommendation from Section Chief Charles Rochat, June 10, 1940; letter of recommendation from Paris Archdiocese, June 10, 1940, PRO FO 371 22940 8235 C 20861.

57. Julius Deutsch, *op. cit.*, p. 316. This assumption was verified after the first release of documents of the British Foreign Office in 1972. Report from the British Embassy, Paris, February 6, 1940, PRO FO 371 24409 6054, No. 94. British Embassy, Paris, to Foreign Office, February 29, 1940, PRO FO 371 24409 6054 C 3246. Foreign Office memorandum, February 29, 1940, PRO FO 371 24409 6054 C 2500/G.

58. Julius Deutsch. *op. cit.*, p. 317.

59. Armistice agreement between Germany and France, June 22, 1940. Auswärtiges Amt, Akten zur deutschen auswärtigen Politik, 1941–1945, Series D, Vol. IX, pp. 554 ff. Carl Misch, "Es fiel die Zitadelle," *Aufbau* (New York), Vol. VI, No. 40 (Nov. 2, 1940).

60. I owe this information to M. Georges Dethan, Curator of the Library of the French Ministry of Foreign Affairs, who told me in July, 1968, that French documents were sent to such distant regions as Warsaw and were to be reassembled as far as they were existent. It was hoped that the results of these endeavors would provide more accurate sources for historic research. According to a report I received from the French Ministry of Foreign Affairs, Archives et Documentations, May 27, 1975, the documents found in Warsaw have no relevance for the Austrian emigration in France. Helmut Andics, *Der Fall Otto Habsburg* (Vienna: Verlag Fritz Molden, 1965), p. 110, states that Otto von Hapsburg was present at the "famous burning of documents" in the French Ministry of Foreign Affairs.

61. It is not without interest that an official publication such as *Austrian Information*, published by the Austrian Cultural Institute in New York, could state in an obituary for Ambassador Dr. Martin Fuchs that there existed an Austrian legion in France.

Chapter III   Austrian Political Emigration
in the United States to America's Entry into the war, 1941

1. Carl Misch, "Die Lager," *Aufbau* (New York), Vol. VI, No. 47 (Nov. 22, 1940), quotes the French law of October 2, 1940, which assigns general internment in work camps for men between the ages of seventeen and fifty-five. See also *Aufbau* (New York), Vol. VI, No. 30 (July 26, 1940).

2. *Aufbau* (New York), Vol. VII, No. 40 (Oct. 3, 1941). The Emergency Rescue Committee, founded for this purpose, and its representative, Valian Fry, did outstanding work. Hellmut Andics, *Der Fall Otto Habsburg,* p. 109, quotes Otto von Hapsburg as saying: "I now had all the Austrians on my shoulders." "The Austrian Emigration and Its Activity," May 7, 1942, OSS 16588 S, states that Otto von Hapsburg could obtain visas for the refugees, who later repaid him by working for his goals. Letter of British Embassy, Lisbon, and memorandum, September 29, 1940 PRO FO 371/24409 6054 C 10586.

3. (Hans Rott), memorandum from Walter von Schuschnigg, Lisbon, September 24, 1940, folder "Free Austrian Movement."

4. U.S. State Department File 863.01/631.

5. Julius Deutsch. *op. cit.,* p. 315.

6. Martin Fuchs, *op. cit.,* p. 248.

7. (Hans Rott), Wilhelm Wunsch, Secretary General of the Free Austrian Movement to Hans Rott, November 27, 1941, folder "Free Austrian Movement." British Embassy, Paris, to Foreign Office, October 20, 1939, PRO FO 371 23104 8395 C 17025: "The splitting up of the Austro-Hungarian Monarchy was not a practical or even a possible solution."

8. (Hans Rott), Wilhelm Wunsch to Hans Rott, Nov. 27, 1941, folder "Free Austrian Movement." "Organization and Status of the Free Austrian Movement in Canada," September 18, 1941, PRO FO 371 30910 8264.

9. (Hans Rott), Wilhelm Wunsch to Hans Rott, November 27, 1931, folder "Free Austrian Movement." Kurt Hellmer, "Wandlungen der österreichischen Sozialisten," *Aufbau* (New York), Vol. X, No. 11 (March 17, 1944).

10. (Hans Rott), Wilhelm Wunsch to Hans Rott, November 27, 1941, folder "Free Austrian Movement": Wunsch disagrees with the appointment of Baron Hano Friebeiss as deputy to Rott; he refers to the agreement of Lisbon.

11. Robert Rie, *Die Entwicklung der Anerkennungspolitik der Vereinigten Staaten von Amerika im 18. und 19. Jahrhundert,* Archiv für Völkerrecht, edited by Hans Jürgen Schlochauer (Tübingen: Verlag J. C. B. Mohr, 1964), Vol. II, Part 3, p. 283. E. Wilder Spaulding, *The Quiet Invaders* (Vienna: Österreichischer Bundesverlag für Unterricht, Wissenschaft und Kunst, 1963).

12. E. Wilder Spaulding, *op. cit.,* p. 46.

13. E. Wilder Spaulding states reasons for the development: *op. cit.,* pp. 1 ff. Vaclav L. Beneš, a modern historian, demonstrates the drawbacks of the Kossuth regime's rule in Slovakia in "The Slovaks in the Habsburg Empire: A Struggle for Existence," *Austrian History Yearbook, 1967* (Houston: Rice University, 1967), Vol. III, Part 2, pp. 346–355.

14. E. Wilder Spaulding, in *op. cit.,* even states that the Austro-American antagonism of 1815 to 1918 had disappeared as a result of the Treaty of St.-Germain. He claims that the end of the First World War was in this respect a happy turning point. This may be the first time that a historian has considered the peace of St.-Germain as a happy event, at least from the Austrian point of view. This opinion is not shared by Gordon Brook-Shepherd in *Dollfuss* (New York: St. Martin's Press, 1961), p. 25.

15. Contrary to present American historical studies, which examine the importance of the old Austro-Hungarian state also in relation to the political circumstances and aims of the present United States. See Andrew J. Whiteside, *Austrian History Yearbook, 1967,* Vol. III, Part 1, p. 200. E. Wilder Spaulding, *op. cit.,* pp. 8, 20. Robert Rie, *op. cit.*

16. Robert Rie, *op. cit.* E. Wilder Spaulding, *op. cit.,* p. 44.

17. Konstantin von Dumba, quoted by E. Wilder Spaulding, *op. cit.,* p. 77.

18. E. Wilder Spaulding, *op. cit.,* p. 44: "Most Americans disliked Austria not only because of Metternich, the Holy Alliance and the Catholicism . . . but because they knew almost nothing about it, and because what they did know seemed to indicate that Austrians and Americans had very little in common."

19. Hellmut Andics, *Der Staat, den keiner wollte* (Vienna: Verlag Herder, 1962), p. 108, quotes the statement of Georges Clemenceau at the Peace Conference of St.-Germain in 1920: "The rest is Austria."

20. (Hans Rott), Memoranda, November 24, 1938, and December 8, 1939, of Prof. Dr. R. Heine-Geldern's and Frank Harand's New York conversations with the former armaments factory

owner, Fritz Mandl: "Mandl further stated that he had not found any interest here among people of influence in the reestablishment of an independent Austria. He anticipates the trend of British policy to take hold here too." Even before, he had pointed out that the interests of Austria were in a bad way in Paris as well as in London (folder "Robert Heine-Geldern").

21. William C. Bullitt to President Roosevelt, September 5, 1939, FDR Library, File PSF France, Bullitt.

22. (Hans Rott), memorandum on a conversation of Prof. Dr. R. Heine-Geldern and Frank Harand with Dr. Lewis Mumford, Inter-Allied Information Center (New York), Nov., 1940, folder "Robert Heine-Geldern." Foreign Research and Press Service, Balliol College, Oxford, "Austria," August 27, 1941, PRO FO 371 26538 6032.

23. Charles C. Burlingham to President Roosevelt, Feb. 17, 1934, FDR Library, File OF 166, states that execution of socialist leaders would shake public opinion in the United States and England, and that it also would endanger the success of the Austrian trade delegation in the United States. Hellmut Andics, *Der Staat, den keiner wollte,* p. 538: "It is simply a fact that Austria is not too popular in London and in Paris, it has no moral credit there. In a decisive moment they will always remember that the Schuschnigg government, which is asking for help, is an authoritarian government. . . . World politics has nothing to do with morals. If London and Paris still had a burning interest in Austria, they would not have preferred peace with Hitler; it would have made no difference to them whether the Schuschnigg regime was a dictatorship or not. This way, however, considering the constant attempts to keep peace at any price, the discomfort with the authoritarian regime in Austria, does play a role."

24. Hellmut Andics, *Der Staat, den keiner wollte,* p. 310.

25. E. Wilder Spauling, *op. cit.,* p. 79: "Czechoslovakia achieved independence to become the favorite in America of all successor states, it was quite clearly 'made in America.' "

26. Gordon Brook-Shepherd, *Dollfuss,* gives a detailed description of the political circumstances that led to the establishment of the authoritarian federal state of Austria. "Austria," Aug. 27, 1941, PRO FO 371 26538 6032.

27. Brook-Shepherd, *op. cit.,* U.S. State Department File 863.01, No. 417. PRO FO 371 26538 6032.

28. Mexico to State Department, March 21, 1938, U.S. State Department File 863.00/1562: "The manner and the circumstances of the political death of Austria constitute a serious transgression of the covenant of the League of Nations and of the sacred principles of international law." Franklin D. Roosevelt, Press conference No. 442, March 15, 1938, Presidential Press Conferences of Franklin D. Roosevelt, FDR Library: The President announced that only the German Ambassador had informed the State Department about the disappearance of Austria as a sovereign country. State Department to President Roosevelt, April 27, 1938, FDR Library, File OF 133, states that the Austrian Ambassador announced on March 17, 1938, that Austria had ceased to exist as an independent nation. "Aufzeichnung des Vortragenden Legationsrates Freytag," March 30, 1938, Auswärtiges Amt, Akten zur deutschen auswärtigen Politik, Series D, Vol. V, p. 693.

29. Otto Bauer, *loc. cit.*

30. "K.H.," interview with Julius Deutsch, "Zwei Emigrationen," *Aufbau* (New York), Vol. VIII, No. 9 (Feb. 27, 1942).

31. "Statement of Policy," *Aufbau* (New York), Vol. VI, No. 21 (May 24, 1940). This was not the case in England, where at least during the war immigration was impossible, and for many people returning to the home country was the goal.

32. U.S. State Department File 863.01/661. "Policy Regarding Free Movements in the United States," U.S. State Department File 800.01/135. "The Free Movements Are on Their Own," *Aufbau* (New York), Vol. X, No. 10 (March 10, 1944): "However, in accordance with most reliable information we would like to reiterate that the State Department in no way changed its attitude, as outlined in December 1941, with regard to Free Movements."

33. The publishing efforts of the Austrian emigration consisted mostly of newsletters of the various Austrian organizations. However, they never reached a circulation comparable to the New York *Aufbau.*

34. *Aufbau* (New York), Vol. VI, No. 48 (Nov. 29, 1940), gives the following information

under "Ein Jahr Wochenausgabe": Sales of 3,000 copies in February, 1939, jumped to 18,000 in November, 1940.

35. Considerable advertising in the *Aufbau*.

36. "Statement of Policy," *Aufbau* (New York), was published from time to time such as Vol. VI, No. 21 (May 24, 1940) and No. 38 (September 20, 1940).

37. The noted journalist Harold Callender made this statement in the *New York Times,* May 21, 1943, under the title "U.S. Germans Fear Splitting of Reich." *Aufbau* (New York), Vol. IX, No. 22 (May 28, 1943), replied: "It is a serious mistake . . . if *Aufbau* and the German-Jewish immigrant community are in any way presented as belonging to the same category as German-Americans who have a different sociological orientation."

38. "In Sachen Habsburg," *Aufbau* (New York), Vol. IX, No. 9 (Feb. 20, 1943). Compare interview of Kurt Hellmer with Otto von Hapsburg in *Aufbau* (New York), Vol. VI, No. 10 (March 8, 1940), with the article by the same journalist in *Aufbau* (New York), Vol. X, No. 11 (March 17, 1944). Compare articles by Kurt Hellmer in *Aufbau* (New York) of 1941/1942 with his reports of 1943/1945 regarding Otto von Hapsburg and the Free Austrian Movement.

39. Hellmut Andics, *Der Staat, den keiner wollte,* p. 81, quotes the Chancellor of the First Austrian Republic, Dr. Karl Renner, before the departure of the Austrian peace delegation for Paris: "The Anschluss is an eternal right which we shall get for ourselves, even if we have to get it from the high heavens." It is true that the idea of the Anschluss was propagated mainly by the Austrian side.

40. Austrian lawyers were invited to join the German Federation of lawyers as full equals. Compare, however, with "Österreicher im Exil," *Aufbau* (New York), Vol. VI, No. 5 (Feb. 2, 1940), which points out the ways in which Austrian exiles were different.

41. (Hans Rott), Ernst Karl Winter, the former vice-mayor of Vienna, to Hans Rott, July 24, 1942, folder "Ernst Karl Winter": He asks Hans Rott's help regarding the loss of his job as visiting professor at New York's New School for Social Research, including a copy of his letter to Dr. Johnson, the president of the school. This letter mentions that he was let go because "he is too much of an Austrian," concerning himself with Austrian problems. Winter mentions that the German faculty members are his political opponents. Hans Rott to Ernst Karl Winters, July 24, 1942: "It is abominable that Johnson states that your Austrian point of view should be the reason for firing you."

42. John C. Wiley, American Consul in Vienna, to State Department, February 19, 1938, U.S. State Department File 762.63/484: This is perhaps the most detailed description of these critical times by a foreign diplomatic observer. Mr. Wiley points out that the Social Democrats had collaborated directly or indirectly with the official labor organizations of the authoritarian regime at that point and that the labor leaders and the membership had supported Schuschnigg's government.

43. (Hans Rott), Conference of Prof. Heine-Geldern and Mrs. Irene Harand with Jan Masaryk in New York, March 30, 1939, folder "Robert Heine-Geldern."

44. Vaclav L. Beneš, *loc. cit.,* p. 392, states: "A remarkable phenomenon in Slovak national life from the end of the nineteenth century on was the impact of the activities of Slovak immigrants in the United States. . . . The activity made itself especially felt not only in the western but also in the eastern areas of Slovakia, where the level of political and national consciousness was relatively low."

45. Otto von Hapsburg to President Roosevelt, August 27, 1942, FDR Library, File PPF 8151, refers to conference of August 26, 1942, and the President's support of Austrians' and Hungarians' efforts. Hellmut Andics, *Der Fall Otto Habsburg,* pp. 124 ff, deals with Otto's attempts to help Hungary.

46. Assistant Secretary Adolf A. Berle, Jr., to President Roosevelt, October 15, 1942, FDR Library, File PSF State Department.

47. E. W. Spaulding, *op. cit.,* p. 47: "Indeed, the reverence in which Italians and Americans have long held the Italian heroes who fought the Austrians in those times has contributed to the Anti-Austrianism in the United States." (Hans Rott), Conference of Prof. Heine-Geldern and Mrs. Irene Harand with Jan Masaryk in New York, March 30, 1939, folder "Robert Heine-Geldern." These minutes state that the Mayor of New York, Fiorello La Guardia, still referred to old

Austria in his speeches as "a peoples' jail." Masaryk said that he would instruct La Guardia to omit insults to Austria in the future. Masaryk even tried to reach by telephone a certain Mrs. Epstein, whom he called La Guardia's left and right hand.

48. Piotr S. Wandycz and Henry Wereszyki, *Austrian History Yearbook, 1967*, Vol. III, Part 2, pp. 261 ff, state that all Polish political parties in the Austro-Hungarian monarchy supported the government from 1867 until the turn of the century; that the majority of Polish political circles defended the monarchy almost up to its collapse; and that they were interested in a lasting connection with the monarchy after the establishment of a Polish national state.

49. "In Sachen Habsburg," *Aufbau* (New York), Vol. IX, No. 9 (Feb. 26, 1943), turns against the sentimental point of view of many emigrants from the Hapsburg monarchy. But the article finally states that "nobody had ever argued the fact that Jews had it better under Hapsburgs than in other countries, but to mix up the Hapsburg question with one of Jews, that would be impossible."

50. Oskar Karbach, *loc. cit.*

51. *Österreichische Post* (Paris), Nos. 13/14 (July, 1939).

52. Joseph Buttinger, *op. cit.*, p. 351. Memorandum of the Coordinator of Information, February 6, 1942, OSS 11314, Foreign Nationalities Branch, p. 3: "The average Austrian émigré and refugee is very poor. Most of them were taken completely by surprise in March, 1938." "A Survey of the Austrian Political Emigration," April 11, 1945, OSS 2853, states that Adler, Bauer, Ellenbogen, Deutsch, and Heinz were designated managers and factual owners of Vorwärts A.G., the publisher of the *Arbeiterzeitung* and of the *Kleines Blatt*. After Bauer's death in 1938 his part was divided among the others. PRO FO 371 30911 8273 C 12767, concerning Rott's financial situation: "The poor old fellow has nothing to live on at all. He gets his coffee from the few contributions which come in from members. In short it is disastrous." OSS 16588 S, "The Austrian Emigration and its Activity," May 7, 1942, contains the remark that Otto von Hapsburg is the one with money.

53. (Hans Rott), Wilhelm Wunsch to Hans Rott, June 17, 1942, folder "Free Austrian Movement."

54. "Wandlungen der Österreichischen Monarchisten," *Aufbau* (New York), Vol. X, No. 11 (March 17, 1944). Hans Rott to Ferdinand Czernin, April 16, 1942, folder "Austrian National Committee."

55. (Hans Rott), newsletter *Free Austria,* No. 1, March 1943, folder "Free Austrian Movement." "Wandlungen der österreichischen Monarchisten," *Aufbau* (New York), Vol. X, No. 11 (March 17, 1944). OSS 19407, "The reorganized National Committee," August 7, 1942, maintains that Rott insisted the Austrian people should have the right to choose their head of government after the war.

56. Julius Deutsch, *op. cit.*, p. 315.

57. U.S. State Department File 863.01/6–2944.

58. (Hans Rott), Curriculum vitae of Dr. Ernst Karl Winter and a letter of July 24, 1942, concerning his being fired by the New School for Social Research after four years of teaching, folder "Ernst Karl Winter."

59. (Hans Rott), Prof. Robert Heine-Geldern, Memorandum (no date), about his relations with the Austro-American Center, folder "Robert Heine-Geldern." "Great Britain and the Austrian Problem," June 25, 1942, Foreign Nationalities Branch, OSS 18165 S.

60. (Hans Rott), Prof. Robert Heine-Geldern, Memorandum, April 3, 1939, folder "Robert Heine-Geldern." The Certificate of Incorporation of the Austrian-American League was not filed until November 3, 1939, OSS 18165 S.

61. (Hans Rott), Conference of Prof. Robert Heine-Geldern and Mrs. Irene Harand with Jan Masaryk in New York, March 30, 1939, folder "Robert Heine-Geldern."

62. *Ibid.*

63. *Ibid.* When conversation turned to Otto von Hapsburg, Jan Masaryk said, "Well, you will have to be careful. The main obstacles are Serbia and Romania; King Alexander for instance said to me, 'If you mention the Hapsburgs to me once more, I am going to shoot you . . . !' And King Carol said, 'Ileana married a Hapsburg and is not allowed to go to Romania, and you talk Hapsburgs to me.' Our Czechs are not ready either. When you talk with Dr. Beneš, be careful

with legitimism, he is not ready yet.'' "Otto von Hapsburg," May 14, 1943, Foreign Nationalities Branch, OSS 34484 S: "The visit of President Beneš of Czechoslovakia brings to mind the person already for years in the United States who is the direct antithesis of all that Beneš represents and whom Beneš himself regards as his ultimate antagonist in the European scene.''

64. (Hans Rott), Conferences of Prof. Robert Heine-Geldern and Frank Harand with Fritz Mandl, Nov. 24, 1939, and Dec. 8, 1939, folder "Robert Heine-Geldern.''

65. (Hans Rott), folder "Free Austrian Movement.'' Appeal, "Free Austrian Movement in Canada," September 18, 1941, PRO FO 371 30910 8264.

66. U.S. State Department File 863.01/652 1/2.

67. Several letters of thanks and telegram from Otto von Hapsburg and Empress Zita to President Roosevelt; Count Heinrich Degenfeld to Grace G. Tully, the personal secretary of the president, November 14, 1944, in which the writer extends thanks for the friendliness shown to the imperial family between 1940 and 1944, FDR Library, File PPF 9036. Otto von Hapsburg to President Roosevelt, November 19, 1942, FDR Library, File PPF 8151. U.S. State Department File 863.0011/74 and 863.0011/75. "Great Britain and the Austrian Problem" June 25, 1942, OSS 18165 S, states that Otto von Hapsburg was the only Austrian in exile who could have brought unity in 1939–1940. British Embassy, Washington, to Foreign Office, March 9, 1940, PRO FO 371 24409 6054 C 4562, with memorandum from John Wheeler Bennett of March 5, 1940, about Otto von Hapsburg.

68. Certificate of Incorporation of Austrian Action, April 5, 1941, PRO FO 371 26537 6027: Ferdinand Czernin became active immediately (April 22, 1941) and wanted to put Austrian doctors at the disposal of the British government when it appealed for a thousand foreign doctors.

69. Hans Rott to Dr. Plöchl, February 17, 1941, Christian Willars, *Die böhmische Zitadelle* (Vienna: Verlag Fritz Molden, 1965), p. 199. Karl-Heinz Mattern, *op. cit.*

70. (Hans Rott), Dr. Willibald Plöchl to Hans Rott, January 12, 1941, folder "Willibald Plöchl.''

71. Article 81, par. 2: "The Federal Chancellor will be represented in his absence by the Vice-Chancellor. Should the Federal Chancellor and the Vice-Chancellor be absent at the same time, then the President will name a member of the government to replace the Chancellor.'' Article 77, par. 1: "If the President is unavailable or disqualified, his duties will devolve on the Federal Chancellor.''

72. Hans Rott, folder "Willibald Plöchl.''

73. Registration statement. State Department File 863.01 B 11. "Österreichische Aktion, Eine neue Kampftruppe österreichischer Emigranten," *Aufbau* (New York), Vol. VII, No. 14 (April 4, 1941): "In New York a group of emigrants formed an Anti-Nazi organization called Österreichische Aktion, whose president will be Count Ferdinand Czernin, the son of the former Austrian Minister of War.''

74. "Grosse Kundgebung des New World Club," February 6, 1941, *Aufbau* (New York), Vol. VII, No. 5 (Jan. 31, 1941).

75. In a conversation with the Undersecretary of State Joseph C. Grew in January, 1945, Ferdinand Czernin referred—without success—to the attempts made by his father to reach a separate peace, which confirms this theory (U.S. State Department File 863.01/1–1145).

76. U.S. State Department File 863.01 B 11. "Austrian to Fight Nazi Spying Here," *The New York Times*, April 9, 1941.

77. Coordinator of Information to Secretary of State, November 10, 1941, U.S. State Department File 863.01/664, 7/14: Czernin says that a certain Bittner has "Otto tendencies.'' "Scratch an Austrian and you find Otto.''

78. U.S. State Department File 863.00/7–645: Czernin says that Czechoslovak Foreign Minister Jan Masaryk claimed that Czernin was the only Austrian whom the Czechs could trust.

79. U.S. State Department File 863.00/4190. U.S. State Department File 863.01/653. U.S. State Department File 863.01/660. Dr. Willibald Plöchl to Sir R. I. Campbell, British Embassy, Washington, September 23, 1941, PRO FO 371 23941 26539 8302. John Wheeler Bennett, "Austrian Political Refugees in the United States," October, 1941, PRO FO 371 26539 C 13169/280/18, is the first attempt to classify the political refugees from Austria. British Embassy, Washington, to Foreign Office, September 26, 1941; and memorandum, September 26, 1941,

PRO FO 371 26538 8296 C 10793, concern the legality of Hans Rott's demands as successor to the Schuschnigg government.

80. U.S. State Department File 863.01/660. U.S. State Department File 800.01/148. U.S. State Department File 863.01/854. Department of State, Division of European Affairs, Memorandum, December 7, 1943, U.S. State Department File 863.01/850.

81. "Österreicher-Protest," *Aufbau* (New York), Vol. VI, No. 40 (October 3, 1941).

82. *Aufbau* (New York), Vol. VI, No. 42 (October 17, 1941).

83. U.S. State Department File 863.01/664, 5/14.

84. Hans Rott to Department of State, U.S. State Department File 863.01/675, announces disbanding of the Austrian National Council and the resignation of Dr. Willibald Plöchl as its representative in Washington. (Hans Rott), Prof. Robert Heine-Geldern to Congressman Eberharter, August 1, 1942, folder "Robert Heine-Geldern."

85. U.S. State Department File 863.01/651. Foreign Secretary Anthony Eden, Circular, June 18, 1941, PRO FO 371 26539 8302 C 4523/2951/18.

86. U.S. State Department File 863.01/651.

87. U.S. State Department File 863.01/652 1/2.

88. U.S. State Department File 863.01/657. PRO FO 371 30911 8273 C 12767.

89. U.S. State Department File 863.01/652 1/2. Joseph Buttinger, *op. cit.*, p. 596.

90. U.S. State Department File 863/01/655. U.S. State Department File 863.01/659. Morgenthau Diaries, Book 449, p. 150, FDR Library.

91. U.S. State Department File 863.01/664, 13/14. PRO FO 371 30910 8264. PRO FO 371 30910 8264 C 158/46/18.

92. U.S. State Department File 863.01/664–1/14. U.S. State Department File 863.01/664–2/14.

93. White House memorandum, March 6, 1940, FDR Library, File OF 166, concerns William C. Bullitt's arrangements for receiving Otto von Hapsburg in the White House.

94. William C. Bullitt to President Roosevelt, September 5, 1939, FDR Library, File PSF France, Bullitt.

95. U.S. State Department File 762.63/484. John C. Wiley, Chargé d'Affaires at interim, to Secretary of State, February 19, 1938, FDR Library. U.S. State Department File 863.01/572. U.S. State Department File 863.01/573. Report No. 68, December 28, 1938, U.S. State Department File, U.S. Legation, Vienna. "Otto von Hapsburg," May 14, 1943, Foreign Nationalities Branch, OSS 34484 S.

96. U.S. State Department File 762.63/484. John C. Wiley, *loc. cit.* U.S. State Department File 863/01/572. U.S. State Department File 863/01/573..

97. Adolf Schärf, *Österreichs Erneuerung* (Vienna, 1955).

98. Otto von Hapsburg to President Roosevelt, August 27, 1942, FDR Library, File PPF.

99. U.S. State Department File 664.11/14: Lyle Kennedy, who belonged to a pro-Austrian American group, thought that Otto von Hapsburg was the main reason for the disunity of the Austrian groups and that he created factions. Alexander Vodopivec, *Die Balkanisierung Österreichs* (Vienna: Verlag Fritz Molden, 1966), p. 314.

100. U.S. War Department File 302.2. *The Rubicon, Criscuolo Newsletter* (Washington, D.C.), December 15, 1942.

101. U.S. State Department File 863.01/631. U.S. State Department File 740.0011 European War 1939/1780.

102. "Versuch einer Täuschung," *Aufbau* (New York), Vol. IX, No. 7 (February 12, 1943). In this article Otto von Hapsburg is blamed by the German writer Emil Ludwig for adopting the name "Otto von Österreich," because this implies the claim to be head of the Austrians.

103. Austrian Labor Committee to Secretary of State Cordell Hull, January 16, 1942, U.S. State Department File 863.01/730.

104. *Aufbau* (New York), Vol. X, No. 37 (September 15, 1944).

105. U.S. State Department File 762/63/484. John C. Wiley, *loc. cit.* U.S. State Department File 863/01/572. U.S. State Department File 863.01/573.

106. Memorandum of a conversation between Otto von Hapsburg and the Assistant Secretary of State, October 16, 1941, U.S. State Department File 863.01/656.

107. U.S. State Department File 800.01/135.

108. (Hans Rott), Conference of Robert Heine-Geldern and Mrs. Irene Harand with Jan Masaryk in New York, March 30, 1939, folder "Robert Heine-Geldern."

109. U.S. State Department File 863.01/663. Memorandum, Foreign Office, PRO FO 371 34353 8428 C 6781.

110. U.S. State Department File 800.01/115. U.S. State Department File 800.01/203. U.S. State Department File 800.01/119–42. Circular of the Foreign Office about the German and Austrian Free Movements, June 18, 1941, PRO FO 371 26539 8302 C 4523/2951/18.

111. U.S. State Department File 800.01/19–42. U.S. State Department File 800.01/203. Foreign Office guidelines for the Free Movements, March 17, 1942, PRO FO 371 30866 8381 C 2013/669/62: Only the Danish Council receives special treatment.

Chapter IV Austrian Political Emigration in the United States after 1941

1. "Summary of Proclamations of the President of the United States of December 7 and 8, 1941, and January 14, 1942, and of Regulations of the Attorney General thereunder, 1942, prescribing the conduct to be observed by Aliens of Enemy Nationality," U.S. Justice Department, Form AR-AE.

2. FDR Library, File OF 133–A, 1941.

3. Methodist Church of Chicago, Commission of World Peace, to President Roosevelt, January 19, 1942, FDR Library, points out the humane treatment of enemy aliens. FDR Library, File OF 10–misc. 1933 to 1942, consists of letters which object to the excessively lenient treatment of enemy aliens.

4. U.S. State Department File 863.01/12–2744.

5. U.S. State Department File 863.01/661.

6. FDR Library, File OF 133–A 1941.

7. U.S. State Department File 811.142/10714. "Registration Austrian Action," U.S State Department File 800.01 B 11.

8. U.S. State Department File 863.01/664, 12/14.

9. *Austrian Action* (Newsletter), February 4, 1942.

10. U.S. State Department File 863.01/733.

11. U.S. State Department File 863.01/730. U.S. State Department File 863.01/3-1042. *Austrian Labor Information* (New York), No. 1 (April 20, 1942). A memorandum of February 6, 1942, OSS 11314, stated that the Socialists have contributed nothing to removing the stigma of "enemy alien" from the Austrians. "Austrian Politics in Great Britain, May 30, 1944, OSS 88818, mentions that also in Great Britain no organization, except the Free Austrian Movement, was willing to assume the stigma of being a refugee organization. This was especially true of the Austrian socialists in London, who, unlike the Free Austrian Movement, wanted to have nothing to do with refugees. Memorandum, March 14, 1944, OSS XL 1244: "They are not interested in organizing the émigrés, but quite the contrary take a very critical view toward them."

12. U.S. State Department File 863.01/668.

13. Edward J. Ennis, Director of Alien Control, to United States Attorney, Knoxville, Tennessee, February 13, 1943; Edward J. Ennis to United States Attorney, Richmond, Virginia, February 10, 1942, U.S. Justice Department File 146–13–016. Hellmut Andics, *Der Fall Otto Habsburg*, p. 121, states that his success was due to Otto von Hapsburg and that the art dealer Kallir, thanks to his connections, had opened the way to the Ministry of Justice. *Austrian Action* (Newsletter), February 4, 1942, takes credit for this organization. *Österreichische Rundschau* (Newsletter), April 11, 1942, takes credit for the establishment of the Austrian National Committee. Memorandum Coordinator of Information: Foreign Nationalities Branch, OSS 11314.

14. Memorandum to Mr. Ennis, Director of Alien Control, January 9, 1942, U.S. Justice Department File 146–13–016. OSS 11314.

15. U.S. Justice Department File 146–13–016.

16. U.S. State Department File 842.00–B/109. FDR Library, File OF 133–A 1941.

17. FDR Library, File OF 133–A 1941.

18. (Hans Rott), Dr. Robert Plank to Hans Rott, March 4 and 30, 1943, folder "Free Austrian Movement."

19. U.S. State Department File 863.00/5–2142. "Austrians are Enemy Aliens for the Draft Board," *Aufbau* (New York), Vol. VIII, No. 23 (June 5, 1942).

20. War Department press release, May 21, 1942, *Aufbau* (New York), Vol. VIII, No. 14 (April 3, 1942).

21. U.S. State Department File 863.00/5–2142. "The German Group Neubeginnen," *Aufbau* (New York), Vol. VIII, No. 26 (June 26, 1942). PRO FO 371 26538 6032.

22. U.S. State Department File 863.00/5–2242. William C. Bullitt to President Roosevelt, June 20, 1938, FDR Library, File PSF France, William C. Bullitt, 1938, praises the exceptional work of John C. Wiley, Chargé d'Affaires ad interim, in Vienna at the time of the Anschluss, suggests rewarding him with the post of Ambassador in Riga, and tries to argue against the negative feelings of the Secretary of State, Cordell Hull, toward Mr. Wiley.

23. U.S. State Department File 863.00/5–2242.

24. U.S. State Department File 863.00/6–642. U.S. State Department File 863.00/5–2142. (Hans Rott), Many letters in which Austrian immigrants request help in reclassification, folder "Free Austrian Movement." Requests of the same kind were undoubtedly sent also to Austrian Action. In the registration of foreigners, the Selective Service System and the American registration offices had registered Austrians as "Austrians," "Germans," and "Stateless persons," reflecting the vague position of the United States toward the Anschluss. Only with the Justice Department ruling of June 11, 1942, had the former Austrian nationals who had been registered as Germans in 1940 been given the opportunity for correction.

25. U.S. State Department File 863.00/7–2042.

26. FDR Library, File OF 166–A.

27. U.S. State Department File 863.01/681. British Embassy, Washington, to Foreign Office, February 18, 1942, PRO FO 371 30942 8374 C 1880. Aide-mémoire, March 5, 1942, PRO FO 371 30942 8374 C 2570.

28. U.S. State Department File 863.01/680. *Österreichische Rundschau* (New York), March 7, 1942. Harrison memorandum, February 21, 1942, PRO FO 371 30942 8374 C 2400. Harrison memorandum, February 27, 1942, PRO FO 371 30942 8374 C 2401/1364/18. Parliamentary question by Mr. Mander, March 4, 1942, PRO FO 371 30910 8264 C 2428. The correct spelling is "Franckenstein," but some American and British documents also use "Frankenstein," see Foreign Office to J. R. Colville, January 23, 1945, PRO FO 371 46593 8438 C 86/6G. OSS 39372 C.

29. U.S. State Department File 863.01/679.

30. U.S. State Department File 863.00/683. U.S. State Department File 863.01/689 1/2. British Embassy, Washington, to Foreign Office, February 18, 1942, PRO FO 371 30942 8374 C 1880, discusses releasing Austrians from the status of enemy aliens. Anthony Eden, "Free National Movements in the United Kingdom," October 7, 1942, PRO FO 371 30911 8273 C 9306/46/18, takes an opposite position.

31. U.S. State Department File 863.00/5–2242. U.S. State Department File 800/01/206.

32. U.S. State Department File 800/01/257.

33. U.S. State Department File 800.01/135. U.S. State Department File 800.01/145 1/2.

34. U.S. State Department File 800.01/148.

35. U.S. State Department File 800.01/148. PRO FO 371 30910 8264. "The Austrian Emigration in Great Britain," July 7, 1944, OSS XL 1615.

36. U.S. State Department File 800.01/148. "Declaration of the Austrian Society in Great Britain," PRO FO 371 26539 8302 C 13372. Foreign Office Memorandum, "Germany Confidential," March 12, 1942, PRO FO 371 30910 8264 C 2281/1364/18.

37. U.S. State Department File 863.01/148. Association of Austrian Christian Socialists in Great Britain to the Editor of *The London Sunday Times,* December 18, 1941, PRO FO 371 26539 8302: the Association states that it is not represented by the Free Austrian Movement.

38. U.S. State Department File 800.01/145 1/2. U.S. State Department File 800.01/257.

39. U.S. State Department File 800.01/135. U.S. State Department File 800.01/257. U.S.

State Department File 800.01/145 1/2. U.S. State Department File 842.00–B/109. Foreign Office to USA, Statement on Free Movements, March 17, 1942, PRO FO 371 30866 8381 C 2013/669/62. Only the Danish Council had the open support of the British government.

40. U.S. State Department File 863.01/721 1/2.

41. U.S. State Department File 800.01/257.

42. *Austrian Action* (Newsletter), February 4, 1942. Hans Rott to Dr. Walter Goldschmidt, New Orleans, February 6, 1942; Hans Rott, Address at the constitutional meeting of the Austrian National Committee, February 14, 1942, folder "Austrian National Committee." *Aufbau* (New York), Vol. VIII, No. 8 (February 20, 1942). British Embassy, Washington, to Foreign Office, May 9, 1942, PRO FO 371 30910 8264 C 13264, reports that the State Department approved the Austrian National Committee.

43. *Austrian Labor Information* (New York), No. 1 (April 20, 1942). British Embassy, Washington, to Foreign Office, May 13, 1942, PRO FO 371 30910 8264.

44. U.S. State Department File 863.01/3–1042. *Österreichische Rundschau* (New York), March 7, 1942. *Aufbau* (New York), Vol. VIII, No. 10 (March 6, 1942).

45. U.S. State Department File 863.01/675.

46. *Austrian Action* (Newsletter), February 4, 1942.

47. U.S. State Department File 842.00–B/109. Hans Rott to Ferdinand Czernin, April 16, 1942, replies to Czernin's letter of March 18, 1942, folder "Austrian National Committee." *Aufbau* (New York), Vol. VIII, No. 16 (April 17, 1942). British Embassy, Washington, to Foreign Office, May 13, 1942, PRO FO 371 30910 8264. British Embassy, Washington, to Foreign Office, August 18, 1942, PRO FO 371 30911 8273 C 8340. Memorandum, "The Reorganized Austrian National Committee," August 7, 1942, OSS 19407: Hans Rott and Guido Zernatto had retired, Dietrich von Hildebrand had resigned. The idea of reorganizing was to make the Austrian National Committee more palatable to the Social Democrats. The Assembly for a Democratic Republic of Austria was founded by younger socialists in New York who were dissatisfied with the policy of Dr. Friedrich Adler and Julius Deutsch and who wanted to renounce the possibility of Anschluss and were willing to cooperate with any group that would guarantee a democratic postwar Austria.

48. U.S. State Department File 740.00/11, European War 1939/19991; see also U.S. State Department File 863.01/685.

49. U.S. State Department File 863.01/7–698.

50. U.S. State Department File 863.00/7–2242.

51. U.S. State Department File 863.00/7–2542. U.S. State Department File 863.00/1818. U.S. State Department File 863.00/1819.

52. State Department press release, July 27, 1942, U.S. State Department File 863.00/1819. "K.H.," "Die Causa Austria," *Aufbau* (New York), Vol. VIII, No. 31 (July 31, 1942).

53. U.S. State Department File 863.00/1819. U.S. State Department File 863.01/648 speaks altogether differently about a "De-jure sovereignty." (Hans Rott), James G. MacDonald, Interview with Otto von Hapsburg. British Embassy, Washington, to Foreign Office, August 8, 1942, PRO FO 371 30943 8378 C 8007, reports that Cordell Hull had made the statement only with hesitation; in fact it meant only a repetition of previous statements. The Free Austrian Movement in Great Britain called for nonrecognition of the Anschluss (Aide-mémoire, July 31, 1942, PRO FO 371 30911 8273 C 7606).

54. U.S. State Department File 863.00/1818. U.S. State Department File 863.00/1819. "K.H.," "Die Causa Austria," *Aufbau* (New York), Vol. VIII, No. 31 (July 31, 1942).

55. U.S. State Department File 863.00/1817. Memorandum, February 6, 1942, Foreign Nationalities Branch, OSS 11314.

56. U.S. State Department File 863.01/3–1042.

57. U.S. State Department File 863.01/709. U.S. State Department File 863.01/711. Anthony Eden, Statement, October 7, 1942, PRO FO 371 30911 8273 C 9306/46/18.

58. U.S. State Department File 863.01/796.

Chapter V.   The Austrian Battalion
in the Army of the United States

1. *The New York Times,* September 15, 1939, and October 10, 1939. William C. Bullitt to President Roosevelt, September 5, 1939, FDR Library, File PPF William C. Bullitt. Joseph Buttinger, *Am Beispiel Österreichs, op. cit.,* p. 597. British Foreign Office to Major-General F. G. Beaumont-Nesbitt, October 10, 1939, PRO FO 371 22940 8235 C 15717 C.

2. Karl-Heinz Mattern, *op. cit.* Christian Willars, *op. cit.,* p. 204.

3. FDR Library, File PPF 9036.

4. Zita von Hapsburg to President Roosevelt, July 20, 1940, and November 9, 1944, FDR Library, File PPF 9036: The Empress thanked the President for his hospitality in 1940, and, in the latter communication, congratulated him on his reelection and recalled their sharing tea at the Quebec Conference.

5. FDR Library, File PPF 9036.

6. War Department General Staff Organization and Training Division G–3, Memorandum, October 25, 1942, U.S. War Department, General Staff WDGCT 320.02 (8–29–42); and WDGCT 320 (10–25–42).

7. U.S. War Department, General Staff WDGCT 320.02 (8–29–42).

8. War Department, General Staff Organization and Training Division G–3, Memorandum, U.S. War Department File WDGCT 320.2 (10–21–42).

9. Memorandum for Chief of Staff, October 25, 1952, U.S. War Department File WDGCT 320 (10–25–42).

10. War Department General Staff Organization and Training Division G–3, Memorandum, September 24, 1942, U.S. War Department File WDGCT 320 (9–24–42).

11. War Department General Staff Organization and Training Division G–3, Memorandum, September 24, 1942, U.S. War Department File 320 (9–19–42). U.S. War Department File 320.2 (9–21–42).

12. Memorandum, September 24, 1942, U.S. War Department File 320 Austria (9–24–42).

13. War Department Organization and Training Division G–3, Memorandum, October 25, 1942, U.S. War Department File WDGCT 320.02 (10–24–42).

14. U.S. War Department File 320 Austria.

15. War Department General Staff Organization and Training Division G–3, Memorandum, Nov. 17, 1942, U.S. War Department File WDGCT 320 (11–17–42).

16. Sumner Welles to President Roosevelt, August 30, 1942, FDR Library, File PSF Sumner Welles.

17. U.S. State Department File 863.01/115.

18. U.S. State Department File 863.01/758. British Embassy, Washington, to Foreign Office, November 26, 1942, PRO FO 371 30911 6051 C 12118, states that neither Cordell Hull nor the British government had been informed about the planned press conference.

19. U.S. State Department File 863.01/721 1/2. Secretary of War Henry Stimson to Secretary of State Cordell Hull, November 2, 1942, U.S. War Department File 320.01. Ambassador Viscount Halifax, Report, November 7, 1942, PRO FO 371 30911 8273 C 11279, declares that Undersecretary of State Berle personally hopes that nothing becomes of the plan for a battalion, and that the War Department is not especially interested in the matter.

20. War Department General Staff Organization and Training Division G–3, Memorandum, November 17, 1942, U.S. War Department WDGCT 320 (11–17–42); U.S. War Department File WDGCT (11–10–42). British Embassy, Washington, to Foreign Office, November 24, 1942, PRO FO 371 30911 8273 C 11642, reports that Undersecretary Berle did not agree; he was not informed, however, that the position of the War Department toward the matter of the battalion had changed.

21. Memorandum, November 10, 1942, U.S. War Department WDGCT (11–10–42). U.S. State Department File 863.01/716. "Aus dem österreichischen Lager," *Aufbau* (New York), Vol. VIII, No. 51 (December 18, 1942), contains Mr. Berle's correction, communicated to the *Washington Post,* to the effect that he had not thought up the Austrian battalion. British Embassy, Washington, to Foreign Office, Nov. 24, 1942, PRO FO 371 30911 8273 C 11642.

22. Secretary of War Henry L. Stimson to President Roosevelt, November 13, 1942, U.S. War Department File 320.

23. President Roosevelt, Memorandum, November 17, 1942, U.S. War Department File 320: "I have every sympathy with your note of November 13, in regard to the advisability of encouraging Americanization in the Army. Therefore, I would agree with your argument were it not for two facts: (a) we already have a Norwegian battalion, Filipino units and a Japanese battalion. Therefore the creation of one or two small units would create no precedent. (b) The memo from Staff points out in the preceding last paragraph that formation of such battalions should be strictly limited to cases where political advantages are to be gained. That is why I hope the matter will be kept open and, of course, I must be the one to determine political advantages, if any. I have no desire for any large unit. Even if the numbers were small enough only for a company, the objective would be achieved, . . . " British Embassy, Washington, to Foreign Office, Nov. 24, 1942, PRO FO 371 30911 8273 C 11642. Austrian Major of the German Army to Archduke Robert, June 23, 1941, PRO FO 371 28537 6027 C 7552, declares he would be satisfied with fifty men for an Austrian troop unit.

24. War Department General Staff Organization and Training Division G–3, Memorandum, U.S. War Department File WDGCT (11–17–42). War Department Bureau of Public Relations, press release, November 19, 1942, U.S. War Department File 320.2. British Embassy, Washington, to Foreign Office, Nov. 24, 1942, PRO FO 371 30911 8273 C 11642.

25. Military Committee for the Liberation of Austria to Secretary of War Henry L. Stimson, November 19, 1942, and his answer of the same day, U.S. War Department File 320.2 (11–19–42). PRO FO 371 30911 6051 C 12118.

26. U.S. State Department File 863.01/717.

27. Julius Deutsch, *op. cit.,* pp. 361, 362.

28. U.S. State Department File 800.01/257.

29. U.S. State Department File 863.01/719.

30. U.S. State Department File 863.01/148.

31. U.S. State Department File 863.00/11–2142.

32. U.S. War Department File 302.2 (11–22–42).

33. U.S. War Department File 320.2 (11–27–42).

34. U.S. War Department File 320.2 (11–27–42).

35. U.S. War Department File WDCSA 320.02 095, Ferdinand Czernin (11–29–42).

36. U.S. War Department File 320.02.

37. U.S. State Department File 863.01/726.

38. U.S. State Department File 863.01/726. British Embassy, Washington, to Foreign Office, February 6, 1943, PRO FO 371 34417 C 1870 Ref. 29/4/43, reported that Secretary Hull had informed the Ambassador he had not been in favor of the Austrian battalion; the decision, however, had been made without his consent.

39. U.S. State Department File 863.01/724. U.S. War Department File 320.02.

40. U.S. State Department File 863.01/724.

41. U.S. War Department File 320.2.

42. U.S. State Department File 863.01/731.

43. *Freiheit für Österreich* (New York), No. 7 (December 15, 1942).

44. Adjutant General's Office, Memorandum, December 7, 1942, U.S. War Department File W 615–63–42. "Der Kampf um das österreichische Bataillon," *Aufbau* (New York), Vol. X, No. 49 (December 4, 1942).

45. U.S. State Department File 863.01/732.

46. War Department General Staff Organization and Training Division G–3, "Die Kampagne gegen den Erzherzog," by S. Gould, C. Sp. USNTS, December 4, 1942, U.S. War Department File 320.02.

47. Secretary of War Henry L. Stimson, press conference, November 27, 1942; War Department Administrative Assistant John W. Martyn to Ferdinand Czernin, December 18, 1942, U.S. War Department File 320.02.

48. War Department Organization and Training Division G–3 to Special Assistant Harvey H. Bundy, November 25, 1942, U.S. War Department File 320.02. British Foreign Office to Brit-

ish War Office, November 18, 1942, PRO FO 371 34420 8403 C 13449/39/18, concerns the possible establishment of an Austrian fighting unit and the use of outside volunteers.

49. Special Assistant Harvey H. Bundy, Memorandum, December 16, 1942, U.S. War Department File 320.02. PRO FO 371 34420 8403.

50. Special Assistant Harvey H. Bundy, Memorandum, November 25, 1942, U.S. War Department File 320.02.

51. War Department Organization and Training Division G–3, November 25, 1942, U.S. War Department File 320.02 WDGCT (11–25–42).

52. Otto von Hapsburg to President Roosevelt, August 27, 1942, FDR Library, File PPF 8151.

53. Karl-Heinz Mattern, *op. cit.* Christian Willars, *op. cit.*

54. Sumner Welles to President Roosevelt, August 30, 1942, FDR Library, File PSF Sumner Welles.

55. U.S. War Department File 320.02 (10–25–42).

56. Undersecretary of State Robert Patterson to Eleanor Roosevelt, December 16, 1942, U.S. War Department File 320: "For your confidential information I may add that the War Department reluctantly agreed to the formation of these national battalions and the emphasis given to Otto in connection with the formation of an Austrian battalion is the result of strong representations made to us by the State Department."

57. Assistant Chief G–3, Memorandum, December 2, 1942, U.S. War Department File, British Embassy, Washington, to Foreign Office, November 26, 1942, PRO FO 371 8273 6051 C 12118.

58. Austrian Labor Committee to Secretary Stimson, December 5, 1942, U.S. War Department File 320. A copy, sent to Secretary of State Cordell Hull, can be found in U.S. State Department File 863.01/730.

59. Memorandum, December 9, 1942, U.S. War Department File 320.02.

60. Senator Claude Pepper to Secretary of War Henry L. Stimson, December 15, 1942; Chief of Staff, Memorandum, December 23, 1942, U.S. War Department File WDGCT 320.02.

61. Secretary of War to Senator Claude Pepper, January 2, 1942, U.S. War Department File WDGCT 320. Foreign Secretary Anthony Eden to Prime Minister Winston Churchill, December 28, 1942, PRO FO 371 30911 8273 C 12132/46/18, draws the conclusion that any Austrian military unit would be possible only if the Austrian political emigration could agree beforehand.

62. Henry L. Stimson to Assistant Secretary of State Adolf A. Berle, Jr., January 8, 1943, U.S. War Department File WDGCT 320. Foreign Secretary Anthony Eden to Prime Minister Winston Churchill, December 28, 1942, PRO FO 371 30911 8273 C 12132/46/18.

63. Franklin D. Roosevelt, Press conference No. 872, Presidential Press Conferences of Franklin D. Roosevelt, FDR Library, Vol. XXI, p. 008.

64. Ferdinand Czernin to Secretary of War Henry L. Stimson, January 28, 1943; Stimson to Czernin, February 9, 1943, U.S. War Department File WDGCT 320.2. Report, January 27, 1943, Foreign Nationalities Branch, OSS 27687, states that three Austrian groups had united in order to proceed further together with the socialists. *Austrian Labor News* (December 20, 1942), however, rejected any lasting connection with Ferdinand Czernin.

65. President Roosevelt's secretary to Ferdinand Czernin, March 8, 1943, FDR Library, File OF 166.

66. John W. Davis, Brief representing Austrian Action as *amicus curiae* in the trial of Paul Schwarzkopf, FDR Library, File OF 166–A.

67. U.S. State Department File 863.01/741.

68. U.S. State Department File 863.01/776.

69. U.S. State Department File 863.01/760.

70. Sumner Welles to President Roosevelt; J. Edgar Hoover, Memorandum, FDR Library, File PPF 8151. Foreign Secretary Anthony Eden to Prime Minister Winston Churchill, December 28, 1942, PRO FO 371 30911 7263 C 12132/46/18, states that, even at this early date, he cannot see any future for the Hapsburgs.

71. U.S. War Department File WDGCT 320.2, Austrian Bn (12–10–42), January 1, 1943.

72. *Freiheit für Österreich* (New York), No. 9 (March 1, 1943).

73. War Department General Staff Organization and Training Division G–3, Memorandum, U.S. War Department File WDGCT 320 (11–20–42).

74. Adjutant General's Office, Memorandum W.615–22–43, February 17, 1943, U.S. War Department File.

75. Assistant Secretary of War, John J. McCloy, Memorandum, February 5, 1943; Memorandum, February 8, 1943, U.S. War Department File.

76. U.S. State Department File 863.01/752. Army War College, Memorandum, March 16, 1943, U.S. War Department File, Headquarters, Army Ground Forces.

77. *Freiheit für Österreich* (New York), No. 10 (April, 1943).

78. Antonin Gazda, *Providence Journal* and *Providence Evening Bulletin,* December 5, 1942, U.S. State Department File 863.01/737. George Kovazevich to Secretary of War Henry L. Stimson, December 6, 1942, U.S. War Department File 320.02.

79. War Department Organization and Training Division G–3, Memorandum, February 27, 1943, U.S. War Department File WDGCT 320.2, Austrian Bn (2–21–43).

80. Adjutant Gerela to Commander-General, Army Ground Forces, March 5, 1943, U.S. War Department File AG 220.31 (3–2–43), OC–E–WDGCT.

81. Adjutant General's Office, Memorandum 615–28–43, March 8, 1943, U.S. War Department File.

82. Army War College, Memorandum, March 16, 1943, U.S. War Department File Headquarters, Army Ground Forces. Memorandum *re* Austrian Battalion, March 20, 1942, U.S. War Department File Headquarters, Army Ground Forces.

83. War Department Organization and Training Division G–3, Memorandum, April 7, 1943, U.S. War Department File WDCSA Austria (4–7–43).

84. U.S. War Department File WDCSA Austria (4–7–43).

85. Army War College, Memorandum, April 1, 1943, U.S. War Department File Headquarters, Army Ground Forces.

86. Memorandum, April 7, 1943, states that the Austrian battalion was reduced to 144 men, with scant hope that it could be brought to full strength; Headquarters Army Forces, Army College, Memorandum, April 1, 1943, states that 25 volunteers were conscripted in March, 1943, and that it would take two and a half years to reach the full strength of 931 men; Organization and Training Division G–3 states that three months of Otto's attempts to recruit men had yielded only 25 volunteers; Secretary of War Henry L. Stimson to President Roosevelt, April 17, 1943, U.S. War Department File WDCSA Austria (4–7–43).

87. Memorandum, April 12, 1943, U.S. War Department File 320.02 (4–12–19). PRO FO 371 34418 9768 C 4080: An official of the British Foreign Office expressed in a handwritten note the hope that the fiasco of the Austrian battalion would have a salutary effect in American official circles.

88. Army War College, Memorandum, March 16, 1943, U.S. War Department File Headquarters, Army Ground Forces. Memorandum, April 12, 1943, U.S. War Department File, Chief of Staff 320.2 (4–12–29).

89. Secretary of War Henry L. Stimson to President Franklin D. Roosevelt, April 17, 1943, U.S. War Department File 320.2.

90. Attorney General Francis I. Biddle to President Roosevelt, April 23, 1943, FDR Library, File PPF 5309.

91. Secretary of War Henry L. Stimson to President Roosevelt (with the signature F.D.R.), April 17, 1943, U.S. War Department File 320.2.

92. Memorandum, May 3, 1943, U.S. War Department File 320.2 (5–3–43).

93. *Freiheit für Österreich* (New York), No. 12 (April 14, 1943).

94. *The New York Times,* September 15, 1939, and October 10, 1939. Joseph Buttinger, *op. cit.,* p. 579.

95. President Roosevelt, Memorandum, November 17, 1942, U.S. War Department File 320.2.

96. Sumner Welles to President Roosevelt, August 30, 1942, FDR Library, PSF Welles Files.

97. U.S. Department of State, *Foreign Relations of the United States: Diplomatic Papers, 1943,* Vol. I (General), p. 761.

98. "Regierungspläne zur Schaffung von Freiwilligenlegion," *Aufbau* (New York), Vol. VIII, No. 11 (March 13, 1942). *Österreichische Rundschau,* September, 1942, p. 10.

99. Ernst Karl Winter to Secretary of War Henry L. Stimson, U.S. War Department File 320.2. (Hans Rott), Ernst Karl Winter to Hans Rott, July 16, 1942, regarding the Norwegian battalion as an example for the Austrian battalion, folder "Ernst Karl Winter."

100. *The Rubicon, Criscuolo Newsletter* (Washington, D.C.), December 15, 1942. U.S. War Department File 320.2.

101. U.S. War Department File 320.2. (Hans Rott), Ernst Karl Winter to Hans Rott, July 16, 1942, folder "Ernst Karl Winter."

102. War Department Organization and Training Division G–3, Memorandum, October 25, 1942, U.S. War Department File, General Staff WDGCT 320.02 (10–25–42). British Foreign Office, January 23, 1945, PRO FO 371 46595 8438 C, C86/6/G.

103. (Hans Rott), Henry Delfiner to Hans Rott: List of the "Peter Paul" group of experts, folder "Austrian Battalion."

104. (Hans Rott), Walter G. Goldschmidt, New Orleans, to Hans Rott, folder "Austrian Battalion."

105. U.S. Satate Department File 863.01/656.

106. Sumner Welles to President Roosevelt, August 30, 1942, FDR Library, PSF Welles Files.

107. Sumner Welles to President Roosevelt, August 30, 1942, FDR Library, PSF Files. (Hans Rott), Circular, September 2, 1942, folder, "Austrian Battalion." "Austrian Action's Branches and Contacts in Central and South America," March 24, 1942, OSS 14268.

108. U.S. State Department File 863.01/854. Ernst Karl Winter to Secretary of War Henry L. Stimson, July 18, 1942, and December 16, 1943, U.S. War Department File 320.

109. Sumner Welles, Letter, August 30, 1942, FDR Library, PSF Welles Files. Henry L. Stimson, Letter, August 20, 1942, U.S. War Department File 320. War Department Organization and Training Division G–3, Memorandum, August 29, 1942, U.S. War Department File WDGCT 320.02 (8–29–42).

110. U.S. War Department File 320.02 (11–27–42).

111. U.S. State Department File 863.01/3–1042. "Regierungspläne zur Schaffung von Freiwilligenlegionen," *Aufbau* (New York), Vol. VIII, No. 11 (March 13, 1942).

112. Ernst Karl Winter to Secretary of War Henry L. Stimson, November 20, 1942, and December 16, 1942, U.S. War Department File 302. U.S. State Department File 863.01/854.

113. "In Sachen Habsburg," *Aufbau* (New York), Vol. IX, No. 9 (February 26, 1943).

114. Sumner Welles to President Roosevelt, August 30, 1942, FDR Library, PSF Welles Files. (Hans Rott), Hugo Moser, Santiago, Chile, to Hans Rott, January 29, 1943, folder "Südamerika."

115. Hellmut Andics, *Der Fall Otto Habsburg,* p. 123.

116. William C. Bullitt to President Roosevelt, September 5, 1939, FDR Library, File PSF France, Bullitt. Austrian Action, Memorandum with special attention to Central and South America, March 24, 1942, OSS 14268, had dealt with this question much earlier.

117. Antonin Gazda, *Providence Journal* and *Providence Evening Bulletin,* December 5, 1942, U.S. State Department File 863/01/737.

118. War Department Bureau of Public Relations, Memorandum to Secretary of War regarding President Roosevelt's press conference of January 5, 1943, U.S. War Department File. Franklin D. Roosevelt, Press conference No. 872, Presidential Press Conferences of Franklin D. Roosevelt, Vol. XXI, p. 008; and Press conference, January 5, 1943, FDR Library.

119. U.S. State Department File 863.00/6–642.

120. Julius Deutsch, *Ein weiter Weg,* p. 362, claims that the battalion was a "very expensively staged action for Hapsburg, which was supported by people of power."

121. Cordell Hull, Statement, December 1, 1942: ". . . there was not enough fighting and too much gossiping going on, and that everybody, every individual and group from any country are invited to get in and fight," U.S. State Department File 863.01/726.

122. Albert Rakovsky, Montreal, to Secretary of War Henry L. Stimson, January 4, 1943, U.S. War Department File, contained the information that he had volunteered and was hoping

that others would follow suit instead of delivering long speeches. Telegram of the Austrian Society in Palestine and Free Austrian Movement in Egypt to Secretary of War Henry L. Stimson, December 1, 1942, U.S. War Department File 320. Free Austrians in Santiago, Chile, to Cordell Hull, January 7, 1943, inquired whether volunteers could report from Chile; and Secretary of State Cordell Hull to Free Austrians, January 19, 1943, U.S. State Department File 863.01/739, replied that only residents of the United States could volunteer.

123. William L. Shirer, *The Rise and Fall of the Third Reich* (New York: Simon and Schuster, 1960), p. 903.

124. Hellmut Andics, *Der Fall Otto Habsburg,* p. 123.

125. William L. Shirer, *op cit.,* p. 903.

126. Hans Rott to Julius Deutsch, March 30, 1945 (reprinted in full in the Appendix), folder "Free Austrian Movement." "Otto von Hapsburg," May 14, 1943, Foreign Nationalities Branch, OSS 34484 S. Viscount Halifax to Foreign Secretary Anthony Eden, April 13, 1943, PRO FO 371 34418 9768 C 4461, includes two memos from John Wheeler-Bennett of March 24 and 27, 1943, "Otto von Hapsburg and His Politics."

127. U.S. Department of State, *Foreign Relations of the United States: Diplomatic Papers, 1945,* Vol. III, pp. 562, 563. U.S. State Department File 863.01/1845. Sumner Welles to President Roosevelt, August 30, 1942, FDR Library, PSF Welles Files.

128. U.S. War Department File 320 WDGCT (11–10–42). U.S. State Department File 863.01/716.

129. Hans Rott to Julius Deutsch, March 30, 1945 (reprinted in full in the Appendix), folder "Free Austria Movement." "Otto von Hapsburg," Foreign Nationalities Branch, OSS 34484 S.

130. Letters to Secretary of War Henry L. Stimson, November 27, 1942, and January 28, 1943, U.S. War Department File 302.

131. Austrian Organizations to Secretary of War Henry L. Stimson, November 29, 1942, U.S. State Department File 800.01/160 A SUPPL.

132. Luigi Criscuolo to Secretary of War Henry L. Stimson, December 19, 1942, U.S. War Department File 320. *The Rubicon, Criscuolo Newsletter* (Washington, D.C.), December 15, 1942.

133. William L. Shirer, *op. cit.,* p. 1095. British Foreign Office, London, to J. R. Colville, Esq., January 23, 1945, PRO FO 371 46593 8438 C 86/6/G. Viscount Halifax to Foreign Secretary Anthony Eden, April 13, 1943, PRO FO 371 34418 9768 C 4461: two memos from John Wheeler Bennett of March 24 and 27, 1943, "Otto von Hapsburg and His Politics." In the latter memorandum Otto is reported to "have given up on the battalion."

134. Luigi Criscuolo to Secretary of War Henry L. Stimson, December 19, 1942, War Department File 320. *The Rubicon, Criscuolo Newsletter* (Washington, D.C.), December 15, 1942.

135. Headquarters Army Ground Forces, Memorandum *re* Army War College, March 16, 1943, U.S. War Department File.

136. "In Sachen Habsburg," *Aufbau* (New York), Vol. IX, No. 9 (February 26, 1943).

137. Bulletin on Austro-Hungarian internal information, January 16, 1945, FDR Library, File OF 198–A. British Overseas Press Service, Daily Digests of War Broadcasts, Memorandum No. 239 (OWI Reports) quotes the Viennese *Kleine Kriegszeitung,* September 12, 1944, to the effect that the Allies will not distinguish between Austrians and Germans. OWI, Group 208, entry 369, box 365, Suitland, Md.

138. U.S. State Department File 711.62114–608.

139. Christian Willars, *op. cit.,* p. 203.

140. Memorandum, December 7, 1943, U.S. State Department File 863.01/854.

141. U.S. Department of State, *Foreign Relations of the United States: Diplomatic Papers, 1945,* Vol. II, pp. 562, 563. Secretary of State Edward C. Stettinius to the United States Ambassador in Paris, March 16, 1945, U.S. State Department File 863.01/1–1845. Dean Acheson, *Present at the Creation: My Years in the State Department* (New York: N.W. Norton and Company, 1959), p. 38.

142. Alexander Vodopivec, *op. cit.,* p. 278. Richard N. Coudenhove-Kalergi, in *The New York Times,* September 14, 1944, PRO FO 371 28858 9268 C 15593: "While the Greek and

Yugoslav governments would express their claims on Italian territory inhabited by Greeks and by Slavs, Austria could not join in these claims because it has no government."

143. U.S. State Department File 863.01/8–2043.

Chapter VI   From the Dissolution of the Austrian Battalion to the Moscow Declaration

1. U.S. State Department File 863.01/799.

2. U.S. Department of State, *Foreign Relations of the United States: Diplomatic Papers, 1943,* Vol. I (General), p. 515. U.S. State Department File 863.01/429. Foreign Secretary Anthony Eden, Memorandum, December 28, 1942, PRO FO 371 30911, 8273 C 12132/46/18, shows the indecision of British government policy concerning the Austrian question. British Embassy, Washington, to Foreign Office, June 4, 1943, with John Wheeler-Bennett, Memorandum of conversation with Ferdinand Czernin, May 29, 1943, PRO FO 371 34418 9768 C 6759.

3. U.S. State Department File 863.01/8–20–43. British Embassy, Washington, to Foreign Office, December 4, 1943, PRO FO 371 34421 8405 C 14311, reports that Otto von Hapsburg had been received by Prime Minister Churchill during the conference in Quebec. Report, July 13, 1943, OSS 38885: "Austrian particularism grows from day to day."

4. U.S. State Department File 863.01/862.

5. U.S. State Department File 863.01/774.

6. U.S. State Department File 800.01/160–A SUPPL.; Dean Acheson, *op cit.,* p. 38. "The Austrian Emigration in Great Britain," OSS XL 1615: "The Austrian Emigration lacks really able leadership, [and there is no] first-rate political leader."

7. U.S. State Department File 800.01/6–2343. U.S. State Department File 800.01/6–2343 EG.

8. U.S. State Department File 800.01/313. British Embassy, Washington, to Foreign Office, June 4, 1943, PRO FO 371 34418 9768 C 6759.

9. U.S. State Department File 863.01/807. U.S. State Department File 863.01/808.

10. U.S. State Department File 863.00/1933.

11. U.S. State Department File 863.01/807.

12. Ambassador Dr. Arthur Breycha-Vauthier, Memorandum concerning a conference with Allan Dulles in Geneva, October 17, 1943, U.S. State Department File 863.01/808. Austrian socialists in Sweden to London Bureau, early July, 1943 (photocopy—original in Bruno Kreisky Archive).

13. U.S. Department of State, *Foreign Relations of the United States: Diplomatic Papers, 1943,* Vol. I (General), p. 515. U.S. State Department File 863.014/29; the expose mentioned, "Die Zukunft von Österreich," could not be found among the unpublished papers. Auswärtiges Amt, Akten zur deutschen auswärtigen Politik 1941–1945, Series E, Vol. I, "Runderlass des Reichsaussenministers von Ribbentrop vom 16. Jänner 1942," p. 231, concerning negotiations by the British Foreign Secretary Anthony Eden with J. V. Stalin in Moscow from December 16 to 22, 1941.

14. U.S. Department of State, *Foreign Relations of the United States . . . 1943,* Vol. I, p. 515. Dean Acheson, *op cit.,* p. 69. Report, July 13, 1943, OSS 38885.

15. U.S. Department of State, *Foreign Relations of the United States . . . 1943,* Vol. I, pp. 549, 550. U.S. State Department File 863.01/429.

16. U.S. Department of State, *Foreign Relations of the United States . . . 1943,* Vol. I, p. 550.

Chapter VII   From the Moscow Declaration to the Armistice

1. U.S. Department of State, *Foreign Relations of the United States: Diplomatic Papers, 1943,* Vol. I (General), p. 741. U.S. State Department File 740.0011 Moscow/10–1943. OSS 54103 R, January 18, 1944. The influence of the Moscow Declaration upon Austria itself was not

too great in the beginning. OWI Bureau of Overseas Intelligence, Central File 1941–1945, Axis 2, 12–417; British Overseas Press Service, Group 208, entry 364, box 363, mentions "deep distrust regarding the intention of the Allies."

2. U.S. State Department File 863.01/846, "K.V.," "The Fate of Austria," in *War and the Working Class* (Moscow: 1943). Fürnberg, Lecture, Moscow, December 14, 1943, U.S. State Department File 863.01/844. Memorandum, digest of the Austrian Communist leaflet "Auf zum Kampf für die Freiheit und Wiedergeburt Österreichs," August 11, 1944, OSS 89420 C. British Embassy, Moscow, Report, November 15, 1943, PRO FO 371 34420 8403 C 13544, concerns Ernst Fischer, "Für ein freies und unabhängiges Österreich," in *TRUD*, November 14, 1943.

3. Ernst Fischer, *op. cit.*, pp. 439, 459. British Embassy, Moscow, Report, Nov. 15, 1943, PRO FO 371 34420 8403 C 13544. Ernst Fischer states that Austria lagged behind other occupied countries in the efficacy of its underground opposition. He was the main commentator of the Soviet European Service in German, according to "Daily Digest of World Broadcasts," OWI, Axis, group 208, box 365. OSS 11991 ascertains the intensity of the Moscow broadcasts and their special Austrian bent. Memorandum "Austrian Communist Party," March, 1943, OSS 33855.

4. "Zwei Jahre österreichische Labor Information," *Austrian Labor Information* (New York), No. 24 (March–April, 1944). Harrison memorandum, January 21, 1942, PRO FO 371 30910 8264 C 1282/46/18, states that Stalin had asked Great Britain to promise a separate Austria as early as December 16, 1941. Vortragender Legationrates Freytag, Notes, March 30, 1938, Auswärtiges Amt, Akten zur deutschen auswärtigen Politik, Series E, Vol. V, p. 693, suggests that the Mexican note protesting against the Anschluss on March 19, 1938, should not be answered with another protest note. "Der Gesandte in Mexico an das Auswärtige Amt," April 8, 1938, Auswärtiges Amt, Akten zur deutschen auswärtigen Politik, Series E, Vol. V, p. 697.

5. U.S. State Department File 863.01 841 1/2.

6. U.S. State Department File 863.01/854. British Embassy, Moscow, to V.N. Molotov, Commissar for Foreign Affairs, December 12, 1943, states that Great Britain will not recognize an Austrian Committee; and V. Dekanosov to British Embassy, Feb. 11, 1944, PRO FO 371 38828 8412 260/12/43. Aide-mémoire, February 2, 1944, PRO FO 371 38827 8409 C 1440/30/3: The importance of an Austrian symbol is acknowledged here.

7. U.S. State Department File 863.01/830.

8. U.S. State Department File, 863.01/850 OSS 54103R of January 18, 1944. OWI, Memorandum No. 139, "Austria," January, 1944, Group 208, box 365. PRO FO 371 30910 8264 C 13264. PRO FO 371 34421 8405 C 14743, December 16, 1943.

9. U.S. State Department File 863.01/850. State Department Aide-mémoire, January 20, 1944, PRO FO 371 38827 8403 Ref. No. 129/63/40. PRO FO 371 38827 8409. British Embassy, Washington, to Foreign Secretary, January 29, 1944, PRO FO 371 38827 8409 C 1338.

10. Political Advisor John G. Erhard to State Department, October 27, 1945, U.S. State Department File 863.00/10–2745. State Department to Renner government, U.S. State Department File 863.00/10–2745. State Department, Letter, Nov. 21, 1945, U.S. State Department File 740.00/19 Control (Austria) 11–1245, notes that there is no objection to naming Dr. Ludwig Kleinwächter ambassador from Austria.

11. U.S. Department of State, *Foreign Relations of the United States: Diplomatic Papers, 1943*, Vol. I (General), p. 801.

12. U.S. State Department File 863.01/7–2744.

13. U.S. State Department File 863.01/7–2744. Hans Rott to State Department, July 27, 1944; and State Department to Hans Rott, August 22, 1944, folder "State Department." "Interview with Prisoners of War," December 1, 1944, OSS XL 2586: Austrian prisoners of war hoped to join the Austrian legion on the Allied side.

14. Political Advisor John G. Erhard to Secretary of State, U.S. State Department File 863.01/10–1845, characterizes opposition in Austria from 1938 to 1945: The Austrian underground groups had not received official help from abroad. U.S. State Department File 863.01/7–2744. Legation, Stockholm, Telegram, July 28, 1944, U.S. State Department File 863.00/6-2844, notes the absence of strong Austrian organizations abroad. Hans Rott to State Department, July 27, 1944, folder "State Department." Österreichische Vereinigung in Schwe-

den (Austrian association in Sweden) to Anthony Eden, April 11, 1945, PRO FO 371 46614 9768 C 1445 criticizes Eden's statement in Parliament of March 1, 1945, in which he mentioned the Austrian underground with condescension.

15. (Hans Rott), Prof. Robert Heine-Geldern to Secretary of State Cordell Hull, November 7, 1943, folder "State Department."

16. U.S. State Department File 863.01/835. U.S. State Department File 863.01/785.

17. U.S. State Department File 863.01/11–2343.

18. U.S. State Department File 863.01/12–3043.

19. U.S. State Department File 863.00/10–1845.

20. U.S. State Department File 863.01/898. U.S. State Department File 863.01/7–2744. "Interview with Prisoners of War," December 1, 1944, OSS XL 2586.

21. Franklin D. Roosevelt, Press conference No. 995, March /13, 1945, Presidential Press Conferences of Franklin D. Roosevelt, FDR Library.

22. U.S. State Department File 711.62114/608. "Interview with Prisoners of War, December 1, 1944, OSS XL 2586. OWI, War Records Group 208, Information of Psychological Warfare Branch, Italian Headquarters, January 15, 1945.

23. U.S. State Department File 711.62114/8–2344. War Office Memorandum, March 30, 1944, PRO FO 371 38828 8412 C 4311, with cable regarding separation of Austrian prisoners of war in the Middle East. High Commissioner of Canada, Memorandum, March 2, 1944, PRO FO 371 38828 8412 Ref. PW 232/18. (Hans Rott), Egon Ranshofen-Wertheimer, Notes on conversation with General Bryan, January 28, 1944. *Austria Libre* (Newsletter of Österreichisches Zentralkomitee für Lateinamerika, Montevideo), No. 2, June, 1944.

24. U.S. State Department File 863.01/884.

25. U.S. State Department File 711.62114/8–2344. *Austrian Labor Information* (New York), No. 20/21 (November/December, 1943).

26. U.S. State Department File 863.01/839. *Aufbau* (New York), Vol. I, No. 17 (April 28, 1944). OSS 2853, April 11, 1945, states that Dr. Friedrich Adler was the recognized head of the Austrian Social Democrats until his resignation in April 1944; from then on it was Julius Deutsch, who took over but who refused to form a united front of all the exile groups in spite of his being more pragmatic.

27. U.S. State Department File 863.01/841.

28. U.S. State Department File 863.01/825. *Austrian Labor Information* (New York), No. 24 (March/April, 1944). Friedrich Adler, "Zwei Jahre Österreichische Labor-Information," Austrian socialists in Sweden to London Bureau, early July 1943 (photocopy—original in Bruno Kreisky Archive).

29. U.S. State Department File 863.01/821. U.S. State Department File 500 C/115/28th Conference/223.

30. U.S. State Department File 863.01/839. U.S. State Department File 863.01/854.

31. U.S. State Department File 863.01/839. U.S. State Department File 863.01/854.

32. U.S. State Department File 863.01/830, Note. U.S. State Department File 863.01/850.

33. U.S. State Department File 863.01/850. Memorandum, "Great Britain and the Austrian Problem," June 25, 1942, OSS 18165S. Department of State, Aide-mémoire, January 20, 1944, PRO FO 371 38827 8409: "Austrian émigrés are totally unrepresentative of present-day opinion in Austria." British Embassy, Washington, to Foreign Office, January 29, 1944, PRO FO 371 38827 8409 C 1338. Aide-mémoire, February 2, 1942, PRO FO 371 38827 8409 C 1440/30/3.

34. U.S. State Department File 863.01/855. PRO FO 371 38827 8409 C 1440/30/3.

35. U.S. State Department File 740.0011, European War 1939–32219. OSS 54103 R, January 18, 1944. Austrian socialists in Sweden to London Bureau, early July, 1943 (photocopy—original in Bruno Kreisky Archive). The author is convinced that this letter dates from the time when the Allies, in preparation for the Moscow Conference, were trying to sound out prominent Austrian emigrants on the question of a reestablished autonomous Austrian Republic. Ambassador Dr. Arthur Breycha-Vauthier was thus questioned. Arthur Breycha-Vauthier, Memorandum concerning a conference with Allen Dulles in Geneva, October 17, 1943, U.S. State Department File 863.01/808. Dr. Bruno Kreisky, because of his good contacts with Swedish government circles, must have been informed about the Allied interest, quite contrary to the London Bureau.

36. U.S. State Department File 863.01/835 1/2. OSS 54103 R of January 18, 1944.

37. U.S. State Department File 863.01/857.

38. U.S. State Department File 863.01/12–3043.

39. U.S. State Department File 863.00/3—745.

40. U.S. State Department File 863.01–3043.

41. U.S. State Department File 740.00119 Control Austria 4–345. U.S. State Department File 863.01/9–1444.

42. U.S. State Department File 740.00119 Control Austria 4–345. U.S. State Department File 863.01/9–1444.

43. U.S. State Department File 863.01/839. "The Austrian Underground, Tactics, Prospectives," OSS XL 2102: The socialist underground movement in Austria wanted to operate cautiously and with due consideration for human lives; the communists advocated aggressive opposition. Also OXX XL 1824.

44. "Hull's Warnung an Österreich" (an interview with Ferdinand Czernin), *Aufbau* (New York), Vol. X, No. 37 (September 15, 1944). "Austrian Intelligence," Oct. 5, 1944, OSS XL 1824. OSS XL 2101.

45. *Aufbau* (New York), Vol. X, No. 44 (November 3, 1944). "The Austrian World Movement," "Austrian Politics in the United States," OSS XL 2102: Ferdinand Czernin's decision to join the Free Austrian World Movement can only be interpreted as his response to a loss of hope about coming to terms with the socialists. OSS 27687, Foreign Nationalities Branch, January 27, 1943. Franz Novy, London, to Dr. Bruno Kreisky, Stockholm, Feb. 28, 1944 (photocopy—original in Bruno Kreisky Archive), states that political warfare of Great Britain unfortunately is behind that of Russia. Free Austrian Movement to BBC Broadcasts, June 23, 1942, PRO FO 371 30911 8273.

46. *Aufbau* (New York), Vol. X, No. 38 (September 22, 1944). PRO FO 371 30911 8273: The London Free Austrian Movement welcomed the call to underground action; in a memorandum of June 23, 1942, it stated that the BBC expected the workers in Austria to oppose the Nazis but not the German occupation.

47. U.S. State Department File 863.01/3–345.

48. U.S. State Department File 863.01/839.

49. *Aufbau* (New York), Vol. X, No. 37 (September 15, 1944).

50. U.S. State Department File 863.01/12–2744. *Aufbau* (New York), Vol. X, No. 47 (November 24, 1944).

51. U.S. State Department File 863.01/3–1045. British Embassy, Washington, to Foreign Office, March 14, 1945, PRO FO 371 46614 9620 C 933.

52. U.S. State Department File 863.01/1–1145.

53. FDR Library, File PSF Austria 1945.

54. U.S. State Department File 863.01/4–545.

55. Ernst Fischer, *op. cit.*, p. 461. Report on Austria's internal situation, March 13, 1945; Declaration of Radio Moscow that the Allies would treat Austria differently than Germany, but that she would have to rise against the oppression, OSS 121899 C. OSS XL 1615, July 7, 1944, and OSS 2853, April 11, 1945: Again and again the reports of the United States Office of Strategic Services stress that according to the Moscow Declaration the slowly emerging underground did not have any national characteristics but seemed only to be directed against the "Prussian" oppressors; it is equally stressed that the socialists abroad did not accept Austria's independence for patriotic motives but only for reasons of political realism. OSS 89420 C, August 11, 1944: Contents of a Communist leaflet by a partisan fighter in southern Austria, which demands a patriotic uprising against Germany. Report, March 22, 1944, PRO FO 371 38828 9768 C 4152, concerns a memorial celebration staged by the Austrian Action and the Austrian Labor Committee in New York, March 11, 1944; the State Department refused to send a representative to this event, as the "base" of the celebration was "too narrow"; the Czechoslovak Consul in New York, Dr. Karel Hudec, addressed the celebration.

56. Ernst Karl Winter, "Die österreichische politische Emigration in den USA," *Die Abwehr* (Graz), January/February, 1950.

57. U.S. State Department File 863.01/869.

58. U.S. State Department File 863.01/844. U.S. State Department File 863.01/846.

59. U.S. State Department File 863.01/7–3144.

60. U.S. State Department File 863.00/3–2045.

61. U.S. State Department File 863.01/4–845. British Embassy, Moscow, to Foreign Office, Report about the broadcast by Radio Moscow "Declaration of the Soviet Government on Austria," April 8, 1945; and Marshal Tolbuchin, Appeal to the people of Vienna, April 6, 1945, PRO FO 371 46614 9620. *Pravda,* April 7, 1945, PRO FO 371 46593 8438. *Pravda,* April 9, 1945. PRO FO 371 46614 9620 C 1453. OSS XL 7839 of April 27, 1945.

62. U.S. State Department File 863.01/2–2145.

63. Franklin D. Roosevelt, Press conference, April 5, 1945, Presidential Press Conferences of Franklin D. Roosevelt, FDR library.

64. U.S. State Department File 863.01/12–2044. U.S. State Department File 863.01/3–345. *Aufbau* (New York), Vol. X, No. 1 (April 28, 1944). Friedrich Adler, "Die Legende vom glücklichen Österreich," *Austrian Labor Information* (New York), No. 20/21 (November/December, 1943). Report, March 14, 1944, OSS XL 1244. "Survey of the Austrian Political Emigration," April 11, 1945, OSS 2853.

65. U.S. State Department File 863.01/4–1045. U.S. State Department File 863.01/7–1145. Dr. Ernst Lemberger believed that the number of Austrian Communists was less than 10 percent of the Austrian population.

66. U.S. State Department File 863.01/3–345.

67. U.S. State Department File 863.01/4–1045. U.S. Department of State, *Foreign Relations of the United States, Diplomatic Papers, 1945,* Vol. III, p. 58. U.S. State Department File 740.00119 EAC 4–545: "Little help from outside [is expected] until the entrance of the Red Army in Austria this month."

68. U.S. State Department File 800.01/6–2343 EG.

69. Alexander Vodopivec, *op. cit.,* p. 278.

70. Julius Deutsch to Franz Goldner, Feb. 7, 1943. Austrian socialists in Sweden to London Bureau, early July, 1943 (photocopy—original in Bruno Kreisky Archive).

71. U.S. State Department File 863.00/1933. U.S. State Department File 863.01/8–2043.

72. U.S. State Department File 863.01/3–2245. Dr. Oskar Pollak, Report, March 1, 1945, PRO FO 371 46593 8438 C 800, states that Austrian committees exist in Debrecen and Sofia; they later faded away without much ado. Report, March 12, 1945, OSS L 53931. Russian broadcast, April 9, 1945, OSS XL 7839, states that the Russians desired the establishment of an independent democratic Austria in the sense of the Moscow Declaration. British Mission in Hungary, Report, July 18, 1945, PRO FO 371 45596 9620 C 4305/8/3, mentions that the Russian political representative in Budapest had been cool toward the Free Austrian Committee in Budapest.

73. U.S. Department of State, *Foreign Relations of the United States: Diplomatic Papers, 1945,* Vol. III, p. 58. U.S. State Department File 863.01/2–845. U.S. State Department File 863.01/3–2145. Report, January 19, 1945, OSS 110492. "Austrian Appreciation," OSS 121908 C, No. 8. Report, March 8, 1945, OSS 122908 S. Report, March 28, 1945, OSS XL 8121.

74. U.S. Department of State, *Foreign Relations of the United States: Diplomatic Papers, 1945,* Vol. III, p. 58. U.S. State Department File 863.01/3–1745. Report, January 21, 1945, OSS XL 5786: Distribution of the parties in the Austrian underground: 10 percent Communists, 35 percent revolutionary Socialists, 35 percent Catholics, 8 percent Legitimists, and 8 percent right-wing radicals. OSS XL 8121, Report, March 28, 1945.

75. U.S. Department of State, *Foreign Relations of the United States: Diplomatic Papers, 1945,* Vol. III, p. 58. U.S. State Department File 863.01/3–1745. *Austrian Labor News* (New York, No. 34 (June 1, 1945). OSS 110492.

76. U.S. Department of State, *Foreign Relations of the United States: Diplomatic Papers, 1945,* Vol. III, p. 58. U.S. State Department File 863.01/3–1745. Report, April 4, 1945, OSS 122706, contains appeal of the POEN to the Austrian people and the leadership of the Austrian underground, calling for an uprising. OSS 110492. British Embassy, Washington, to Foreign Office, April 25, 1945, PRO FO 371 46593 8438 C 1713.

77. U.S. Department of State, *Foreign Relations of the United States: Diplomatic Papers,*

1945, Vol. III, p. 58. U.S. State Department File 863.01/2–845. PRO FO 371 46593 8538 C 1713. OSS 110492.

78. U.S. State Department File 863.01/4–1045. Report, April 27, 1945, OSS XL 7839, declares that the POEN was apparently dominated by Social Democrats and Christian Socialists.

79. U.S. Department of State, *Foreign Relations of the United States: Diplomatic Papers, 1945*, Vol. III, p. 58. Jean Lambert is the pseudonym of Dr. Ernst Lemberger. *Izvestia*, May 31, 1945, PRO FO 371 46594 9768 C 2731, acknowledges participation of all Austrian parties in the administrative takeover by the Russian occupation forces.

80. U.S. State Department File 863.01/7–1945. U.S. State Department File 863.00/5–2945.

81. U.S. Department of State, *Foreign Relations of the United States: Diplomatic Papers, 1945*, Vol. III, p. 58. U.S. State Department File 863.01/3–1745. "A Survey of the Political Emigration," April 11, 1945, OSS 2853. "Resistance Movement," January, 1945, OSS XL 5786.

82. Friedrich Adler, "Die Legende vom glücklichen Österreich," *Austrian Labor Information* (New York), No. 20/21 (November/December 1943). "A Survey of the Austrian Political Emigration," April 11, 1945, OSS 2853, states that Socialists do not want to collaborate with Austro-Fascists and Legitimists. "Austrian Intelligence," October 5, 1944, OSS XL 1824, reports that there exists a readiness in Austria proper to collaborate with other parties: "There is a definite willingness on the part of the underground leaders of the Social Democrats to forget their ancient quarrels with the Christian Socialists and to cooperate with the bourgeois parties."

83. U.S. State Department File 863.01/9–445. British Embassy, Moscow, to Foreign Office, April 29, 1945, PRO FO 371 46614 9620 C 1822.

84. U.S. State Department File 863.01/4–2845. British Embassy, Moscow, to Foreign Office, April 29, 1945, PRO FO 371 46614 9620 C 1822. British Embassy, Moscow, to Foreign Office, April 26, 1945, PRO FO 371 46614 9620 No. 1557.

85. U.S. State Department File 863.01/4–3045. U.S. State Department File Control Austria 4–945. British Embassy, Moscow, to Foreign Office, April 27, 1945, PRO FO 371 46614 9620 C 1744/205/G.

86. U.S. Department of State, *Foreign Relations of the United States: Diplomatic Papers, 1945*, Vol. III, p. 58. U.S. State Department File 863.01/4–2645.

87. U.S. State Department File 863.01/5–145. PRO FO 371 46614 9620 C 1744/205/G.

88. U.S. Department of State, *Foreign Relations of the United States: Diplomatic Papers, 1945*, Vol. III, p. 58. U.S. State Department File 863.01/4–2645.

89. U.S. State Department File 863.01/9–445. British Embassy, Moscow, to Foreign Office, April 26, 1945, PRO FO 371 46614 9620 No. 1557.

90. U.S. Department of State, *Foreign Relations of the United States: Diplomatic Papers, 1945*, Vol. III, p. 58. U.S. State Department File 740.00119 Austria 10–2645.

91. U.S. State Department File 863.01/10–1645. U.S. State Department File 863.01/10–1745. U.S. State Department File 863.01/5–1545. U.S. State Department File 863.01/10–3045. Dr. Bruno Kreisky, Address as Chairman of the Austrian Society in Sweden, Stockholm, April 29, 1945, on the occasion of the establishment of Renner's provisional government; Oskar Pollak and Franz Novy, the London Bureau of Austrian Socialists, to Dr. Bruno Kreisky, May 3, 1945 (photocopy—original in Bruno Kreisky Archive).

92. U.S. State Department File 863.01/11–145.

93. U.S. State Department File 863.01/12–2744. "A Survey of the Austrian Political Emigration," April 11, 1945, OSS 2853. "Austrian Association of Christian Socialists in Great Britain," PRO FO 371 46596 9768 C 9438/8/3, announces closing of the organization on Dec. 7, 1945. PRO FO 371 46596 9768 C 4291: An Austrian Peoples' Party was established only on July 3, 1945, in Great Britain, by followers of the old Christian Socialist Party.

94. Julius Deutsch, *op. cit.*, p. 364. London Austrian Representative Committee to Foreign Office, Dec. 20, 1944, PRO FO 371 46593 9620 C 54/E3.

95. Franz Goldner, "Die Wirtschaftspolitische Bedeutung der Wiedergutmachung," *Austrian American Tribune* (New York), Vol. 5, No. 11 (June, 1947); Franz Goldner, "Opfergleichheit," *Ibid.*, Vol. 6, No. 11 (August, 1947). "Über die politische Situation in Öster-

reich,'' April 2, 1946, OSS XL 46435, reports an editorial in *Arbeiterzeitung* (March 27, 1946), which stressed that only one-sixth of the 34 million war victims were Jews and that they therefore did not require special consideration.

Chapter VIII Epilogue to the History of Political Emigration in the United States

1. Julius Deutsch, *op. cit.*, p. 362. Franklin D. Roosevelt, Press conference, January 5, 1943, Presidential Press Conferences of Franklin D. Roosevelt, FDR Library.

2. Ernst Fischer, *op. cit.*, p. 364. Karl Vogelmann, ''Die Propaganda der österreichischen Emigration in der Sowjetunion für einen selbständigen österreichischen Nationalstaat, 1938–1945'' (Ph.D. Dissertation, University of Vienna, 1973).

3. Julius Deutsch, *op. cit.*, p. 315. ''Austrian Intelligence,'' Oct. 5, 1944, OSS XL 1824.

4. *Aufbau* (New York), Vol. X, No. 47 (November 24, 1944).

5. Alexander Vodopivec, *op. cit.*, pp. 314, 315.

6. Hellmut Andics, *Der Fall Otto Habsburg*, pp. 148, 149. British Embassy, Vienna, to Lord Halifax, March 9, 1938, PRO FO 371 22318 8218 R 2964. John W. Wheeler-Bennett, Memorandum, Oct. 7, 1943, PRO FO 371 26539 8309 C 13169/280/18, shares my opinion that Otto von Hapsburg is to be viewed as a refugee of World War I.

7. Hans Kelsen, *Österreichisches Staatsrecht* (Tübingen, 1923). Hellmut Andics, *Der Fall Otto Habsburg*, pp. 53–58.

8. Sumner Welles to President Roosevelt, August 30, 1942, FDR Library, PSF Welles Files. William C. Bullitt to Secretary of State, Nov. 9, 1939, U.S. State Department File 863.01/631.

9. ''Keine Einigung der Österreicher in New York,'' *Aufbau* (New York), Vol. XI, No. 16 (April 20, 1945).

10. Hans Rott to Julius Deutsch, and replies, March 9, 13, 23, 24, 26, 28, and 30, 1945 (reprinted in full in the Appendix), folder ''Free Austrian Movement.''

11. *Aufbau* (New York), Vol. XI, No. 16 (April 20, 1945).

Chapter IX The Austrian Emigration in Great Britain

1. U.S. State Department File 863.01/850. U.S. State Department File 863.01/8–2644. U.S. State Department File 863.01/830, Note. Foreign Secretary Eden to Viscount Halifax, March 12, 1942, PRO FO 371 30942 8474 C 2281/1364/18. Foreign Office, ''Germany Confidential,'' Nov. 16, 1942, PRO FO 371 30911 8273 C 11239/46/18. ''Resolution of the Austrian Committee,'' June 12, 1944, OSS 88820. OSS XL 2102.

2. Harold Callender, ''Watchful Britain Shuns Showdown,'' *The New York Times*, Feb. 13, 1938. Ferdinand Kuhn, Jr., in *The New York Times*, Feb. 16, 1938. Auswärtiges Amt, Akten zur deutschen auswärtigen Politik, Series D. Vol. I, p. 494. Foreign Research and Press Service, Balliol College, Oxford, Memorandum, August 27, 1941, PRO FO 371 26538 6032, explains in detail Austria's development up to the Anschluss, stating that the Anschluss was the least natural solution of the Austrian problem.

3. Joseph Buttinger, *op. cit.*, p. 641. Foreign Research and Press Service, Balliol College, Oxford, Memorandum, August 27, 1941, PRO FO 371 26538 6032. ''Great Britain and the Austrian Problem,'' June 25, 1942, Foreign Nationalities Branch, OSS 181655, states that the Labour party saw Austria as occupying a natural place within the Reich territory and criticized BBC broadcasts to Austria with an All-German and socialist tone. In a report by Labour leader Franz Novy to the Austrian socialists in Sweden, regarding the possibility that the Swedish-Austrian exile Gustav Moser might join the London Bureau of Austrian Socialists, Novy declared that the socialists had refused to give the communists a statement subscribing to lasting Austrian independence. Résumé for Dr. Bruno Kreisky, August 1, 1944 (photocopy—original in Bruno Kreisky Archive), about the negotiations concerning Gustav Moser.

4. Hellmut Andics, *Der Fall Otto Habsburg*, p. 107. Foreign Research and Press Service, Balliol College, Oxford, Memorandum, August 27, 1941, PRO FO 371 26538 6032.

5. PRO FO 371 4768 C 6782/1870/G. *Aufbau* (New York), Vol. VI, No. 4 (January 26, 1940): The tribunals worked extremely well; established in October, 1939, the checkup was finished several months later; only 120 persons had been interned. Memorandum, Nov. 5, 1939, PRO FO 371 24106 8230 W 17510: The Austrian Center, established in March, 1939, and originally considered unpolitical and above party, was soon taken over by Communist party sympathizers. The cofounder, Count Kurt Strachwitz, was asked to withdraw; the founders, Professors Hertz and Bosch, resigned, and all socialists left the organization. PRO FO 371 23101 C 17786/13409/18, Nov. 2, 1939: Eva Kolmer, who later became the principal speaker for the Austrian Center, declared that the organization was unpolitical. PRO FO 371 23104 8395 C 14823, Sept. 15, 1939: Independently of the Austrian Center, there existed a Committee of Austrians, later called Council of Austrians in Great Britain, founded in September, 1938, under the leadership of Prof. Hertz. According to a public announcement of Sept. 11, 1939, the Committee declared itself to be the sole representative of all Austrians who did not recognize the Anschluss. The Committee, or Council of Austrians in Great Britain, however, from the very beginning was not a mass organization but a nonpartisan organization of all those who opposed the Anschluss. Furthermore, there had existed since early 1940 a Club of Austrian Socialists in Great Britain as well as an Austrian Labour Group, and Austrian Trade Unionists. "Great Britain and the Austrian Problem," June 25, 1942, Foreign Nationalities Branch, OSS 181655, states that the reason for regarding Austrians as enemy aliens was Chamberlain's policy of not committing himself to any postwar destruction of Germany. This was also the policy of Churchill and Eden for a long time, in spite of Churchill's Mansion speech of Nov. 9, 1940, and his speech of Feb. 18, 1942. "Austrian Organisations in Great Britain," OSS 47683 S, states that the Austrian Center and the Council of Austrians in Great Britain were nonpolitical in the beginning. The Austrian Council, then called the Committee of Austrians, and the Austrian Committee later were fused into the Austrian Center and were put under the leadership of Communist party members. The London Bureau of Austrian Socialists and the Group of Austrian Trade Unionists, under the leadership of John Svitanics, were founded in early 1941.

6. *Aufbau* (New York), Vol. VI, No. 29 (July 19, 1940).

7. *Aufbau* (New York), Vol. VI, No. 30 (July 26, 1940).

8. *Aufbau* (New York), Vol. VI, No. 41 (Oct. 11, 1940).

9. *Aufbau* (New York), Vol. VI, No. 50 (Dec. 13, 1940).

10. "Glänzende Kämpfer," and "Ein Lob der Refugee Pioniere in England," *Aufbau* (New York), Vol. VII, No. 2 (Jan. 10, 1941). Foreign Office to J. R. Colville, Esq., Jan. 23, 1945, PRO FO 371 46593 8483 C 86/6/G, gives a detailed description of the attempts to concentrate Austrians serving in pioneer units into special units that were purely Austrian, beginning with the first attempt in 1940; this attempt was regarded as a fiasco.

11. U.S. State Department File 863.01/113. "Austrian Emigration," OSS 47683 S: The Austria Office was founded in January, 1940, by Count Huyn, the former Press Secretary to the Austrian Embassy in London, Heinrich Allina, and Dr. Franz Klein, and by monarchists and socialists who had left the Austrian Center; Heinrich Allina was therefore banned from the Club of Austrian Socialists. Austrian Center to Foreign Office, July 30, 1941, PRO FO 371 26538 6032 C 8561. Foreign Secretary Anthony Eden to Viscount Halifax, March 12, 1942, PRO FO 370 30942 8374 C 2281/1364/18: It is stated here that the Austrian Center, which later developed into the Free Austrian Movement, consisted mainly of nonpolitical members but was led by communists. The reason for its not being recognized was that neither the Socialist nor the Christian Socialist parties were represented by the Free Austrian Movement.

12. "Pionierdienst der Refugees in England," *Aufbau* (New York), Vol. VI, No. 8 (Feb. 23, 1940).

13. U.S. State Department File 800.01/148. Council of Austrians and Austrian Center on a joint letterhead to Foreign Office, July 30, 1941, PRO FO 371 26538 6032 C 8561, announces unification for the planned Free Austrian Movement.

14. U.S. State Department File 800.01/148. "Declaration of the Austrian Associations in Great Britain," Dec. 3, 1941, PRO FO 371 26539 8302 C 13372. Association of Austrian Christian Socialists in Great Britain to the *London Sunday Times*, Dec. 18, 1941, PRO FO 371 26539 8302, includes the statement that the group is not represented by the Free Austrian Movement.

Foreign Office memorandum, Jan. 7, 1942, PRO FO 371 30910 8264 C 212, concerns a conference with Heinrich Allina, Eva Kolmer, and Dr. Müller-Sturmheim, representing the Free Austrian Movement, about its aims. Foreign Office memorandum, Jan. 27, 1942, PRO FO 371
30910 8264 suggests that the Austrian question should not be approached hastily. Foreign Office
memorandum, Jan. 27, 1942, PRO FO 371 30910 8264 C 1282, refuses to recognize the Free
Austrian Movement, as neither Christian Socialists nor socialists had joined it because it was led
by communists and because 90 percent of its members were Jews.

15. U.S. State Department File 863.01/825. U.S. State Department File 863.01/8–2644.
American Embassy to State Department, PRO FO 371 30910 8264 C 1282, concerns the "Declaration of the Austrian Society in Great Britain"; it did not mention that the Association of Austrian Christian Socialists in Great Britain had not joined in the declaration. "The Austrian Emigration in Great Britain," July 7, 1944, OSS XL 1615, gives a detailed description of the
development of socialist émigré organizations since the meeting of exiled socialists in Brussels in
April, 1938. The exiled socialists had secured a so-called inland mandate, electing émigré organizations by the underground Revolutionary Socialists. Until the fall of France the headquarters of
the émigré socialist office were in Paris. Only Dr. Oskar Pollak went to England; most members
moved to the United States. Because of the proximity of London, the London Bureau of Austrian
Socialists demanded leadership in the policies of the exiled socialists. Early in 1941, the London
Bureau of Austrian Socialists as well as the Group of Austrian Trade Unionists was founded,
while the Club of Austrian Socialists embraced exiled former Austrian Social Democrats and
Revolutionary Socialists in London. The London Bureau of Austrian Socialists, led by Dr. Oskar
Pollak and Karl Czernetz, referring to the inland mandate, viewed itself as party leader and the
leading organization, in contrast to the members who had emigrated to the United States. The
Group of Austrian Trade Unionists was headed by John Svitanics, who was later joined by Franz
Novy. Report, March 14, 1944, OSS XL 1244, states that the London Bureau of Austrian Socialists neither wanted to gain new membership, as it considered itself to be the party leadership, nor
planned to organize the émigrés. Its attitude toward the émigrés was unfriendly and critical; it
regarded racial emigrants as politically interested only accidentally; they did not want to be
regarded as refugees. OSS 30310 reports that no new members were accepted in the Club of Austrian Socialists. According to OSS XL 1615, the Labour party recognized the London Bureau of
Austrian Socialists and the Group of Austrian Trade Unionists in Great Britain on May 3, 1944,
as bona fide representatives of the Austrian inland party and inland trade unions. Karl Stadler,
"Das London Bureau der Österreichischen Sozialisten" (Paper read at the Internationales Symposion zur Erforschung des österreichischen Exils von 1934 bis 1945, Vienna, June, 1975). Sir
George Franckenstein to Carl Buchberger, August 14, 1944,.

16. U.S. State Department File 800.01/148. Report, July 7, 1944, OSS XL 1615: "The Austrian political emigration lacks really able leadership." Anthony Eden, "Germany Confidential,"
Nov. 16, 1942, PRO FO 371 30911 8273 C 11239/46/18, states that the Austrian people are
represented neither by the "unrepresentative and ill-assorted collection of monarchists, communists and Jews who make up the Free Austrian Movement, nor by the socialist émigrés who, it
may be recalled, are for the most part refugees not from Hitler, but from Dollfuss," and that the
Austrian people will not recognize them as its representatives. Home Secretary Herbert Morrison
to Foreign Office, Feb. 2, 1942, PRO FO 371 30910 8264 C 1283: Morrison turned against the
Free Austrian Movement. Anthony Eden to Ernest Bevin, Feb. 10, 1942, PRO FO 371 30910
8264 C 1542/46/18, asks Bevin not to accept an invitation of the London Bureau of Austrian Socialists. PRO FO 371 30911 8273 C 7606: Memorandum of visit of Dr. E. Müller-Sturmheim,
Heinrich Allina, and Leopold Hornik, July 31, 1942, attempting to achieve agreement between
the Free Austrian Movement and the London Bureau of Austrian Socialists. Report, March 13,
1944, OSS XL 1244.

17. (Hans Rott), Secretary of the Austrian Monarchist World Union to Hans Rott, Sept. 3,
1944, folder "Grossbritannien." "A Survey of the Austrian Political Emigration," April 11,
1945, OSS 2853.

18. U.S. State Department File 863.01/825. U.S. State Department File 863.01/831. PRO FO
371 34420 8403 C 13142: Foreign Office memorandum about the visit of Eva Kolmer, the
speaker for the Free Austrian Movement, on Nov. 5, 1943. Austrian Representative Committee

to Foreign Secretary Anthony Eden, Nov. 9, 1943, PRO FO 371 34420 8403 C 13340. *Austrian News*, No. 16 (Nov. 12, 1943), PRO FO 371 34420 8403, concerns the "Vorbereitendes Komitee" of the Free Austrian Movement. Foreign Office memorandum, Nov. 29, 1943, PRO FO 371 34421 8405 C 14257, rejects Sir George Franckenstein as trustee for Austria. Foreign Office to Major T. L. Dugdale, M.P., Feb. 1, 1944, PRO FO 371 38827 8409 C 1107/30/3, states that neither the Free Austrian Movement nor the Austrian Representative Committee is recognized by the British government. Report, June 12, 1944, OSS 88820.

19. "Zwei Jahre Austrian Labor Information," *Austrian Labor Information* (New York), No. 24 (March–April, 1944). "Saboteure der Einheit," *Austria Libre* (Montevideo), No. 6 (October, 1944): This aritcle accuses Friedrich Adler, Pollak, and Czernetz of being saboteurs of the united front.

20. U.S. State Department File 863.01/825. Foreign Office to Major T. L. Dugdale, M.P., Feb. 1, 1944, PRO FO 371 38827 8409 C 1107/30/3. Association of Austrian Christian Socialists in Great Britain, Letter, Jan. 12, 1944, PRO FO 371 38827 8409 No. 419/30/3 C 561, concerns Professor Dr. Josef Dobretsberger. The suggestion was made in a letter of Jan. 8, 1944.

21. U.S. State Department File 863.01/4–345. "Gerbot der Stunde," *Austria Libre* (Havana), Circular letter No. 10/11 (July/August 1944).

22. (Hans Rott), Free Austrian World Movement to Hans Rott, July 28, 1944, folder "Südamerika." Report, Free Austrian World Movement, OSS XL 2102.

23. U.S. State Department File 863.01/11–1544. (Hans Rott), Free Austrian World Movement to Hans Rott, July 28, 1944, folder "Südamerika."

24. U.S. State Department File 863.01/11–1544. *Austria Libre* (Montevideo), No. 2 (July, 1944). *Austria Libre* (Montevideo), No. 4 (August, 1944). *Austrian News* (London), No. 4 (May, 1944).

25. *Austrian News* (London), No. 4 (May, 1944). *Austria Libre* (Montevideo), No. 4 (August, 1944). PRO FO 371 38830 8416.

26. U.S. State Department File 863.01/11–1544. *Austrian News* (London), No. 4 (May, 1944).

27. Gustav Gluck, Secretary of the Free Austrian Movement, Buenos Aires, Memorandum, Dec. 27, 1944, U.S. State Department File 863.01/12–2744.

Chapter X   The Austrian Emigration in Sweden

1. William L. Shirer, *op. cit.*, pp. 556, 557. Auswärtiges Amt, Akten zur deutschen auswärtigen Politik 1941–1945, Series D, Vol. IX, pp. 209–212, 492, 493, 512. According to the memorandum in OSS 23072, on the other hand, the right of passage gave the Allies and Swedish circles friendly to them a chance to contact Austrian members of the Wehrmacht who were passing through. They could establish facts at first hand. This report states that "all" members of the Wehrmacht of Austrian origin who wanted to pass through Sweden south of Kirkenes in occupied Norway were searched and disarmed before their departure. The report draws conclusion as to the nonreliability of the Austrian soldiers. Later these contacts were widened when the number of Austrian deserters rose as the war dragged on and especially after the Moscow Declaration. Another memorandum, PRO FO 371 46493 9620 C 56/6/3, states that at least one hundred deserters had offered themselves to the Austrian Society in Sweden as guides in the northern Italian and Austrian Alps. United States Legation, Stockholm, Memorandum, April 13, 1944, OSS 75791, mentions that frequent clashes occurred between the Austrian troops stationed in Norway and the German units.

2. William L. Shirer, *op. cit.*, pp. 556, 557. Alexander Werth, *Russia at War, 1941–1945* (New York: E. P. Dutton & Co., 1964). Helmut Muessener, *Exil in Schweden: Politische und kulturelle Emigration nach 1933* (Munich: Carl Hanser Verlag, 1974).

3. U.S. State Department File 800.01/207.

4. U.S. State Department File 800.01/115. U.S. State Department File 800.01/135. U.S. State Department File 800.01/148. U.S. State Department File 800.01/119–42.

5. Hans Rott, "A Survey of Austrian Organizations Abroad," London, July, 1944, folder

"Free Austrian World Movement." Helmut Muessener, *op. cit.*, pp. 223. Austrian socialist clubs existed in Sweden before and after the victory at Stalingrad. They had been established as cultural and social centers; but in 1943 they began to have political aims. Up to the Moscow Declaration concerning an independent Austria, they followed and adopted the line of the London Bureau of Austrian Socialists, with which the Swedish socialists were in close contact. It is obvious from the letter of early July, 1943, from Swedish socialists to the English socialists in the London Bureau of Austrian Socialists, in the Bruno Kreisky Archive, that even before the Moscow Declaration the Swedish socialists must have been informed that Allied negotiations were taking place which could "be of great importance for our country," as the letter stated. At this time—in October, 1943—Austrian émigrés in Switzerland were also being questioned by Allen Dulles regarding their opinion on the Austrian problem, according to Ambassador Dr. Arthur Breycha-Vauthier (see note 35, Chapter VII). Dr. Bruno Kreisky, at that time one of the most prominent and active émigré socialists, thanks to his standing with the influential Swedish cooperatives and his entrée to Swedish government circles, seems to have judged the political situation correctly. Besides, during the summer of 1943 Sweden switched from a pro-German neutrality to a position closer to the Allies, as is obvious from her new attitude on the passage of German members of the Wehrmacht. OWI, "Power of a Neutral," August 13, 1943, British Information Service, Vol. II, No. 14, group 108, box 365. After the Moscow Declaration and with the defeat of the German Wehrmacht clearly to be expected after the battles of Orel and Belgorod in 1943, Sweden changed to a neutrality openly friendly to the Allies. Memorandum, November 17, 1943, OSS 55730 R, reports on a meeting of Austrian Social Democrats in Stockholm on the twenty-fifth anniversary of the founding of the Austrian Republic.

6. Resolution of the Austrian Social Democrats, December 13, 1943, PRO FO 371 34421 C 15376/39/18, welcomes the Moscow Declaration on Austria. U.S. State Department File 863.01/867. "A Survey of the Austrian Emigration," April 11, 1945, OSS 2853: "In view of the preponderance of the Social Democrats and the Communists, all the other groups in the emigration have tended to gravitate around these two parties." And, in Sweden especially, right-wing circles had kept away from the dominant parties.

7. U.S. State Department File 863.01/884. Report on Austrian, Sudeten-German, and Czech organizations in Sweden, March 31, 1944, OSS 65053, states that while the collaboration of Communists and Social Democrats in Sweden has to be called not too close, it is nevertheless more successful than that within the German groups. The Moscow Declaration had not given much of a choice to the socialists in Sweden, who followed Bauer's line, except for an independent Austria, while the communists had adopted this plan a long time ago.

8. U.S. State Department File 863.00/1942. Arvid Fredborg, "Probleme der Zukunft Österreichs," *Svensk Tidskrift*, No. 2, Vol. 30 (1944). "A Survey of the Austrian Emigration," April 11, 1945, OSS 2853, states that the socialists in Sweden were in close touch with their colleagues in Great Britain and that they followed the directions of the London Bureau of Austrian Socialists until shortly before the Moscow Declaration. This is also obvious from the July, 1943, letter from Austrian socialists in Sweden to the London Bureau of Austrian Socialists (photocopy)—original in Bruno Kreisky Archive). Up to the break in early 1945, there was a desire in Sweden to affect a unified stand. Since the beginnings of the political emigration, the socialists had played a decisive part in the Austrian political emigration, in the founding as well as the leadership of the Österreichische Vereinigung in Schweden. This was due largely to the political instinct of Dr. Bruno Kreisky and to his leadership ability. Carl Buchberger to Franz Goldner, July 16, 1973. Helmut Muessener, *op. cit.*, p. 230.

9. U.S. State Department File 863.01/7–344. Report, July 13, 1944, OSS 96782 C. Report, June 22, 1944, OSS 80929S. British Embassy, Stockholm, to Secretary of State; S. C. Parrot to British Embassy, Stockholm, about conversation with Dr. Bruno Kreisky, July 5, 1944, PRO FO 371 38829 8414 C 9234/154/6/44. OSS 2853, April 11, 1945, stressed that Kreisky had declared that the founding of the Österreichische Vereinigung in Schweden was a political act initiated by the socialists but that it could be traced back to the activities of Carl Buchberger. Helmut Muessener, *op. cit.*, p. 224.

10. U.S. State Department File 863.01/7–1244. United States Legation, Stockholm, to Secretary of State, July 12, 1944, OSS 91470, with Resolution No. 2 by Carl Buchberger. This second

resolution advocates establishing local Austrian representative committees with a central committee in London, instead of an Austrian Congress in London.

11. U.S. State Department File 863.01/11–744. Report, March 31, 1944, OSS 65053: Dr.
Bruno Kreisky received permission to interrogate Austrian refugees and deserters in Sweden.
United States Legation, Stockholm, to Secretary of State, Nov. 14, 1944, U.S. State Department
File 47 C. OWI, British Information Service, Vol. II, No. 14, group 208, box 365. Dr. Bruno
Kreisky to Dr. Oskar Pollak, the London Bureau of Austrian Socialists, Dec. 5, 1944 (pho-
tocopy—original in Bruno Kreisky Archive): He intimated that the policy of the latter was not
very fortunate.

12. U.S. State Department File 863.00/1942. *Aufbau* (New York), Vol. VII, No. 1 (January
3, 1941).

13. U.S. State Department File 863.01/689 1/2. U.S. State Department File 863.01/8–2644.
U.S. State Department File 863.00/1942. "The Austrian Emigration in Great Britain," July 7,
1944, OSS XL 1615: Sir George Franckenstein, however, did not have the influence he was
thought to have at the beginning of the war. He was known as Winston Churchill's friend, but
was considered an aging monarchist without political influence in Austria. Carl Buchberger
evidently wanted to gain time to gather information about the Free Austrian Movement, as is obvious from a letter to me of July 16, 1973.

14. U.S. State Department File 863.01/2–2045. U.S. State Department File 863.01/3–1545.
U.S. State Department File 863.01/850. OSS 2853, April 11, 1945, reports that the socialists
warned that they would withdraw from the Österreichische Vereinigung in Schweden if it should
join with the Free Austrian Movement. British Press Secretary, Stockholm, to Political Intelligence Department, London, January 10, 1945, PRO FO 371 46595 9620 C215, concerns
conversation with Dr. Bruno Kreisky and his idea of contacting the Austrian communist, Hon-
ner, who was active with Tito's partisans, rather than the Austrian communists in Moscow. The
British author of the memorandum thinks that in spite of his being a Social Democrat, Dr. Bruno
Kreisky wanted to establish contact with the communist-led Freedom Front.

15. State Department File 863.01/4–945.

16. *Dagens Nyheter* (Stockholm), March 31, 1945. Report, March 31, 1944, OSS 65053. Carl
Buchberger to Franz Goldner, July 16, 1973, states that "we in Stockholm had no idea about the
POEN."

Chapter XI   The Austrian Emigration in the Soviet Union

1. Karl Vogelmann, "Die Propaganda der österreichischen Emigration in der Sowjetunion für
einen selbständigen österreichischen Nationalstaat 1938–1945" (Ph.D. dissertation, Faculty of
Philosophy, University of Vienna, 1973), p. 1. Vogelmann includes among Austrian political
émigrés the Austrian prisoners of the First World War who remained in Russia, as well as communist émigrés of the 1920's and 1930's in the Soviet Union.

2. Auswärtiges Amt, Akten zur deutschen auswärtigen Politik 1941–1945, Series D, Vol.
VIII, p. 439: "The Soviet Union demanded an end to the German deportation activity to Russian
territory and gained the promise that such actions would not be undertaken in the future."

3. "A Survey of the Austrian Political Emigration," April 11, 1945, OSS 2853, states: "Moscow is said to set the policies for the émigré Austrian communists within the Austrian underground." In spite of this, the American OSS report praises Soviet propaganda in one aspect:
"An attempt to inculcate a much needed and hitherto nonexistent sense of nationalism in the Austrian people is thus indicated." Karl Vogelmann, *op. cit.*, believes that the Austrian communists'
propaganda for the reestablishment of Austria's independence goes back to 1936 and that it is a
sign of the independent policy of the Austrian Community party. United States Legation, Vienna,
to Department of State, May 11, 1935, U.S. State Department File 863.01, no. 417, including a
memorandum on the conversation of the U.S. chargé d'affaires ad interim, Mr. A. W. Kliefoth,
with the then newly accredited Soviet Ambassador Mr. Lorenz proves that already at this time the
main objective of the Soviet Union was the weakening of the German Reich. The Soviet diplomat
confirmed in this conversation that the Soviet Union would support the independence of Austria

even with military force, disregarding the authoritarian character of the regime, and that it would keep communists in Austria under control.

Chapter XII   The Austrian Emigration in Latin America

1. Julius Deutsch, *op. cit.*, p. 328.
2. (Hans Rott), Report, Jan. 12, 1942, on regional groups of the Free Austrian Movement; Anton Retschek to Hans Rott, Dec. 16, 1941; A. Jacob von Kantstein to Hans Rott, Oct. 16, 1941, folder "Free Austrian Movement." Federación Austriacos Libres en Bolivia, eds., *Festschrift* (La Paz, Bolivia: July, 1944). British Embassy, Bogota, to Foreign Secretary Anthony Eden, Dec. 12, 1942, PRO FO 371 34417 C 382, reports that the Comité de los Austriacos Libres in Colombia had requested the annulment of the Anschluss as early as September 1, 1942.
3. U.S. State Department File 863.01/113. U.S. State Department File 863.01/4–345. U.S. State Department File 800.01/160A. "Organization and Status of the Free Austrian Movement in Canada," Sept. 18, 1941, PRO FO 371 30910 8264: According to this memorandum there were thirty-eight branches of the Free Austrian Movement in the world, the majority of them in South America. British Embassy, San Jose, Costa Rica, to Foreign Secretary Anthony Eden, August 7, 1941, PRO FO 371 26538 8296 No. 65. "Austrian Action," March 24, 1942, OSS 14268, gives a summary of contacts of Austrian Action, especially in South America. There is little doubt that none of these organizations functioning in South and Central America reached the membership of the Austria Libre movement.
4. (Hans Rott), "A Survey of Organizations Abroad," London, July, 1944, folder "Free Austrian World Movement."
5. *Austria Libre* (Buenos Aires), Newsletter, July 1, 1943. *Austria Libre* (Montevideo), No. 1 (April, 1944).
6. U.S. State Department File 863.01/12–2744. (Hans Rott), Anton Retschek, President of the Committee, to the Free Austrian Movement, New York, June 18, 1944; Free Austrian World Movement, "A Survey of Organizations Abroad," London, July, 1944; Dr. Rudolf Aladar Metall to Hans Rott, April 9, 1941, folder "Südamerika," British Postal and Telegraph Censorship, Oct. 27, 1943, PRO FO 371 34420 8403 C 11591/39/18.
7. U.S. State Department File 863.01/12–2744. (Hans Rott), Anton Retschek to Hans Rott, June 18, 1944, folder "Südamerika."
8. U.S. State Department File 863.01/10–3045.
9. (Hans Rott), Anton Retschek to Hans Rott, June 18, 1944, folder "Südamerika."
10. (Hans Rott), "A Survey of Organizations Abroad," London, July, 1944, folder "Free Austrian World Movement."
11. U.S. State Department File 863.01/5–2645. British Postal and Telegraph Censorship, Dec. 9, 1942, PRO FO 371 30911 8273 C 12767. Foreign Office to Le Roy Lewis, Censorship Department, Jan. 11, 1943, PRO FO 371 30911 8273 C 12767/46/18: "This memorandum is a mine of information." British Postal and Telegraph Censorship, "Free Austrian Activities Abroad," May 21, 1943, PRO FO 371 34418 9768 C 5967/39/18.
12. (Hans Rott), Free Austrian Movement, Report, Jan. 12, 1942, folder "Free Austrian Movement." (Hans Rott), Asociación Austria Libre to Hans Rott, July 23, 1942, folder "Südamerika," includes excerpts from the statutes and membership list.
13. (Hans Rott), Asociación Austria Libre to Hans Rott, July 23, 1942, folder "Südamerika." *Austria Libre* (Havana), Newsletter No. 7/8 (April/May, 1944).
14. U.S. State Department File 800.01/206. U.S. State Department File 800.01/189. British Embassy, Caracas, to Foreign Secretary Anthony Eden, Nov. 15, 1943, PRO FO 371 34421 8405 C 14326.
15. U.S. State Department File 863.01/4–345.
16. (Hans Rott), A. M. von Schocher, president of Legion österreichischer Patrioten, to Hans Rott, Nov. 2, 1942; Alianca Austriaca and Legion österreichischer Patrioten to Free Austrian Movement, New York, Nov. 24, 1942, folder "Südamerika." Foreign Office to Le Roy Lewis, Censorship Department, Jan. 11, 1943, PRO FO 371 30911 8273 C 12767/46/18.
17. Hans Rott to the Alianca Austriaca, Asunción, Jan. 7, 1943, folder "Südamerika."

18. (Hans Rott), Alianca Austriaca, Asunción, to Hans Rott, Nov. 24, 1942, folder "Südamerika."

19. U.S. State Department File 863.01/4–345. *Austria Libre* (Montevideo), No. 1 (April, 1944).

20. U.S. State Department File 800.01/213. U.S. State Department File 863.01/770. (Hans Rott), Enrique Faltisek to Hans Rott, Oct. 27, 1942, folder "Südamerika." *Austria Libre* (Montevideo), No. 1 (April, 1944). Foreign Office to Le Roy Lewis, Censorship Department, Jan. 11, 1943, PRO FO 371 30911 8273 C 12767/46/18. British Postal and Telegraph Censorship, "Free Austrian Activities Abroad," May 21, 1943, PRO FO 371 34418 9768 C 5967/39/18.

21. U.S. State Department File 863.01/11–1544. *Austria Libre* (Montevideo), No. 1 (April, 1944). British Postal and Telegraph Censorship, "Free Austrian Activities Abroad," May 21, 1943, PRO FO 371 34418 9768 5967/39/18.

22. U.S. State Department File 863.01/11–1544. U.S. State Department File 863.01/12–274–4. British Embassy, Montevideo, Report, Sept. 4, 1944, PRO FO 371 38830 8416 C 13295, states that Austria Libre under the new leadership had a definitely leftist character.

23. U.S. State Department File 800.01/160 A. U.S. State Department File 800.01/143. U.S. State Department File 863.01/4–345. (Hans Rott), Report, Jan. 12, 1942, folder "Free Austrian Movement." (Hans Rott), Hugo Moser, Santiago, Chile, to Hans Rott, Nov. 6, 1942; Hans Rott to Paul Fuchs, Buenos Aires, Jan. 28, 1943, folder "Südamerika." *Austria Libre* (Santiago, Chile), Newsletter No. 20 (August 6, 1943). Foreign Office to Le Roy Lewis, Jan. 11, 1943, PRO FO 371 8273 C 12767/46/18. British Postal and Telegraph Censorship, "Free Austrian Activities Abroad," May 21, 1943, PRO FO 371 34418 9768 C 5967/39/18.

24. *Austria Libre* (Santiago, Chile), Newsletter No. 20 (August 6, 1943). Foreign Office to Le Roy Lewis, Jan. 11, 1943, PRO FO 371 30911 8273 C 12767/46/18.

25. U.S. State Department File 863.00/11–945. (Hans Rott), Report, Jan. 12, 1942, folder "Free Austrian Movement."

26. U.S. State Department File 863.00/1562. Der Gesandte in Mexico an das Auswärtige Amt (April 8, 1938), Auswärtiges Amt, Akten zur deutschen auswärtigen Politik, Series D. Vol. V, p. 697.

27. (Hans Rott), Ing. Hans Altmann to Dr. Richard Schüller, February 19, 1943, folder "Südamerika." British Postal and Telegraph Censorship, "Free Austrian Activities Abroad," May 21, 1943, PRO FO 371 34418 9768 C 5967/39/18. In order to complete the list, let us state that there also existed in Mexico the Acción Republicana Austriaca, under Social Democratic leadership, and the Austrian Action Committee for Mexico. A bulletin, *Austria Libre,* was published.

28. U.S. State Department File 863.01/654. (Hans Rott), Report, January 12, 1942, folder "Free Austrian Movement." Foreign Office to Le Roy Lewis, January 11, 1943, PRO FO 371 30911 8273 C 12767/46/18.

29. U.S. State Department File 800.01/114.

30. U.S. State Department File 863.01/654. Hans Rott, Report, January 12, 1942, folder "Free Austrian Movement." Other Austrian organizations were the Acción Republicana Austriaca and the Austrian Revolutionary Club.

31. U.S. State Department File 800.20210/6–2344. U.S. State Department File 863.01/4–345. U.S. State Department File 863.01/6–944.

32. "Pässe für Österreicher," *Aufbau* (New York), Vol. X, No. 6 (February 11, 1944). "Pizzarellos Pässe," *Aufbau* (New York), Vol. X, No. 8 (February 25, 1944).

33. U.S. State Department File 800.20210/6–2344. U.S. State Department File 863.01/1–3145.

34. U.S. State Department File 863.01/4–1245. (Hans Rott), Silvio Pizzarello von Helmsburg and Dr. Emil Schaale, representative of the Free Austrian Movement in Costa Rica and delegate of the Austria Libre Movement, exchange of letters, folder "Südamerika."

35. "Einigung der Österreicher—auf welches Ziel?" *Austrian Labor Information* (New York), No. 6 (September 20, 1942).

36. Federación Austriacos Libres en Bolivia, eds., *Festschift,* July, 1944, p. 36. OSS XL 1615: "The unpolitical people are the real nationalists" (meaning Austrian nationalists).

Index of Names

ACHESON, Dean Gooderham, 91, 94, 96
ACKERMAN, Manfred, 15
ADLER, Dr. Friedrich [Fritz], 15, 25, 57, 72, 98, 99, 103, 110, 113, 125, 126, 148, 150, 151, 158, 183, 188, 197
ADRIAN-WERBURG, Dr. Leopold von, 124
ALEXICH, George M. V., 49, 65, 77
ALLINA, Heinrich, 124, 125, 202, 203
ALTMANN, Hans, 143, 208
ANDICS, Hellmut, 86, 88, 180, 182, 186

BABOUCZEK, Anton von, 140–41
BAUER, Dr. Otto, 15, 24, 25, 63, 96, 120, 148–49, 161, 183, 205
BENEŠ, Dr. Edvard, 12, 21, 33, 37, 43, 47, 116, 117, 119, 126
BENEŠ, Vojta, 74
BERLE, Adolf A. Jr., 46, 59, 60, 62, 64, 65, 70, 72, 73, 74, 76, 77, 79, 85, 89, 95–96, 104, 106
BEVIN, Ernest, 203
BIDDLE, E. Francis, 56
BISMARCK, Prince Otto von, 37
BITTNER, Dr. Karl, 133
BLUMENFELD, Kurt, 174
BREITNER, Hugo, 57
BREYCHA-VAUTHIER, Dr. Arthur, 95, 195, 197, 205
BUCHBERGER, Carl, 122, 130–34 passim, 206
BULLITT, William C., 17, 26, 31, 43, 50, 86, 177, 187
BURLINGHAM, Charles C., 121
BUTTINGER, Joseph (pseudonym Gustav Richter), 3, 5, 15, 21, 23–25, 26, 27, 40, 49, 51

CALLENDER, Harold, 182
CAMPBELL, Sir R. I., 62, 70, 77
CAROL II, King of Romania, 183
CHARLES I., Emperor of Austria, 43
CHAMBERLAIN, Arthur Neville, 120, 202

CLAYTON, James, 94
CLEMENCEAU, Georges, 180
COLVILLE, J. R., 187, 202
COUDENHOVE-KALERGI, Count Richard N., 4, 49
CRISCUOLO, Luigi, 194
CZERNETZ, Karl, 15, 203
CZERNIN, Count Ferdinand, 43, 45, 46, 47, 49, 53, 55, 61, 63, 65, 79, 86, 89, 92, 93, 102–106 passim, 108, 115, 116, 182, 184, 195, 198
CZERNIN, Count Ottokar, 43, 45

DALADIER, Edouard, 22, 178
DAVIS, John W., 59, 79
DEGENFELD, Count Heinrich, 66, 184
DELFINER, Henry, 193
DETHAN, Georges, 179
DEUTSCH, Dr. Julius, 14, 17, 20, 21, 23, 24, 25, 26–27, 30, 41, 43, 49, 57, 63, 65, 72, 78, 86, 88, 95, 103, 104, 105, 107, 110, 116, 117, 119, 132, 134, 136, 147, 148, 151–57, 160, 161, 164, 166, 183, 188, 197
DOBRETSBERGER, Dr. Josef, 126, 204
DOLLFUSS, Dr. Engelbert, 2, 3, 34, 35, 64, 117, 122, 133, 139, 203
DUBINSKY, David, 79
DULLES, Allan, 195, 197, 202
DUMBA, Konstantin von, 180

EBERHARTER, Congressman, 48, 64, 185
EDEN, Sir Anthony, 65, 78, 96, 120, 121, 152, 197, 202, 203
EDWARDS, J. H. General, 68, 69, 70
EIGRUBER, August, 91
EISLER, Dr. Arnold, 139
ELLENBOGEN, Wilhelm, 72, 183
ENGEL-JANOSI, Dr. Friedrich, 64
ENGELS, Friedrich, 149
ENNIS, Edward J., 186
ERB, Baron Ferdinand, 141